Trumpet I:
– an orchestral life

Bram Gay

Thames Publishing
London

for Margaret, PJN, Sugarlump, and Jonny,
who know what it cost.

Contents

Overture

Once there died a second violinist: one who had served faithfully but unrecognised on the back desk of a great symphony orchestra all his days. He awoke to find himself in a lift, travelling rapidly downwards and getting warmer. He was not a bit surprised, having long known that heaven is a quartet and that ordinary fiddlers can't get in. Imagine his astonishment to find, when the door opened, that beyond lay a great and beautiful foyer, richly carpeted, and that here to greet him was an archangel complete with golden trumpet.

'Come along', said the Angel. 'We've been waiting for you for ages. Rehearsal has started. There's just time to choose your Strad before the second movement begins.'

Our friend was led to a vast room containing hundreds of the finest creations of the Cremonese master, each accompanied by a priceless Tourte bow. 'Yes', said the Angel, smiling at his amazement, 'folks are always taken aback; but the old boy has been with us a long time. We have rather more fiddles than there are fiddlers coming down, nowadays. Just help yourself.' Spoiled for choice, our bemused friend picked up the nearest masterpiece and pronounced himself well pleased. He was led to the concert stage of a sumptuous auditorium where he found a place waiting on the fourth desk of firsts. 'Really', he said, 'I can't sit there. I'm not up to it.' 'Fear not', encouraged the Angel, 'You are much better than you think you are. Just sit down and try.'

So, with many a sidelong glance at the wondrous collection of players around him, he began to play. Paganini was leading, naturally. Practically every leader ever born was there, not to mention the best horn, trumpet, timpani, and woodwind players of all times. Only two seats were empty and waiting in that wonderful orchestra – there was a shortage of harpists, it seemed. The performance was devilishly fine; playing was so easy. It was always easier, of course, to play with good players. Perhaps 'the others' had been the problem all his playing life? So it seemed. Never had the *Fantastique* of Berlioz sounded so well.

The conductor — was that the tip of a forked tail peeping from beneath his tail coat? — was a master: the sort the player seeks in vain through the years, and appreciative too. At the end of the breathtaking finale he said, without putting down the stick, 'Yes, my friends, when the conditions are perfect we really can play better and better. Let's do it again!' And so they did. Even better it was, next time. The orchestra could not be restrained from another *Da Capo*. Over and over they played the piece. Better and better it went. Marvellous! Such playing has never been heard on earth.

After the sixth — or was it perhaps the seventh? — run-through our hero, feeling a growing fatigue in his bow-arm, turned to his colleague and asked in a whisper 'I say — what time is the tea break?'

Was there just a twinkle in the eye in response?

'Tired, are you?'

'Yes. As a matter of fact, marvellous as all this is I have to admit I'm more tired than I've ever been in ...'

'In your life, you were going to say?'

'Yes, I was.'

'I know the feeling well, my friend. But that's the whole point. Everything else about this job is utterly perfect. If only we could stop when we are tired of playing, that would be Heaven.'

This book is dedicated to that violinist and to all his colleagues and mine, past and present. May his conductor discover Stravinsky's *Symphony of Psalms*, in which there are no violins. And when my turn comes, perhaps Mozart in G minor?

CHAPTER 1
Beginnings

I am a Welshman from Treorchy, a mining village near the top of the Rhondda Valley. My fair hair and blue eyes betray the influence of the Cornish influx into the valleys at the time of the coal boom.

In my childhood the Rhondda was famous for coal and music. The coal was the world's best. It fuelled the navies of Europe and the ironworks of Merthyr, all going great guns at that time. The music was mainly of two sorts. We had our male-voice choirs and our brass bands. These still thrive.

To be a Welshman is to have a special relationship with music. Whether or not it is true that all Welshmen are musical and can sing is debatable; but all Welshmen believe themselves to be musical and to have a natural affinity with Placido Domingo. In our schools, music was not a fringe activity limited to a selfconscious few. A music period was a singing period. Teacher played the piano and we all sang Welsh folk-songs in Welsh with the gusto for which Cardiff Arms Park is still famous and with much more accuracy. They are wonderful songs. I am glad to say that this happy practice still goes on. There is no better training, so long as those in charge pay due attention to intonation and diction. As I remember, through my rose-tinted specs, these things came naturally to us. If they still do, we may perhaps concede musicality of a generalised kind to my countrymen.

Instrumental training was for the family to arrange and pay for. Many did. As I look around our orchestras today I am constantly reminded of the influence of the South Welsh on musical life: a reflection of the selflessness of my parents' generation. True, lessons cost only half-a-crown, but miners were paid only thirty-two-and-sixpence a week.

My father was a miner, and his before him. So were my uncles. These were numerous, my mother being one of ten children. All these chaps were Salvationists and played in the Salvation Army Band, so my early training cost nothing apart from the price of the instrument. A cornet was bought on my third birthday for six pounds, and put away carefully in Mother's sideboard until I could develop the puff for blowing it. Three, by the way, was the age at which the Rhondda sent kids to school in the 'thirties. Three is young for cornets and for school but it worked in both cases. At eight I had read a lot of Dickens, and at six I could blow.

Dad failed to teach me. He was short of fuse in both patience and temper and the thing came to tears. Mother was more successful, having watched more subtle teachers among her family. Taking the instrument out casually one day while dusting, she showed me how to put it to my face and 'make a noise like a moo-cow'. A noise of a vaguely bovine kind ensued. I built on it, largely untutored for some years, and my moo-cow provided me with a reasonable living and gratifying applause, here and there, for quite a long time.

I had from the start a lucky knack of making an interesting and expressive sound. I think that physiology, which is genetic and acciden-tal, has a lot to do with this. If that is true then Mother deserves extra credit for making not only the production but the machine itself. All I know for sure is that from a very early age I could throw the instrument up to my face and without conscious thought make a happy musical sound on it. This became harder with time and teaching but my early playing days were what today's youngsters would call a 'piece of cake'. For this reason my parents assumed that I had a talent. This talent was encouraged almost to the point of abuse, I think; but in the Rhondda of my childhood talent usually was.

This was natural. Since there was no work but mining in the Valleys other than for shopkeepers, bankers, teachers and preachers (and my word, we enjoyed a profusion of preachers in all varieties), a talent was a passport to another world: one which escaped the six o'clock hooter, the cage, the pick and shovel, the long afternoon walk home in the pit-dirt, the daily tin bath in front of the fire, and in the end the dust which killed my grandfather. The brainy were to *think* them-selves out of the Valley via university, or at least by the teacher training college. I was required to blow myself clean over Treorchy mountain.

My grandfather had a wind-up gramophone and a collection of records specialising, for my benefit as I now realise, in virtuoso cornetists. These were fed to me with my mother's milk, literally, since the gramophone was the only music we had. As I grew to the point of choosing among them for myself, I was shown style and musicianship by simple comparison between these old records. The fact that my family understood these things is surprising but I am grateful for it.

The band in which my father and his friends played was our pride and joy, and one of the two best in Wales. Rivalry with neighbouring Bargoed was of long standing but in Bargoed, it was well known, they blew too hard and could therefore not be taken seriously. We had also a thriving junior band, and for this I was auditioned when I was six-and-a-half. This fearsome experience (the first of my many auditions) took place in my grandmother's kitchen. I offered as the peak of my achievement a hymn tune called *Rimington*, usually sung to the words *Jesus shall reign*, and I was duly accepted with the usual dire warnings about the need for regular attendance and hard work. These were unnecessary. I had taken to the mouthpiece as certain young ladies take to the wimple, and much younger. I had given up the world for the cornet.

Salvationist children are not christened; the appropriate ceremony is called a *Dedication*. The word is well chosen. The young Salvationist of the 'thirties was dedicated, to the point of obsession, to the work of that extraordinary organisation. Most churches hope for Sunday observance with perhaps weekly choir practice for the musical and an evening's bellringing for the energetic. At 'The Army' there was always 'something on'. From the cradle I thought it quite normal that besides carrying me to the Citadel three times on Sundays my parents spent most evenings there. Twice-weekly band-practice, once-a-week Songsters, at least one evening for a musical service or festival home or away – South Wales brimmed with Salvationism. General Booth kept us on the straight and narrow path largely by depriving us of the time, the energy and the means for the crooked one. A clever man he was, and a first-rate man of business too; but I sometimes wish he had left us time for an education of sorts.

So, off to band practice, quite unprepared for the technical demands of the music. This is, and I hope ever will be, the way the young brass player first meets the brass ensemble. It is the very best way because it teaches the first essential immediately: the basic need not to start too soon and not to stop too late. By this means unwanted and embarrassing solos are avoided. This is the foundation of ensemble playing, and I often wished, while listening to orchestral auditions at Covent Garden, that our music colleges understood this and that it might be taught to string players at the same stage. Alas, ensemble skills are the last shown to budding Heifetzes. Our orchestras, consequently, teach them while paying salaries.

Since my teaching had been primitive I soon found that band music had too many sharps and flats for me. This I tried to remedy by sideways glances at the fingers of my friends, by which means I could find the right note given a time-lag of half a second. My stratagem was soon spotted and forcibly discouraged. Scales, I was told, were the answer; I must learn to play the instrument itself rather than to play pieces on it. Here is the heart of instrumental wisdom. Fingers which have learned a sequence by unremitting repetition never forget it. The 'machinery' runs itself, with instant communication between eye and hand, much as one rides a bike. I took this advice to heart and found it profitable. Even now, many years out of practice, my fingers can still play the scales faultlessly. I wish I could say the same for my lips and lungs.

When I was seven, somewhere between the Abdication and the Coronation, I met the Royal Family. The new King brought his Queen and their two offspring to Cardiff for a great gathering of Welsh youth at Cardiff Arms Park. Our band was invited. I remember a long, hot parade through the streets, the complete impossibility of playing my cornet while trying to march — at seven, can you believe? — and a long stand on the Rugby ground waiting for the magical figures to pass. From a height of three feet the field seemed as big as Salisbury Plain. To my great surprise, though to no-one else's because I was the tiniest person present, the Queen stopped, pointed out my cornet to the Princesses, patted my curls, smiled the smile which has endeared her to generations, and walked on. No doubt the Queen remembers this as clearly as I do — the day I decided to marry Princess Margaret Rose. Unlike the young Mozart in the presence of Marie Antoinette, I did not announce my intention at the time. I could not have spoken, as they say, if Hell had me.

My playing developed. Quite soon I began to play solos in public, usually to audiences of middle-aged ladies gathered in chapels and churches. To these, sentimental hymns played on a cornet by a curly-headed tot were quite irresistible. I became accustomed to applause, and the ease with which I have been able, as a soloist, to face audiences of all sorts must owe a lot to this early training. It is an odd fact, but true, that while certain occasions in the orchestra have provided me with as bad a dose of 'the pearlies' as can be imagined, I have never found it hard to get up on my hind legs and deliver a trumpet concerto.

When I was nine I was given my first real lessons. The conductor of the local brass band, one Reginald Little, was chosen. The first lesson was delivered on his doorstep. My knock was tentative. He opened the door.

'What sort of knock is that, young man? Aren't you a musician?' Optimistically I replied that I was.

'Well, musicians don't knock on doors like postmen, you know! Try again, with rhythm!

I essayed a more organised knock. It was not enough for Little. 'Again! Play it as though you mean it!' So I delivered a more convincing

Marziale moderato

This pleased him. 'Everything has a rhythm. Rhythm makes the world go round. Never forget it!'

Little was a fine teacher. About that time there passed through his hands a number of youngsters who were afterwards famous. One, a Royal Academy professor now, still plays at Covent Garden. Little looked first and always for a beautiful sound and he exercised it through a style largely vocal. We learned all the popular Victorian ballads, with their words — how else could one phrase? — and in that way developed not only musicianship but the physical means of expressing it. Technique he left to grow naturally as required, realising that anyone can develop finger and tongue given sufficient time and determination, while musical style must be instilled early and improved by constant example. These things are easier today, when the best of everything can be heard electronically. Things were very different in the thirties.

By this time the Salvation Army had promoted me all over the land. I had played to an audience of some thousands in London. The onset of Hitler's war actually extended my activities. I was for ever on trains or buses (the motor car was a luxury rare to me in my first ten years) and forever late for school on Monday mornings.

My scholastic performance hardly matched my musical one. All I wanted was to play.

My family had not the first idea what was to be done with me other than to encourage like mad and keep their fingers crossed. A family friend offered advice: 'Show young Bram to Harry Mortimer and he'll know what to do.'

So I met the King — then the Crown Prince — of the brass band at the Belle Vue band contest of '43. He was to adjudicate, and I was taken with my cornet to visit him in the manager's sanctum. He was utterly charming and put me at my ease instantly. He asked me to play. I played an aria of Handel, breathing in all the right places. He took from his bag the waltz song from Gounod's *Romeo and Juliet* and asked me to play at sight. I played a phrase or two. Then he took out his own cornet and showed me a phrase of his own.

'You are saying this', he said, giving a first-rate impression of my delivery, 'and I wonder if you can say this instead,' giving something far more interesting. I could indeed, in a miniaturised way. This interested him. The reason I became one of his very few pupils was my ability to copy Mortimer's own playing. It came very easily to me. His advice was that I should immediately come to live nearer to his home in Cheshire so that I could work with him and join Fodens Motor Works Band as its youngest ever member.

CHAPTER 2
Apprenticeship

Sir Adrian Boult once offered the Brass Band Movement as proof positive of the innate musicality of the British. The band which I had joined was the finest flowering of that movement. Its members had played together for more than a decade with hardly a change, and had developed the sensitivity of a chamber-group. Its conductor, Fred Mortimer, was a true natural musician. I have never, in later and more sophisticated musical life, heard his teaching contradicted. Where I was concerned he set himself the role of hard taskmaster and applied himself to it in a characteristic dry Yorkshire fashion. In an ensemble where every other member was old enough to be my father − otherwise they would have been away fighting Hitler − this was an obvious need. It cannot have been any easier for them than for me to cross the generation gap.

For seven years after, nothing mattered to me but Fodens Band. School went to the dogs. My school head was kind − perhaps too kind. The band was all. It was a wonderful band, and amazingly busy, providing wartime entertainment in a land starved of live music. There were radio concerts every two weeks or so, and at least fifty concerts each year. The travel was astonishing. We played everywhere from Aberdeen to Plymouth. I loved it.

Playing with Harry Mortimer was a musical education of the most practical kind. He was a rare artist: the first player to promote the proletarian cornet into the aristocracy. His innate musicality had been carefully nurtured by his remarkable father and polished by years of work in the Hallé and Liverpool orchestras under Beecham and Harty. All this was still at the service of Fodens Band. His leadership − and he did indeed lead as a great orchestral leader leads − was the factor which had raised this amateur group to their incredible level of performance.

Mortimer made the cornet sing, and with such a golden sound as I have never heard from the instrument since. He was to the cornet what Kreisler had been to the violin. To the young BG it was as though all the brass-playing previously heard had been in black-and-white; here was a gorgeous palette of previously unsuspected resource. There was nothing 'amateur' about HM nor about that band and conductor, except the fun they derived from playing together and the sacrifices they made for Fodens Band. Those sacrifices were considerable. The band rehearsed twice weekly. There was always a concert of some sort at the weekend, and often two. Absence, even lateness, was unheard of. The individual level of performance could not have been sustained without at least one hour's practice during free evenings. Families were organised around the band. Nothing less serious than bereavement justified 'letting the band down', and on those occasions Mortimer would cancel band-practice rather than face an empty chair. Here was a professional level of commitment by factory-hands working an eight-hour day.

It was in the brass band that I met my first conductors of the sort who conduct great orchestras. Before the jet plane made their lives a travel-agent's delight these people found time, unthinkably today, for brass-band conducting. Sir Malcolm Sargent, then conductor of the Liverpool Philharmonic and always at his best with amateurs, revelled in concerts of four massed brass bands. I remember Barbirolli conducting the *Water Music* of Handel, transcribed for the orchestra by Harty and then from that score into the brass band by his first trombonist, Sam Holt, with a hundred brass at Belle Vue, Manchester. The circus elephants provided the 'noises off'. JB was not disturbed by these, since all his Hallé concerts were held at Belle Vue until the bombed Free Trade Hall was rebuilt. 'If my orchestra could play that so well', he said at the end of the slow movement, 'I would be the happiest man in Manchester'. Above all I remember Sir Adrian Boult, who was to turn up at intervals in my life for many years. He conducted Elgar's *Severn Suite*, written for the Championship of 1930, an occasion of glorious memory for Fodens Band.

After sitting next to Harry Mortimer for two years I found myself doing the job for which I had been imported and nursed. HM's BBC appointment meant the end of Fodens Band for him. In future his brass-band activity was limited to the rostrum, where he would become even more famous than his father. Now the pressure was on me and it was unremitting. There was so much music. The band knew it all; there was honestly nothing in the repertoire they could not knock up and polish in two hours. I had it all to learn, and so little time.

The Old Man was hard, and hardest when I thought I was doing well. 'Good', he would say, 'Very good indeed. Good enough for any other band. Not half good enough for Fodens Band.' And on another occasion, when there was general pleasure — carefully suppressed by the band — at something I had done really well, 'Yes. But to play that properly we really need a cornet player like our 'arry, don't we?' No doubt it was good for me, but it was very very hard to take. I depended on audience reaction for reassurance. This was plentiful, and it was because of that plenty that Fred kept up the pressure. He had a very clear idea of the effect of constant applause upon fifteen-year-old boys. I know now that 'Our 'arry' had suffered the same treatment. HM never understood until long after his retirement from playing that his father had thought him even a fine player, still less the greatest cornetist of all.

I was now out of school and working for 'the firm'. Fodens thought it best to put me through a complete course of training which would make an engineer of me. As matters turned out I got through only the first six months of this, which were spent, logically enough, in the foundry where the basic bits and pieces were made. The work was dirty, hot, in some ways potentially dangerous — one developed a healthy respect for liquid aluminium at 1100 degrees — and thoroughly enjoyable. Perhaps it is not surprising that musicians, who spend their lives producing an intangible, get a kick out of working with their hands. Among my colleagues have been first-rate motor mechanics, furniture makers and designers, bookbinders, artists and of course violin makers. I got a great deal of pleasure from the foundry. We went to work at crack of dawn on a pile of sand on the foundry floor, and with the help of wooden forms and patterns formed boxed sand-moulds. Into these, near the end of the day, we poured the hot metal. Just before the whistle the mould was opened and — with luck — out came a gleaming silver-pink gearbox-housing, or perhaps even a crankcase for the new Foden diesel engine. No doubt the craft — almost an art — of sand-moulding has long since been overtaken by technology. It is difficult to mourn the loss of a job which was done in an atmosphere so obviously killing, but I loved it; and not the least good thing about it was the quality of the men who did it.

The band was a constant subject of factory jokes, a cover for the pride of all concerned. It was hard for these hard-working chaps to take seriously an apprentice who might vanish into thin air without notice when required by the BBC or for a concert tour. Leg-pulling was inevitable, but the only days when we bandsmen felt that our workmates disapproved of us were the ones on which we *failed* to win the National Brass Band Championship. In the eyes of the firm, winning that prize was what the band was all about. Some people quite reasonably complained that this sometimes seemed to be what the company itself was all about; but in a firm whose managing director had played the euphonium in the first Fodens Band of 1900, such treasonable thoughts were quickly suppressed.

At this time a seed was sown which would ripen only ten years later. My father, trying to keep me in touch with academic matters, introduced me to the music-master of our local grammar school, a splendid musician and pianist. Browsing through my music he found Mozart's *Voi che sapete*. This was not known to me. We played it together. Thus I met Mozart. He and I have been in touch ever since. And over supper that wise man played to me a recording of Bach's Third Suite, made by the LSO with one George Eskdale playing the trumpet. Suddenly I realised that the trumpet could speak with a voice I had not heard and that there might be excitements in store of which I had not yet dreamed. My mentor wanted to say, I think, 'Forget the brass band and the cornet; take up the trumpet, cram for university; learn music rather than brass technique; aim much higher.'

No-one would have listened.

The big decisions, though, are rarely ours. Somewhere in the War Office a gnome had decided that a career in motor engineering and amateur music was not for me. Upon my doormat dropped a message in a small brown envelope, inviting me in pressing terms to serve His Majesty King George the Sixth as a conscript in the Army.

This was unexpected. We had thought Fodens Motor Works better organised than to allow their solo cornetist to be kidnapped in this careless fashion. There was, though, a more comfortable option than real soldiering. The bands of the Brigade of Guards were avid for first-rate brass players. I was offered my choice of the five. I took advice of those already serving and discovered that there were only two options for a civilised musician. I must join the Scots Guards or the Welsh. I met both Directors of Music and took instantly to Sam Rhodes, of the Scots Guards. I offered my services to him confident that I would be able to purchase my discharge from the Army after two years, as the custom then was. Alas, on the day of my enlistment our nation was struck by one or other of its small national emergencies and this privilege was withdrawn. The die seemed to be firmly and most unpleasantly cast.

CHAPTER 3
Bearskin and Boots
(Allegro Marziale)

I took the King's Shilling in February 1949, making my escape with the blessed permission of his daughter in 1953, five months early.

Most old soldiers, even those who hated the whole thing at the time, think of the Army as having been a good thing. It was truly good for me. The Army was a first-rate crash course in growing up. I did that very quickly in the band of the Scots Guards. Happily for me, the regiment was much kinder to musicians than to Guardsman-recruits. Not for us the dreaded Caterham Depot, with its endless squarebashing under man-eating Sar'n't-Majors. I was billeted with the Corps of Drums of the Welsh Guards at Wellington Barracks. These gentlemen were entrusted with the task of teaching me foot drill, that being the only military skill required of the Guards musician in my time.

Drummers usually enlist as boy soldiers. Many of those who made up my daily drill-squad were still boys in army terms. They were very streetwise young men and they taught me a lot. Beside the routine survival skills of brass 'shining' (easy), and toecap polishing (an art, believe me), I learned to press tomorrow's kit by sleeping on it. If badly done this could result in double creases and an appearance before the Regimental Adjutant on a charge of 'Idle sleeping'. Like thousands before me I learned to salute anything which moved and to blanco anything which did not, and to get the mandatory one foot on the floor within thirty seconds of Reveille, often without waking up. I also learned never to leave my locker open when out of the room. Darwin's theory of the survival of the fittest was very well taught at Wellington Barracks. I got fit and I survived, just.

At five feet three inches I was a formidable challenge for the quartermaster who kitted me out. The result of his work was striking, especially when dressed in the long grey-blue winter overcoat and topped off with the famous bearskin cap. The coat ended six inches above my boots, its pockets barely within reach. My bearskin was enormous. On seeing my uniformed reflection in the mirror for the first time I decided that the Brigade of Guards had no sense of humour. I was wrong; among many valuable things I was to learn from the Guards was a capacity for silent and po-faced amusement.

Once dressed, on with the drill. Our drill was not pretty. One memorable morning we were spotted at a distance (we could not always find a secluded place in which to practise) by an appalled d ill-sergeant who decided, in the national interest, to 'sort us out'. Ten minutes of embarrassing agony ensued. When both he and we were exhausted he delivered a blistering lecture on the British infantryman's essential need to know the right foot from the left, ending with the rhetorical gem ' 'Orrible, that's what you are, 'orrible! Gawd, oojer fink you are? The Regimental Band?'

From this I gathered that once off the drill square I would not be too much troubled by drill. This was true. The military achievement of the Guards' bands, all five, was very limited indeed. True, we had people who had been near as dammit soldiers, having joined line regiments as youngsters and graduated by promotion to the Guards. One such told me in the course of an argument that he had been in Baghdad when I was in Dad's bag. But at least half our membership were, like me, civilians who wanted nothing to do with guns and were simply trying, during their military service, to preserve their musical skills. Drill, and the spit-and-polish inseparable from it, adjusted to a common level. We civvies did our best and the old soldiers consciously relaxed. The result might have been described as a vaguely polite gesture to good order and military discipline.

The ethos of the Guards' musician was once well summed up by our Director of Music: 'Some of us play concertos; some play the piano at Buck House investitures; some can blow through Trooping the Colour without permanent damage to their embouchures; some are good for nothing but shining buttons, polishing boots and keeping us all out of trouble on inspection days. The band has a job to do and you all contribute.'

A remarkable thing was the way this common purpose formed friendships between men of widely different backgrounds; between the orphan soldier-boy who had known and would know nothing but the Army, and the gifted son of a middle-class family, polished by a grammar school and the Royal Academy of Music and destined perhaps for the Royal Philharmonic on the day of his discharge.

Our Director, Lieutenant-Colonel Rhodes, known to us as 'The Guv'nor' or when safely out of earshot as Sam, was a character so extraordinary as to invite caricature or even ridicule. If the first is almost irresistible the second would be unfair. Rhodes was a remarkable man of great integrity in an insulated world where the abuse of power was all too easy. If he was by some standards a freak, then he was made such by the inevitable conflict of two arts — the military and the musical. Sam Rhodes loved music. Whether he loved the Army or nor — he had been a bandboy and knew no other life — he recognised a total obligation to it. A lifetime's determination to reconcile the two had produced a unique personality fit for nothing else but to be Senior Director of Music in the Brigade of Guards. This job he discharged with awesome efficiency.

There was simply nothing Sam did not know about the military band and its repertoire. A bass player, he had learned his skill from the bottom up: the classical way. No more complete product ever passed the gates of the Royal Military School of Music. His ears were superb, missing nothing, so that intonation and precision in 'The Scots' was legendary. His stick technique was not pretty but it never failed; no, never. His knowledge of music in general was encyclopaedic.

Among his known recreations was playing the classical repertoire on his double bass from memory to accompany orchestral broadcasts. Yet with all this technical command he produced no music from that band, packed though it was with fine players. The reason was simple and military: Sam did not conduct; he commanded. Every entry, every phrase, every detail of his performances was done precisely to order and at his exact direction. He gave every entry, literally. Woe betide the man who missed one, having been fed with it. Equally unfortunate the man who made one before it was given; he would of course be wrong. Sam never was. He aspired to the complete control of an organ-grinder. Nothing moved unless he moved it. But when a conductor demands of musicians only notes to order, that is all he will get. Sam produced technical perfection by musical drill movements; military music.

Among the more eccentric foibles retained from his early life in 'the line' was a need to know, when a mistake was made, the identity of the criminal — because to Sam he was no less. We were obliged to 'own up' in performance by making some sign. Punishment, other than a characteristic and tigerish snarl, was rare, but *Sam had to know.*

A raised finger was enough to satisfy him, though some of my friends preferred to raise their right hands in the manner of a schoolboy wishing to leave the room. This was equally acceptable. There came a magic occasion, inevitably, when a mistake was admitted but not heard. The look of panic on Sam's face was wonderful to see. the poor man instantly doubted the most important tools of his trade — his ears. There were nose-blowings and ear-pullings galore. This was great fun. At last we had found a discipline-proof means of pulling the Guv'nor's leg. When life needed pepping up, thereafter, all we had to do was to raise a finger and laugh — but silently.

Sam rarely laughed, and since a massive inferiority complex caused him to assume that he was the cause of any amusement exhibited by anyone within a four-mile radius we never laughed when he was about. I was myself the cause of a rare near-collapse of this collective discipline on my first appearance with the band. It was within a week of my enlistment; the occasion a Rugby International at Twickenham, where we supplied the warmup music before the match. The sight is familiar; the band formed in a circle around the centre spot, the Director of Music walking from the tunnel to begin. As he arrives the band is called to attention, the Band Sergeant-Major salutes and is saluted. On this occasion Sam approached from an angle which screened me from his view. Turning to salute he enjoyed his first sight of my remarkable ensemble, from bearskin to boots. Undeniably his face cracked. Perhaps indeed only his brass kerbchain, screening the vital part of his craggy face from view, saved the day. The band, watching him carefully, moved not a muscle, nor was so much as a chuckle heard. I hope today's regimental musicians are capable of such discipline.

That occasion left one other impression on my mind, or, to put the case more accurately, on the side of my head. I had done no drill at that time, so I was carefully tucked away in the middle of the band for marching. My instructions were simply to follow the man in front and never to move without everyone else. Came the match-interval, came the march and countermarch on the pitch. I made all the right moves but one. No-one had warned me to give the bass drum a wide berth as it passed. I am a small man. Our bass drummer was not. My head was accurately aligned with the centre of the drum. The blow struck my kerb-chain, a feeble shock-absorber. The brass was simply thumped into my face. My head was still spinning when the match ended.

Once through the preliminaries the life of a Guards musician was one of relaxed, nearly professional music-making interspersed with periods of military activity which could be very uncomfortable indeed. I use the word 'nearly' because music-making can never be entirely happy nor relaxed when a mistake can cost a week's loss of liberty. Curiously this rarely happened in the Scots. Sam's personal grip on his band was so complete that the Regimental Adjutant was rarely troubled with disciplinary proceedings.

Our working week, barring interference from the War Office — which had a troublesome habit of disturbing our almost civilian existence with the odd recruiting tour to Scotland or a week or two with a battalion in Tripolitania — was a very civilised one. Unless called for a military occasion on Monday (and with five bands sharing Guardmounting at Buck House and the Guard changing only every two days we were not much troubled in that way) we were always free. This was a traditional arrangement owed to the routine of the music-hall orchestras, then a very important part of London's musical life, which demanded a Monday morning rehearsal. Many among us were busy in that way and Birdcage Walk could not have held on to the best of its talent had the concession not been maintained. For the rest of the week we practised each morning for two hours, from ten o'clock. Thursday was clear for pay-parade. Sunday could mean Church at the Guards' Chapel — another duty shared by five bands in rotation — but we were little troubled by parades except during the early summer, when Trooping the Colour meant work of the worst kind.

Trooping, the Queen's Birthday Parade, was a killer: a day on which the Regimental Bands were put through a military hoop worse than that endured by the battalions on parade. They were fit. We were not. It was the day, I suppose, when we earned our five pounds a week.

It was a Trooping which provided the ultimate demonstration of Sam's military-musical skills. At one of the early rehearsals for this parade the officer in charge remarked that the massed bands were untidy; it was not acceptable, he thought, that the trombones, placed as they were at the forefront of the massed bands, should go in and out at different times. Trombones ought to move together and preferably out on the left foot and in on the right.

A lesser Director of Music would have pointed out that the slides are at the disposal of the composer and beyond the control of a bandmaster. Not our Sam. Away went the trombone parts, to return completely rescored. Now the trombonists moved in and out at the same time; not necessarily on the feet asked by the General, but at least together. From the musicians' viewpoint, lunacy; from another, professionalism; perhaps, after all, Sam had a sense of humour.

The 'First Band', with the best twenty-five players, was known as the Plum Band. We Plums were constantly busy with concerts and broadcasting. For this work we were paid, so as not to offend the Musicians' Union. The pay was pitifully small, and for me membership of the Plums was a mixed blessing. Since I was very much the junior soldier throughout my service — turnover in the Plums being slow indeed — I was the inevitable choice for the duties of 'music orderly', with the privilege of transporting the band's music wherever it went. Repertoire was contained in massive leather binders. The binders lived in an immense wicker skip. There was often no transport and certainly no money for taxis. I have a vivid memory of hauling that basket from Chessington station to the Zoo and back in July heat, clad in red tunic and serge trousers. No joke.

Each regiment had a 'String Band'. Polite musical society might euphemistically have called it a salon orchestra. Besides strings it used the best of the Plum wind and brass. Since we had but few string players, and these were at best second-study people, the string band's performance was, to put it mildly, less than professional. Sam was a good double-bass, a better string player than any we had. Consequently his fuse burned short and fast on String-Band days. To make matters worse, these were usually prestigious occasions when we ran the risk of serious scrutiny. We played often at Government receptions and on occasions of state at the Palace.

Investitures, interminable mornings, were the worst. We were shut into the organ-loft above the milling throng before the business began, to entertain the apparently endless crocodile of those to be honoured with selections from *The Maid of the Mountains, The Chocolate Soldier*, and many another long-dead epic of the West End stage. Even *Chu Chin Chow* was not unknown. Our defensive trick was to use the wind and brass to cover the awful deficiencies of the string-playing. This, unfortunately, pushed up the volume of the music. Then the telephone would ring and the Guv'nor would be told to shut us up. It became a game, creeping up on that faceless man at the other end of the line, to see whether we could reach a tolerable *mezzoforte* without being stopped. He always won.

Minor royals would sometimes creep into our eyrie to see some friend or some favourite of stage and screen tapped with the sword, rising from the knee with the certainty that restaurant-tables and seat-reservations would now be more easily available – though at the cost of much larger tips. By the end of the morning we felt that we were ourselves due for a gong or two. Our reward was very different. Yes, we were given refreshment, in the servants' hall. There we would find, laid out upon scrubbed bare boards, a loaf of bread with a knife, a pound of butter, a pot of jam, with a bottle of beer for each of us; neither more nor less. The Queen's housekeeping was meticulous. We always spent five minutes in arranging these luxuries in an ingenious if precarious pyramid before leaving for the nearest pub.

People went to extraordinary lengths to avoid the String Band. Many creditable second-study string players spent their entire pensionable service in the regimental band without being found out, while making a decent sort of living from fiddle or viola in the music-hall.

We had very little money but we all managed to rent bedsits, it being thought very bad form for a musician to live in barracks, a very uncomfortable option in any case. Some of us did a lot of practice. Others developed a talent for snooker within the facilities kindly provided, in Trafalgar Square, by Lord Nuffield for members of HM Forces. To study music was easy; the finest teachers in the kingdom were within reach, often quite cheaply or even free at the various centres of learning. It was an easy life, and an ideal one for the lazy; something one could easily do for twenty-two years or so and emerge with a pension. For me it was simply a civilised prison. I wanted nothing, from the day I got in, but to get out. I thought the whole thing a great waste of public money in the sense that all the duties of the five bands of the Brigade could have been done in comfort by one band of ninety rather than five of sixty members each. All I can say in its favour, as I look back over the years, is that it gave training to a number of wind players who went on to become pillars of our orchestral establishment. I am sure, though, that the benefit they gained in this way was not so much musical nor technical but personal. They learned to make the best of direction which was often very crude; if not quite to suffer fools gladly, perhaps to suffer them politely and with self-restraint. This can be a useful skill in the orchestra, where the wrong man on the rostrum can so easily drive the less disciplined personality over the temperamental top, often with disastrous professional results. Yes, it was good for me.

I practised, then, as never before. It was a defensive measure because the military band was bad for me as a player. The sheer physical slog – nearly everything we did was out of doors – and the musical navvying which composed our programmes, were light-years away from the sophisticated brass-playing of my former life. I studied hard too, using the Guildhall School. It is impossible for a young musician however limited his background, to spend five years in London without absorbing by osmosis a great deal of music. In those days the Philharmonia, in its first incarnation under Walter Legge, vied for primacy with the Royal Philharmonic. Listening to both I was excited by their wonderful trumpeters. Harold Jackson of the Philharmonia was a product of the Black Dyke Band, I knew. While Fodens Band was still important to me – and I travelled there whenever I could – I began to interest myself in the trumpet at the expense of my faithful cornet. I bought one. I worked at transposition and at the difficult passages of the orchestral repertoire. My mistake was to hesitate. Most of my Army service was spent within two miles of the Royal College of Music, yet I never climbed its steps to meet its fabled trumpet professor, Ernest Hall.

Curiously, people began to feed me work with the trumpet; nothing glamorous, of course, but I learned from it. Naturally I was given the dates at the tail end of the market, the unwanted ones. My first truly professional job in the orchestra was a performance of *The Tales of Hoffman* in the Corn Exchange, Ipswich. Then in a little while I was given a plum by accident. John Tobin, an early enthusiast of what has now become authentic Handel, gave a performance of *Messiah* at St Paul's with the London Choral Society and a very fine 'scratch' orchestra. Only when rehearsal had begun did I realise that we were in for *Messiah* complete with the *da capo* arias, and that I must face the dreaded *Trumpet shall sound* not once but twice that evening. This was the reason the date had been passed down the line of refusals until it arrived at my door. I survived, just, with the help of a generous second trumpet who played a few life-saving bars of the aria for me. It has been good to see my rescuer spend a happy and successful career in the BBC Symphony Orchestra, and now comfortably retired. A Samaritan indeed.

This was the beginning of good things for BG, trumpeter. The performance was repeated. It was played at the Royal Festival Hall and on the radio. It is hard to imagine, in these enlightened days, that *da capo* Handel, with cadenzas and counter-tenors, could cause such a stir. Anyway, it advertised me, and it obliged me to work at the trumpet. The BBC gave me a performance of the Haydn Concerto with its Concert Orchestra. I played my first Mozart symphony in Studio One at Maida Vale, the young Colin Davis conducting. Colin was also a soldier then, in the Life Guards. I must ask my friend one day whether a clarinetist wearing a steel helmet and cuirass, sitting on a horse and vainly trying to get music out of the wobbling instrument, feels as big a chump as he looks. The mounted bands are pure circus.

Time passed, slowly at first and then *accelerando*, in the way it does for soldiers, convicts and the aging. Discharge, for so long regarded as paradise, now loomed as a practical problem. One would be rid of the boots but one still had to live. Fodens Band was doing well enough without me. None of the others seemed attractive. The orchestra presented itself not as an option but as a necessity. I began to audition. This was less terrifying for me than for most of my colleagues; I had always been better at solo performance. Unfortunately I was ill-equipped in terms of orchestral know-how. A well-prepared concerto was one thing, and much enjoyed by the listening panels. They were surprised to find me stumped by a few bars of a popular ballet or a symphony of Vaughan Williams. After many disappointments the BBC took pity on me and promised me something in the Concert Orchestra. Not the Philharmonia, perhaps, but work.

Happy with this promise I set out for a long summer season with the Guards. Returning weeks later to London I found the offer had evaporated with a change of managerial policy. Disaster! Then a friend telephoned to say that while I had been away the City of Birmingham Symphony Orchestra had advertised for a first trumpet. Why not apply?

There were many good reasons, chief among them the fact that I was hopelessly unqualified for the work, but I had nothing to lose. I wrote a letter. On the following morning came a telephone call to say that the CBSO had long since finished auditioning. A choice had been made, but they were not completely satisfied nor committed. If I could get to Birmingham before two o'clock that day, when Rudolf

Schwarz, their Music Director, must leave for his holiday in Sweden, I would be heard.

I had the day off. I grabbed my trumpet, on which I had not practised for six weeks, ran for the train, pausing only to buy a piano-score of the Haydn concerto at Boosey's in Regent Street, and presented myself at the Town Hall at one o'clock.

CHAPTER 4

Out of the Frying-Pan

Rudolf Schwarz was waiting, smoking a small cigarette, seated at a concert grand in the centre of the stage. A slight, dapper figure in a grey pin-stripe suit, silver hair carefully combed back, blue eyes above high cheek-bones looking directly but kindly into my own, he was the archetypal Viennese Jewish musician. The resemblance to Gustav Mahler was lost on me at the time since I knew nothing of Mahler, but I have never since been able to look at a Mahler photograph without being reminded of this marvellous man.

We were introduced, and shook hands while he stubbed out his cigarette. I offered my piano score. He received it gracefully and put it down unopened on the piano top. We tuned, and he began to play the slow movement of my Haydn concerto from memory. I had never before played with a pianist of such sympathy and musicality. Getting the job, I knew, was unlikely; but it had been worth coming here to play like this. The work over, Schwarz made the briefest comment; it was a byword in the CBSO. 'Nice', he said. 'Now some passages from the orchestra'. I resigned myself to the inevitable. But I was lucky today. The CBSO was on holiday, the in-house library was very limited, and the special material brought in for trumpet-auditions had been returned to publishers. Very little was available with which to put me through the hoop. I was shown Rimsky's *Scheherazade*, which is technically difficult but no trouble to a brass-band expert, Bax's *Tintagel*, which is strenuous but needs little purely orchestral expertise, and some parts of Strauss' *Rosenkavalier*, mercifully in the concert suite version which is easy to read. All went extremely well. After the first extract Schwarz walked away and to the back of the hall. I realised that he had twigged a weakness; my inability at that time to project sound at symphonic volume. This could not be hidden. He would accept it and hope for improvement or he would discard. It was down to the man and his judgement.

Returning, he asked me about my orchestral experience. I came absolutely clean; just as well, since he had already assessed it as practically nil. 'Mr Gay,' he asked, 'you can play the trumpet, but experience is necessary in the symphony orchestra of course. Why do you think you can do this job?'

I gave the only answer possible. 'I can play the trumpet. I can read music. I am not afraid of audiences. I learn very quickly. Why not?'

He was unconvinced. 'Tell me, do you know the *Leonora* trumpet call?'

From various collections of orchestral material I knew that there were several possibilities here. 'The B flat, or the E flat from the Second overture?'

He smiled kindly, recognising my gamesmanship. 'The B flat will be enough'. So I played it.

Still he hesitated, tempted but even more aware of my handicap than I was. 'One more thing. I will write it down for you.' Taking a pencil he carefully drew a stave on the back of my still unopened Haydn and wrote:

This also I recognised from a collection of 'hard bits' published for students. It's from the coda of the first movement of the second symphony of Brahms; one of the nightmare passages for trumpeters before the machines themselves improved so helpfully. 'Ah', said I sagely, 'Brahms ...' In another second I would have added 'three'. This might have cost me the job. My hesitation saved me. I was not even required to play the passage. Schwarz smiled broadly. 'All right, Mr Gay. Welcome to the CBSO! But be careful to prepare everything. You and I are taking a big risk together!'

I was now the youngest salaried first trumpet in the British profession; out on a swaying limb and living and playing by my wits.

I have met Brahms in D major many times since, and never without wondering whether I could have played that passage that day. It's never been easy.

CHAPTER 5
Splash!
(First subject, with some development)

In the swim, then! Not at the deep end, but still out of my depth and without the waterwings which even a year at the RCM would have provided. In this perilous situation the state of the water was crucial to my survival. Let's look at my new environment.

Until the creation of the BBC Symphony in 1930, Britain had only one 'permanent' orchestra: the Bournemouth Municipal.

Yes, the Hallé will claim its centenary and more. The Royal Liverpool and the Royal Scottish Orchestra claim long and glorious histories; even the CBSO will point to first performances of *Elijah*, conducted by Mendelssohn, and *Gerontius*, conducted by Elgar, as evidence of an orchestral tradition in Birmingham; but in the sense that the important continental centres possessed permanent orchestras – and indeed opera houses – throughout the 19th century and many of them earlier than that, such claims are feeble. Until late in the second world war all our regional orchestras were created seasonally, playing weekly through the autumn and winter, and dissolving in spring.

Manchester came closest to the continental ideal, perhaps because it was during the last century a very German town. When Hallé formed his orchestra, first for an exhibition and then for his 'Gentlemen's Concerts', he was doing something he thought obviously necessary, however extraordinary the notion may have seemed to Lancashire at large. His first season showed a profit of half-a-crown, an unsubsidised feat which would be universally applauded today. But Hallé did not pay his players permanently. They went to Buxton, Scarborough, Bath, or Hastings for the summer.

As in Manchester so it was in Liverpool and Glasgow. Seasonal orchestras, playing perhaps from October to May, dispersed to the seaside or to various spa towns for the rest of the year. On the pier or in the pumproom new talent was assessed and dead wood identified before the symphony orchestras reassembled, often very much changed, in the autumn.

This is not always a bad system. Most of the symphony orchestras of the USA still work in that way, and many old hands in the UK remembered it with affection; but it does not amount to the building of a properly constituted orchestra serving its home city the year round. That is, and always will be, a large public undertaking; one fraught with financial risk and usually loud with the grinding of political axes.

In London the situation before 1930 was actually worse than in the provinces. Henry Wood's orchestra laid the foundation of London's orchestral life on an *ad hoc* basis; it almost collapsed in 1904 when 'Timber' refused further to allow the deputy system, rife within it. Its members could not afford to sacrifice their other work in the good cause of better performances at the Queen's Hall. The London Symphony Orchestra, our first orchestral republic, resulted. It is a marvellous orchestra, and one with a unique spirit. It's interesting to watch, as the century wanes, the way in which the deputy system which gave it birth gives way to the demand for consistent performance. Perhaps by its centenary the circle will be complete? This loose association of players formed the lasting pattern of the London orchestras. The Philharmonia, the Royal Philharmonic and the London Philharmonic all became self-managing as promptly as their original sponsors left them to their financial fate. All still thrive. Their resilience is amazing.

The BBC Symphony, then, was unique at its formation. It offered to principal players as much as fifteen pounds a week, with sick pay and two weeks' holiday each year. In 1930 such a sum would have paid eight coal-miners. such security had never before been dreamed of by orchestral players. They queued to get in.

The effect on other orchestras was severe; so much of the best talent was suddenly denied to them. Hamilton Harty, the Irish genius who had made the Hallé the best of our orchestras, resigned in protest not only at the blow to 'Hallé's Band' but at radio's threat, as he and many others then believed, to live music. Yet it is to the BBC that we owe not only its own permanent orchestras but many others. In Manchester, Hallé players for many years provided a small studio band for broadcasting. Then in 1943 the BBC decided to set up a second symphony orchestra, the Northern, today's BBC Philharmonic. Hallé players were obliged to choose, and they chose – to the consternation of a Hallé management then hovering on the brink of the formation of a permanent orchestra of its own — the BBC.

The formation of the permanent Hallé is another story, but it was part, too, of a general organising of orchestras throughout the UK. The wartime ENSA, which entertained fighting men the world over, having become in due time the Council for the Encouragement of Music and the Arts, finally emerged from that chrysalis as The Arts Council of Great Britain. The Arts Council had money — little enough, as it still has — for orchestral subsidies. Manchester, Liverpool, Bournemouth, Glasgow and Birmingham all held out their begging bowls, received their pittances and set to. Music Directors were appointed, players were sought and auditioned. As the Second World War ended a whole new orchestral world was created.

What kind of orchestras were they which erupted into being in what we then called the provinces? Two factors conditioned them: the talent available and the skill of their choosing among that talent.

There was a dearth of good players. The fit were still away fighting. The music-schools were not geared up for mass-production. In Manchester, Barbirolli, tempted home from New York with the promise of the prewar Hallé as a basis for rebuilding, found himself with little more than a handful — the remainder having opted for the BBC. He was reduced to auditioning among, as he loved to recount, 'the lame and the halt'. A fine orchestra emerged, composed of some of the most likeable unlikely characters ever found on the concert platform. In Birmingham the young George Weldon was given the task of forming a new permanent symphony orchestra with the advantage of better civic support than that of Manchester. His disadvantage was in serving a populace which in those days seemed almost to take pride in philistinism.

The provision of an orchestra, even a seasonal one, in Birmingham must always have been an uphill task. The young Adrian Boult had done pioneering work there until the BBC tempted him away to their irresistible symphony orchestra. The talented Leslie Heward succeeded him, but Birmingham had never developed the experienced symphonic body, albeit a seasonal one, which was found in Manchester or Liverpool. In putting his orchestra together, Weldon relied too much on local talent which lacked real quality.

His reputation grew, nevertheless. Weldon seemed positively to enjoy that repertoire which the public demanded as part of its immediate post-war diet: a wave of Tchaikowsky, Rachmaninoff and Grieg. There was in those days an apparently insatiable appetite for romantic piano concertos, and economics demanded bums-on-seats. To be fair to Weldon it must be said that he was an enthusiastic advocate of British artists and British music, and encouraged both when his budget permitted it. Walton, Bliss and Elgar were among his 'good things'. His public was large and loyal.

It was not long, though, before the CBSO looked for a change of direction. Their choice, when it came, was controversial. Rudolf Schwarz was an Austrian Jew. A promising career in his own country had been cut short by the rise of Fascism. After suffering terribly in the Holocaust he recuperated in Sweden, from where he had been invited to rebuild the Bournemouth Municipal Orchestra. His success with both orchestra and public had been complete. Birmingham's decision was fine and far-sighted, but Schwarz was not a natural choice for Birmingham; not an easy figure to sell to orchestra nor public in a city parochial to the point of chauvinism.

When I arrived Schwarz had been in Birmingham for two years already; years during which he'd become no more popular with the old guard of orchestra and public for his determined removal of the more obvious weaknesses among the players. Fortunately for me he had provided a marvellous first trombone in Denis Wick, who immediately organised a first-rate trombone section. Before this team inevitably removed itself to the LSO it gave me a fine model for my own orchestral style and also strong moral support in a difficult situation among the trumpets. One of my colleagues had been demoted to make room for me, while the other had expected the place given to me. Each confidently expected my failure. Three weeks was the life predicted for me in that seat, I believe. Happily these people were polite to me and did me no practical harm since I was oblivious of their feelings and totally absorbed by the challenge of the work.

The challenge was immense. The CBSO had enlarged, that year, by ten players — a feat made possible by the generosity of a local shoe-maker, who had donated ten thousand pounds annually for three years. Schwarz' repertoire, never modest, looked to new horizons. His programmes would have caused any London concert promoter to blanch. This has been the case in the regions, to some extent, ever since. Those orchestras, with their serial bookings, loyal audiences, and lack of local competition, have always been on safer ground than metropolitan ones with regard to programme planning.

During the first four days, when we gave advance rehearsal to the season's most interesting new material, I was force-fed with Strauss' *Don Juan* and *Don Quixote*, Hindemith's *Mathis der Maler* Symphony, Vaughan Williams' *Antarctica*, and Elgar's *Falstaff*. The worst was yet to come, though. Over the first weekend we played concerts out-of-town as a warmup for the Birmingham season and as these were of basic repertoire they were done on very cursory 'corner-turning' rehearsals; not even a complete run-through of the work. In that way I played in public the Fourth of Tchaikowsky, the *New World* of Dvořák and − terror of terrors − Sibelius' Second, none of which had I even heard before. Lucky it was, as I had told Schwarz, that I could play the trumpet, read music, and was not afraid of audiences. I was reduced at times to learning tomorrow's repertoire, note by note, while travelling home each night. Commuter trains in those days had no corridors and fortunately they rattled and shook much less than they do today. With the aid of a mute I was often able to sort out difficulties in transit. But the strain, mental, physical and emotional, was no joke.

Such a state of affairs is quite impossible to imagine today. Nowadays an advertisement by a symphony orchestra for a first trumpet meets a response of perhaps fifty bright young graduates, all thoroughly genned-up on the repertoire, any one of whom would have played me comfortably out of my opportunity. Yes, I *could* play the instrument, and perhaps more musically than most of today's RCM output. But no sensible Music Director would today make the choice Schwarz made then. The safe alternatives would be too tempting. As a manager I would say, too, that I would not willingly put a young player under such a strain. I know what it cost me.

It was a little late for study now, but it was very necessary: a fact recognised by my new employers, who kindly added ten shillings a week to my contractual sixteen pounds so that I might travel to London monthly for the purpose. At last I met Ernest Hall. The great man, teacher of almost every first trumpet in the land at that time, must have questioned the sanity of a management which had passed over half-a-dozen ready-made and Hallmarked products in my favour. Still he was kind. He admired my technique, which, brass-band trained, took most orchestral passagework at a gallop, and he showed me what a royal sound the trumpet can make and how much of it. He was convinced from the outset that a chap of my size could never make sound on his own scale, and that my approach must be different from his own. This argument I refused to accept. Polished small-scale stuff I could provide without difficulty and without further teaching; but all my playing life conductors would demand *quantity*. The fact that I struggled for it shows that EH was right about my potential but wrong about the wisdom of accepting my limitation. He was certainly right about everything else in the world of the trumpet, and I am grateful that I learned from him, just in time, what trumpeting can be.

CHAPTER 6
The Teacher
AND
The Daddy of Them All

My new job was an ideal one for any young musician with talent and enthusiasm to exchange for experience. Much more than a conductor, Rudolf Schwarz was a natural teacher of the art of music, an art which so often eludes experts in its theory and technique.

There is a story that while working as assistant to Georg Szell in a German opera house Schwarz had seen Toscanini conduct, had realised that all his work as a conductor so far had been mistaken, and had tendered his resignation to Szell. Szell persuaded him to continue, learning from the Toscanini experience. Certainly there was in Schwarz, as in Toscanini, a rare dedication to the composer. It was not enough that he did what he believed the composer wished; it was important to him that we all knew and understood *why*.

This is where ordinary conducting parts company from the work of the teacher.

It is also where hard cases in the orchestra part company with enthusiastic youngsters. So there were two attitudes to Schwarz within the CBSO, in roughly equal measure. We who wished to learn were educated and inspired by him. Those who wished merely to make a living found him hard work.

Rudi was easy to knock if that was what one wished, because in the physical sense he was unusually limited. Whether, as we suspected, he had been cruelly deformed by the Nazis I do not know; but his arms were never seen to extend fully. This made for an odd technique. Players for whom 'a clear beat' is the beginning and ending of conductorship wrote him off, as they would presumably have written off Furtwängler, Klemperer and Goodall on that account. They have a case of a primitive sort, and that case is strengthened as the pressure of work on the player increases. This may explain why Schwarz, after succeeding in Birmingham and Bournemouth, failed to carry the judgement of the London public and critics. But that was in the future. In the early fifties Birmingham was his platform, and well he served it.

The knockers had another tool to hand: a bent one, but convenient. It was hardly possible for a Jewish soloist to appear in a CBSO programme without some orchestral wit observing that here was 'yet another fine old English Gentleman'. This was xenophobia, I'm sure, rather than anti-semitism. It is difficult to think of today's cosmopolitan Birmingham as a tight, provincial, England-for-the-English community; but forty years ago, with the dust still settling on its bombed sites, such it was. Again, Weldon's orchestra had a warm personal affection for Weldon, a very English Englishman. Schwarz' appointment was more disliked because of Schwarz' nationality than for his race.

This attitude could not long survive, given the nature of the man, the wealth of his talent, and the generosity of his giving. Music was truly his life. It was as though he felt his own miraculous preservation to be meaningless except as the vehicle for his talent. Conducting as an ego-trip was unthinkable to him, perhaps because he had seen with what ease the ego is extinguished. Long before his departure he had achieved the unanimous support of his orchestra and the love of his public. He had become, in a sense, the CBSO. It was my privilege to be part of that happy process.

Rudi's rehearsals were a unique combination of practice and discussion. Our early philistines used to ask 'What time is tomorrow's lecture?' He did indeed talk a great deal, smoking the while. Utterly nicotine-dependant ('I am sympathetic to the cigarette but not to the sweet-paper'), since he never had time to smoke a complete cigarette while rehearsing, he carried a case of very cheap ones, cut into halves, for rehearsal use. These he smoked gracefully through his cigarette-holder while discussing the music.

He liked to begin with a complete run-through of a movement. This was usually followed by a minutely detailed verbal critique, amounting to total demolition, invariably concluding with a polite and encouraging smile and the words 'Otherwise nice!'. This catchphrase we applied to disasters of all kinds, including road-accidents observed from the bus while on tour.

There is a theory, propounded by amateur commentators, that conductors belong either to the Furtwängler (espressivo, rubato, untidy but rather fetching) school or to the Toscanini (precisely rhythmic, dogmatic, back-to-the-autograph-and-concede-nothing) varieties. If this has any truth at all then Rudi was certainly of the second. He very much disliked questionable tradition (Mahler's *Schlamperei*) and would say of such things 'Where did you find that *ritard*? Is Tchaikowsky so stupid or so lazy that he could not write *ritard* if he wanted one? No! He is a careful man!' And so we would cheerfully demolish a tradition taught by Nikisch in Leipzig 70 years earlier, and translated by his pupil Boult to these very boards in the 'thirties.

Schwarz' English, in the early days, could be quaint. To a fourth horn, struggling with a phrase in the *Dutchman* overture, he once said diffidently 'Forgive me, but I can find no other word and to me it sounds *lousy* ...'

That this brought a chuckle from us all, not excluding the player concerned, speaks volumes for the feeling we had for the man and his problem.

With the Viennese classics Schwarz was at his very best, and above all with Schubert. His Great C Major was superb. His instinct for tempo was infallible, and here is a work in which so much depends on tempo. Schumann wrote of its 'heavenly length'; the orchestra knows how easily it can become hellishly tedious. In Schwarz' hands the first movement surged with optimism, the second sang with natural ease, the scherzo danced. The finale did not so much consume the energy of the orchestra as generate its own. The effect was of a turbine, of flywheel-momentum so irresistible that there seemed no way of stopping it. When it ended we were left with the feeling that somewhere Schubert's spinning cosmos went on and on. So it will, so long as such musicians live to give him life.

Long in advance of today's critical acceptance, he believed Schumann to be a great symphonist. His Schumann was heavily edited, though stopping well short of Mahler's re-orchestrations. He excelled in Dvořák and Smetana, and on lighter occasions he revelled in the *Rumanian Rhapsodies* of Enesco and the *Hungarians* of Liszt. Of Wagner he played very little other than the *Siegfried Idyll*, leaving opera for my future discovery. In those days, when Bartok was still a freak, he gave Birmingham the kindest of introductions, the Second Piano Concerto.

Schwarz was a tireless worker, too, in the cause of British music. We had not, in the 'fifties, today's thriving horde of young composers.

Britten was still an oddball, Tippett even more so. Schwarz rejoiced in both, and suffered many lesser talents charitably. For him no programme was complete without something British. The orchestra got a little tired of this enthusiasm for the new, and one day we asked him whether he really enjoyed it. He seemed to find the question surprising. It was not necessary to enjoy it, he said. It would be just as dishonest to play new music because one enjoyed it as to ignore it because one did not. The orchestra was in the position of the curator of the City Art Gallery. Can such a man refuse to hang a picture because he does not like it? Of course not. One must ask, simply, if this is a work of integrity from an honest artist who has something truthful, even if possibly disagreeable, to say? If so yes, we play it. It is for the public to accept or reject. The public, on the whole, came to the right conclusions in the past. We leave these matters to them. Meanwhile we must not impose on them work which we believe to be superficial or dishonest, even when our colleagues come to different conclusions. There was room for opinion, and plenty of new music for us all.

To all his work Schwarz brought endless patience, meticulous care, and absolute conscience. The title *Kapellmeister*, honourable in the time of Haydn, is now often used as a polite denigration of the routine house-conductor. In the better sense that he was entrusted with the musical care of a great community, Schwarz was a great Kapellmeister in Birmingham. He it was who convinced the city that music was a social essential rather than an elitist fad; that a fine orchestra could be a delight to the town and a source of fame nationally.

Announcing his impending departure for the BBC, he told us that he must go because he had been offered the best job and the greatest honour open to a British conductor. He must go now or stay for ever. He did not believe in absolute permanencies. They were bad for everyone: 'So I must give up this happy job, this good orchestra in which I have so many friends.'

I think he was never so happy again in his own orchestra. But there remain, throughout British orchestras, many Birmingham 'graduates' of 40 years ago, each of us aware of the debt we owe to the man and of his great and typically unobtrusive influence on our national music-making.

*   *   *

Once I asked my trumpet professor, Ernest Hall, to name the finest conductor with whom he had ever worked. Since he'd been at the very top of the profession since 1920, Ernest had more than a few to consider. His routine reply to the question, I knew, was to offer Nikisch, the Russian with whom he spent his early days in the LSO and who had, with that orchestra, narrowly escaped a watery grave when the Cunard Line failed to find room for them on the *Titanic*. Nikisch was Ernest's escape route, beyond recollection by anyone else. But the reply came without hesitation: 'Bruno Walter! Walter was a hundred per cent genuine, the most sincere man who ever stood on the box. Never thought of himself, only the music.' Walter, he said, had 'taught me to play the trumpet' as first trumpet in his Covent Garden *Ring* of '24. The end of that cycle had been among his saddest experiences, because he knew when he closed the book on the second *Götterdämmerung* that nothing so wonderful would ever happen to him again.

What was it that made Walter so special?

'Sincerity', he said. 'Walter was the most sincere musician I ever met.'

I asked him for a comparably sincere conductor. A much longer thought now, and then 'Only Sir Adrian'.

Since Sir Adrian Boult was a constant friend, adviser, and welcome guest-conductor for the CBSO throughout my days there and after, this may be as sensible a place as any for his first appearance here. In remembering him I draw on 30 years of recollection.

It is impossible to overstate the debt we owe to Boult, a father-figure to British orchestral music and musicians for 70 hard-working years. First making a reputation in Birmingham — I hesitate to say that he 'founded' the City Orchestra because the permanent band came much later — he was snatched away by Lord Reith to become, as BBC Head of Music, founder of the BBC Symphony Orchestra. He made a magnificent job of this. Yes, he had all the advantages: the first regular salaries, good conditions, a consistent orchestra and, when the orchestra was ready, the finest guest-conductor list ever seen in London; but his basic orchestra training and discipline were at the root of the matter. There is film of his early orchestra — fascinating stuff; to see that huge ensemble, crammed with youthful faces known to us today, if still living, only as elder statesmen of 20 years ago, is a thrill in itself. To see and hear the machine galvanised into marvellous precision by the whiplash of that long stick at the end of those enormous arms is wonderful. Such a sense of youthful disciplined gusto has never been found in a British orchestra, or perhaps any other before or since.

The recordings still exist, and precious they are. I cherish especially those made with Toscanini, an admiring visitor who described Boult's orchestra as 'one of the best orchestras I have ever conducted.'

So for a decade there was at Broadcasting House a world-class orchestra. Many famous visitors thought it the very best in the world and I believe that it was. If so, then it was owed to the 'sincere' Boult; a musician, the last to advertise and the first to praise, who founded a British tradition of truth to the composer and loyalty to 'the job'.

Sir Adrian was the best friend for whom the CBSO or any other orchestra could possibly hope. Once when we were embarrassingly marooned between chief conductors he stood in for a year, telling the orchestra that he was simply 'holding a paternal umbrella over the CBSO for a little time'. That wide and generous umbrella was made available to the entire British orchestral community for a long life-time, and few are the orphans of the storm who have not sheltered beneath it.

Boult was English as Toscanini was Italian, bringing to music the essence and best of the British character. It is almost true to say that his attitude formed the British professional and made him what he is today; perhaps one ought to say rather what he was, at his very best, during the forty years following the foundation of the BBC Symphony Orchestra.

Boult was 'a gentleman', a son of the leisured class who turned to music as a vocation as he might equally well have turned to the Law or to the Church. Had he turned to the Army his immense height, erect bearing, military moustache and direct glance would have fitted him for the Guards. The military life, though, was far from Boult's mentality. His total command of the orchestra came from within, needing no bolster.

In his early years at the BBC he is said to have been a hard and sometimes volatile taskmaster. I believe it, having witnessed superb eruptions much later; yet the essence of his attitude to the orchestra was polite responsibility.

Good manners went a long way with Boult; they covered not only the more obvious professional necessities like being there, ready and tuned, at the time appointed, but the further responsibilities of being in tune and counting one's bars so as not to miss entries. I always felt, when I made a mistake in a Boult rehearsal, that my crime had been not so much musical and technical as social; I had wasted his time, and that of my colleagues, and this was not permitted. Boult wasted not a second of orchestral time in the whole of his ninety years.

Sir Adrian was the great economist; he played no unnecessary note nor spoke a superfluous word in rehearsal. He had studied with Arthur Nikisch in Leipzig, where Nikisch conducted the Gewandhaus. The Nikisch style was a response to a condition of employment there, which permitted the attendance of members of the Gewandhaus Society at rehearsal. Neither players nor conductors enjoy public criticism, so it had been necessary for Nikisch to rehearse with the minimum of chat. Boult recognised the enormous value of the wordless rehearsal to the British orchestra, then as now starved of funds and rehearsal time, and developed Nikisch's style to its ultimate expression. He was not the only Leipzig student to seize upon this gift, which was used with equal effect by Rudolf Kempe, a Leipzig oboist-conductor of a later generation. Long may it thrive in the interest of orchestral sanity.

This skill demands an articulate stick-technique. Boult's stick has been criticised by those who worked for him late in life when he could be − to put the matter as politely as he would himself have done − unclear. From film of his early BBC rehearsals it is obvious that in his thirties and forties he was pikestaff-plain; magisterial. The point of the stick contained all the necessary information about ensemble and phrase, while the left hand, sparingly used ('If you can find nothing useful to do with your left hand', he used to tell his students, 'please put it in your pocket'), indicated dynamic and instantly corrected any temporary looseness. On his best form these qualities were equally in evidence 30 years on. My own view, and I write as one who saw him in 1946 and in his eighties, is that the looseness which developed in advanced age was partly a consequence of a continued wish to refine, to boil down, to reduce to the absolute minimum the visible effort made with the stick. He would conduct nothing which would 'go by itself' − a valuable principle − but he sometimes overestimated the orchestra's capacity to conduct itself. Still, Boult rarely put the *musicians* in the orchestra at risk; to the others — and there are always others, alas — his work could be, in his late years, a minefield. If I show little concern for those others it is because I believe the orchestra to be a place for musicians rather than note-makers. When Sir Adrian knew precise direction to be essential he could be the safest conductor alive. How many can begin the *Eroica* scherzo with such confidence? One small gesture, the hands moving no more than six inches, and the strings were away in perfect ensemble and at exactly the tempo he wished; and tempo with Boult was never miscalculated.

His rehearsals, given middle-of-the-road repertoire, always followed the same plan. He would play through a complete movement without stopping, despite sometimes severe accidents, before discussing the changes and corrections he wished to make. That discussion was always of an objective, almost an abstract, kind, avoiding the blame factor completely. The music was under discussion rather than our failure to deliver it according to his wish. Only his polite address to the individual player, usually by name, linked what he had heard to us as personalities. 'Mr Gay', he would say while discussing the finale of Tchaikowsky's Fifth, 'that is a very German semiquaver you are giving me in the brass. Can you perhaps find something a little less precise and more characteristic?' He would not, if it could be avoided, play the whole movement again once detail had been tidied up.

He had a keen appreciation of the physical wear-and-tear of orchestral playing, never playing-through the finale of the Schubert Ninth, for instance, on the day of performance. He would attack the first bar with demonic energy and complete precision, then stop. 'No orchestra', he would say, 'ought to play all that twice in a day'.

There was very little deliberate wit from Boult, and that little was very dry. At a sour-sounding wind player he once aimed a real gem: 'I can't say I like that, Mr .....; it's flat, or sharp, or something!' His face remained so very composed that we managed not to laugh. He might just have been serious; bad intonation was bad manners, like a bad smell, to be ignored by a man of breeding unless intolerable.

In his play-through there was an element of assessing what we had to offer. The outline and scale of the work was for him to decide but he gathered much subtle detail from the orchestra, his appreciation of the experienced orchestra being very great. He once observed that any conductor who imagined that he knew more of a mainstream symphony than did the consensus of a fine symphony orchestra was not very intelligent. That must be true; few conductors have played the first of Brahms as often as has a busy symphonic musician, and we learn from each performance, even the dimmest of us. That experience was used by Sir Adrian to good effect. It was a resource.

Often he exploited it spectacularly. I remember an occasion when, at the end of a Hallé week, he was obliged to give the *New World* in place of the current Brahms. He asked only for an hour to rehearse, and when all was ready he said to us 'Well, ladies and gentlemen, I expect you know this work quite well and so do I. There are just three points to be made in it. Let's begin.' We played the first bar, learning without words that he would beat a big four, not the customary and safer eight. Then he asked for the beginning of the famous *Largo*, showing us only the attack on the first chord before stopping. 'Now the Finale' he asked. The long right arm, with its substantial stick, whiplashed the movement into life. He stopped within a bar. 'I'm sure that will be splendid this evening. Thank you.' Off we went to our fish-and-chips.

Now the *New World* is not really so simple. There are booby-traps galore. Boult knew that we were aware of them, and that we would be awake at those points. All he had to do was conduct to the limit and all would be well. In the event all was more than well; I remember few performances of the work so fine, so spirited, or so spontaneous. A good orchestra reacts marvellously to a vote of confidence. We like conductors to be as professional as we are.

Had any one of us failed him, though, the reaction might have been dramatic. Sir Adrian's urbane charm was, I believe, the product of considerable self-restraint; good manners again. When the safety-valve blew the results could be Vesuvian. Seldom has sloth in the orchestra been so effectively blasted from the rostrum as by the irate Boult. His reprimand, when at last it was forced from him, was all the more terrifying because it was perfectly calculated and delivered in impeccably precise language − and rarely beyond the bounds of propriety. Only once did I hear him overstep the mark. It was a splendid occasion, treasured by the orchestra.

We'd been on tour for a week. There was a soloist of oriental origin, his concerto being the same on each day. Naturally the piece was rehearsed briefly in each hall during our short rehearsal call, for his benefit only. Our visiting artist, no doubt through a series of misadventures, managed to arrive late on four consecutive afternoons.

On three occasions Sir Adrian received his apology with a charming 'Think nothing of it, my dear sir!' But at last the storm broke. Arriving at the rostrum to find himself once more without a pianist he turned to the empty hall, hands gripping lapels in the much-copied gesture which always boded ill, and roared 'WHERE IS THAT DAAAAAAAAMNED CHINAMAN?'

I wonder if the poor chap has ever since been late for rehearsal?

Boult has been called, unfairly, a superficial conductor. He was certainly not a superficial man or musician; rather a creature of the conditions under which the British orchestra has always worked, where the need to prepare two hours of music in three hours' rehearsal is ever with us. But I agree he was not a musical psychoanalist; not a man to put Rembrandt under an X-ray. He allowed us, players and listeners, to come to some conclusions of our own, crediting us with the intelligence required. Never, except in exceptional luxury at the BBC, was he given endless rehearsal time – the exceptions including the historic first British performance of *Wozzeck* with the BBC Symphony in 1934, when he was given three months: two-and-a-half longer than the most demanding operatic wizard would ask or need at Covent Garden today.

He admitted at least once to not knowing what to do with a surplus of time. While rehearsing *The Planets* in Birmingham he told us that he had recently recorded it in Vienna. There he had been given four days to rehearse. The Philharmonic had done excellently in three hours. Boult asked the leader of the orchestra what was to be done with the remainder. The answer was that he should rehearse, of course. So – when in Rome etc., – Boult rehearsed. 'Do you know, Ladies and Gentlemen', he told us, '*it improved!*'

His surprise seemed genuine. With Boult one could never be quite certain where lay the sting. About one other occasion we still wonder. We were at work on *Tod and Verklärung* of Strauss, and the matter was one for a very loud cymbal-crash. This effect is not as easy as it may look. It requires a strong pair of arms, fine judgement and exquisite timing. It's not an easy matter, anyway, for a lady percussionist unless of masculine build. Our percussionist was a marvellous performer, but small; and she was – let's say – unusually sylphlike of figure. This can be an advantage in that job, since a large bust combines badly with short arms and large cymbals. On this occasion, though, the instruments chosen were just not big enough for Boult, who looked for a cataclysm.

Looking up kindly from the rostrum he politely asked 'My dear Miss ... *is that really the biggest pair in Birmingham?*' Needless to say, the double-entendre was purest accident.

CHAPTER 7
A Thunderbolt ...

The great conductors, as the bandroom joke has it, have only one thing in common: they are all dead. This is not really a joke at all. Experienced orchestral musicians rarely find themselves in the presence of any stickwagger meriting the description 'great', and when it happens they invariably put the man into perspective by invoking the memory of a long-dead giant. The reason is simple. When, as inexperienced youngsters, we meet fine conductors for the first time, we are overwhelmed. This is natural. Ten years on we might find the same man less exciting. But, thank heaven, talent still comes down from Olympus to remind us that music is worth something.

My second season in Birmingham was notable for the number and quality of visiting conductors. As a management achievement it was remarkable though, as it turned out, premature. The orchestra was by no means ready for what we now call the jet-set; and the jet-set, disappointed, never returned. But for me it was a wonderful year in which I met a number of great conductors just before they vanished for ever.

Sir Thomas Beecham stood apart, his art technically unrelated to that of any other conductor I have since seen. Among my colleagues and friends are many who served under him in the Royal Philharmonic, an orchestra hand-picked by him on the principle, as he often said, of employing ninety of the finest players in the world and leaving them to get on with the job without interference. For them there was no-one half so much worth playing for as Tommy; indeed there was no other conductor. Forty years on, for them this is still true. But they were seasoned professionals. The electric charge which invigorated them was much more than I could comfortably earth. I played in two of his concerts almost paralysed with nerves. I remember little of them except the tension; but I remember the rehearsals vividly.

Beecham had the natural command of the upper crust of his generation; one which believed without question that some were fitted to lead and others fortunate to be so well led. Those who think of him today — and many mistakenly do — as an eccentric gifted amateur with an acid wit and an adequate supply of money with which to buy performances have not read his autobiography. This is a revelation. Such a profusion of gifts have rarely inhabited a musician; so broad a view of life, art and music has seldom been granted to a conductor.

He brought the first symphony of Schubert, some extracts from the opera *Irmelin* by his friend Delius, some Mozart and Dvorak's *Symphonic Variations*. He began rehearsal with the Schubert, then the Mozart, then into the Dvorak. To our surprise he made little comment, seeming only to play through the repertoire as quickly as possible, and looking up very rarely. The general effect was of a deflating lack of interest in the City of Birmingham Symphony Orchestra.

The Delius he left until late in the morning since it required a bass clarinet, an exotic luxury coming by train from the North. At the appropriate time TB suggested with an urbane smile that we might now 'take a little refreshment and await the arrival of our esteemed colleague from Manchester.'

The tea-break was a subdued one. We resumed rehearsal fearing that the great man, famously impatient with the second-rate, could not be bothered even to apply the whip. Then back to the music; not Delius, but Schubert again, and Schubert transformed. This time his eyes were on us; such eyes, and set in such a mobile face. It was not so much the stick nor the hand which was expressive but the whole man. We had not then invented the term *body language* but that was how he communicated. Most of all the message was in his face and especially in his eyes. So, by Beecham's personal alchemy an orchestra which had been ditchwater at 10.45 was, at 12.15, fine wine; a feat which, as one of my colleagues remarked, had only one historic precedent.

I had seen for the first time what can be done by the first-rate artist on the rostrum, and with what ease. Happily for me this experience has renewed itself many times, but this first time was a revelation. The immediate difference lay in a tightness of ensemble and attack and a clear, bright texture. A slack and lifeless feel was replaced by precision, lightness and vitality. Schubert danced and Beecham smiled. the smile was in the eyes. Then the most remarkable gift of all arrived; his ability to play phrases through the orchestra. His eyes held every one of ours, leaving only a glance for the written score. He seemed never to look at his own. And through the eyes came the music. People played solo phrases that morning in ways which had never before occurred to them. Surprise was all around, mingled with an atmosphere of mounting enthusiasm and joy; there is no other word for it. A young orchestra, we were given a glimpse of the pot of gold at the end of the rainbow.

Beecham's response to the change seemed one of mildly sardonic pleasure, his success with the orchestra giving him as much amusement as satisfaction. To him it had been a foregone conclusion. If the orchestra fell short of his ideal, then he made no concessions to it. He did not so much demand performance as presume it.

His Sibelius, rehearsing for the second concert, was revelatory not only of the music but of the orchestra's potential. Two features stand out vividly in my memory: the velocity of the scherzo and the drama of the recitative which followed it. That scherzo simply flew. We could not play the notes. We did, though. If the keywork of the woodwind had actually melted, one felt, Beecham's day would have been made. It was, on one level, a game at our expense. We played during that extraordinary week at speeds and dynamics previously unknown to the Town Hall, Birmingham. The miracle was that a performance resulted. The great orchestral recitative with which the finale of that symphony begins is a technical minefield for the conductor. Beecham gave only the simplest of indications, direct, clear, and unmistakeable, with the stick. We arrived without mishap at the three climactic tenuto notes for the strings which precede the run from top to bottom. These were produced by three separate commanding gestures in the direction of the ceiling, reinforced by Beecham's own remarkable vocal contribution. Then came the descent. Here he simply scrubbed the air with his stick, rather as one might clean a window pane, but much more quickly. The result was a musical cataract of complete accuracy and unanimity. A flick of the left wrist for the punctuating pizzicato and we sat, in the ensuing stunned silence, amazed at our own virtuosity. The eyes sparkled. How he must have loved that trick. Circus? Perhaps; but since audiences, like players, must look at conductors, there is nothing wrong with gestures that mirror the music, surely?

Musicians in general sing decently or not at all. Beecham's singing voice, often heard over the orchestra in rehearsal, was – to state the case politely – limited. The violist Bernard Shore has described it as 'somewhat inadequate for the opening phrase of *Ein Heldenleben*;' a charitable description, I think. The first two bars of *God Save the Queen* would have given him trouble.

That tune was a speciality of Beecham's. Few orchestras play it well. Of all the many orchestrations none seems to 'work' convincingly. In those days every orchestral concert began with the Anthem, and for Beecham this was more than a gesture. He was a patriot; perhaps in some ways − especially in his dislike of British conductorships for foreign conductors − a chauvinist, if so cosmopolitan a personality can ever be so described. It is said that he never rehearsed the Anthem. Certainly he did not in Birmingham. Yet his concerts were as memorable for this tune as for all the other music. His walk to the rostrum was stately, with plenty of time for a long crescendo of applause. His bow was signified and leisurely. He turned to the orchestra; a gesture to the percussion for their roll, and away into a majestic three-four with a triumphant crash of cymbals. The tempo was not exaggerated nor pompous but exactly right. It might easily have been sung; yet it was given its full expansive due. The climb to the last phrase was majestic in its increase − where did all that sound come from? − and the final bars gloriously affirmative. God, one felt, would indeed save Queen Elizabeth the Second, since His failure to do so would give serious offence to Sir Thomas Beecham, Baronet. No monarchist I, following five years in the Guards, yet I wish TB had recorded the tune for posterity. It was among his great achievements.

... and two Olympians

The Concertgebouw Orchestra − now the Royal Concertgebouw − of Amsterdam was the creation of a great orchestral engineer, Willem Mengelberg, and it is to Mengelberg and his school that we owe not only a great orchestra but an approach to orchestral conducting quite unlike that practised elsewhere. Mengelberg I never saw. I have heard veterans of the pre-war BBC Symphony speak of him as simply boring; a man who spent an hour tuning the orchestra, a tactic guaranteed to drive it mad; useless too, because at the end of that time one would have to start all over again, rather like painting the Forth Bridge. The conductor's ears cannot be substituted for those of the player. Almost certainly, though, these were the methods Mengelberg used in building his own orchestra, and the results, solidified now into a great national tradition, are beyond criticism.

We are indebted to Mengelberg too for his championship of Mahler at a time when Vienna would have none of him. Again, a tradition was formed which still provides us with perhaps the most authentic and certainly some of the most exciting and polished performances of that repertoire today.

The war and the occupation were disastrous to Mengelberg's reputation. He was succeeded by his pupil, Eduard van Beinum. In the early 'fifties I was fortunate enough to hear van Beinum with the Concertgebouw at the Edinburgh Festival in Brahms' first symphony. Now he brought that symphony to Birmingham. Like Beecham, the great Dutchman spent some time listening to the orchestra before applying himself to it. Unlike Beecham, whose approach to the music, to the orchestra and perhaps to everything else seemed extemporary and inspired, he was a conviction musician and a methodical orchestral trainer.

His rehearsal began with the *Freischütz* overture of Weber. This started badly with a roughish unison and a nervous horn quartet. He pressed on, apparently undisturbed. The ensuing *allegro* was undistinguished. He stopped for the first time just before the C major *fortissimo* which transforms the mood of the overture. Here, on ideal ground, he did battle.

Like Mengelberg at the BBC − though doubtless with more reason − he tuned the orchestra, starting with the strings. When he was satisfied that the instruments were in tune he addressed the chord itself, listening to each string section before combining them. When the tuning was right he encouraged the sound quality; then improved the balance. Then to the wind, with the same painstaking treatment. Finally to the brass. Only an organ-like blend would satisfy him. Then the full orchestra was balanced, and discrepancies between sections corrected. After perhaps 15 minutes of dismantling and reassembling of the orchestral structure he seemed better pleased.

One refinement remained. He asked for 'one centimetre higher, the first trombone, and one half-centimetre the second trumpet please'. My colleagues demurred; they were now certain that the chord was in tune. He agreed. 'Yes, in tune. Now it must be more exciting. This note must be just a little bit sharp. It will be C major *major*!'

Then to the attack on the chord. 'I will beat four. Play the chord.' This was done. It was a healthier sound now, lacking only punch. 'We will do it many times — once again, after four!' Many times it was done, and each time with better ensemble and increased volume. As the result developed, his own contribution became more and more energetic. Soon our C major chord became November the fifth. Finally 'Good! Now we play to the end of the piece please!' The coda of the overture was a joyful affirmation of tuneful orchestral confidence.

Returning to the beginning of the piece, we played through. His corrections were few. In common with nearly all the great conductors he talked little. He collected eyes when he needed them and transmitted instructions without words. This was a different *Freischütz*, from a different orchestra. He was pleased with us and, I think, for us. Closing the score he said with a great warm smile 'So, my friends! Three times so good the orchestra! And for the same money, too!'

Van Beinum had given the CBSO an overdue reminder of the fundamentals of performance. Until we are in tune, together, balanced, and accurate in notation we are not ready for the composer. Fortunately these qualities come all at once, given one condition. The entire orchestra must *listen*. Listen for tuning and the balance improves. Listen for balance and the ensemble becomes tighter. Listen for ensemble and the notation becomes unanimous. Ears are the essential tool!

He was puzzled by our Brahms, a work we knew really well from Schwarz' performances. Technically we were on very safe ground, but our Brahms was the product of an intellect very different from his. For some time he struggled for expansion and warmth, using his preferred equipment, his hands alone. In the end, nearly exasperated but realising where lay the root of the problem, he said 'My friends, I do not understand your Birmingham Brahms. It is so small!' Then, striking his heart with his fist, 'Brahms is a *man's* music!' With this he began the symphony again. Now bow-arms discovered uncharted horsehair, wind players new freedom, brass and horns reserves of sonority. Here was big, bearded, cigar-smoking, black-coffee-drinking Brahms.

The orchestra itself sounded twice as big as yesterday. It was certainly twice as much fun to play in. Our enjoyment gave him equal pleasure. He *joined* the CBSO for ten days, taking a great fancy to some of the characters around him and providing constant good-humoured comment. To the violas, who seemed at one point reluctant to accept technical advice — violas being a race apart — he said 'I know what I'm talking about. I am a viola player' (he pronounced it *vie-ola*) and then, with a big grin, 'I am the worst viola player in Holland!' He got his own way, of course. He was all heart, all encouragement, and exactly what we needed. Truly he was what every orchestra needs, a technical master with a fine musical instinct. Above all a human being; an artist who realised that the orchestra, like the composer, serves humanity and not vice-versa.

His own humanity, sadly, caught up with him soon after his time with us. While in Birmingham he complained of difficulty with his heart. Doctors found no cause for concern. We understood that the great man was a hypochondriac, convinced that his healthy heart was in trouble. He had simply to be reassured. In the meantime he did everything possible to guard against a condition everyone else believed to be imaginary. Then, one day, rehearsing his beloved Brahms with the Concertgebouw, he collapsed almost into the arms of his Leader and died.

Some years later in Amsterdam I met a member of the Concertgebouw Orchestra and over a beer told him of our affection for the man and our admiration of the musician. He was puzzled. 'I don't know why you found him so interesting', he said. 'Van Beinum knew nothing. He was just a viola player from Arnhem'.

Our British failure to honour the native prophet is not, it seems, unique.

After van Beinum, the *Chef Cordon Bleu*: Pierre Monteux of glorious and happy memory for all those fortunate thousands who played for him during a long, successful and obviously happy life. Already an old man — he was approaching 80 when I first had the delight of playing for him — he brimmed with vitality and gallic wit. Again, like Beecham, a short man; but a really *wide* one. Behind his magnificent walrus moustache his face was alive with interest and energy. A happy man, as one saw at a glance, he set about the job of making us happy with the zest of a popular uncle at a birthday party. His menu was ambitious. The second symphony of Beethoven (why is this so often a choice of touring conductors? Is it perhaps because resident maestros luxuriate in their 'personal' odd-numbered Beethoven and dislike having it disturbed?) with Strauss' *Till Eulenspiegel* and the Debussy *Nocturnes*. It was no easy ride for me and even less so for the first horn. As luck would have it our first horn fell ill, leaving the third player to cope with the rehearsal day while some superman would be brought from London in time for the concert. We were won over immediately by the consideration the old maestro showed for our player. He was rewarded with playing so fine that at the end of the day Monteux refused to accept a change. This was the making of the player. That's how this very strange game can work, when talent and guts combine.

Like all the best chefs Monteux was practical. Yes, there was spontaneous magic, but much more of plain commonsense. He had spent more time in touring than had most important conductors, and he knew how to get the best from orchestras of all kinds. In his youth he had worked with Diaghilev. A good school, the ballet theatre, for a conductor with a strong stomach. He had learned from it.

His beat was simple and clear, and his solutions were immediate. At the start of the Beethoven, where lesser men toil without reward over the little note before the bar, he simply said 'Don't worry — play it *on* the bar!' Wisdom indeed; there are no bars for the listener until the sound begins.

His style was lyric and expansive. No nit-picker, Monteux, but a man to luxuriate in life and music and to make performance very easy indeed. Somehow there was always just time to play the phrase; always a comfortable approach to the dangerous corner for the wind soloist. And when we failed, no reproaches; a relaxed suggested solution to the problem, and on with the work.

It was in rehearsal with Monteux that I made the most spectacular *faux pas* of the goodly number in my debit account. It happened in the *Nocturnes*, in the famous passage for three muted trumpets. We three had done a lot of work on that. It's not easy, however it's done. Though it is written with *legato* signs over each group it is invariably played with the tongue because this is much easier and safer; and since there is in all conscience little distinction between a real *legato* sign and a triplet-bracket in some print, no doubt our teachers felt justified in adopting the safe course. Well, the safe course was the one we took. Since it is the one adopted everywhere, I think Monteux was not surprised. He decided to correct it, nevertheless.

'Do you not have a *legato*, trumpets?' he asked.

I replied that I had been taught to play the passage the other way; not, believe me, to debate the matter but simply to pass the buck to my absent teacher. Monteux's response was devastating. 'My young friend, it should be *legato*. There is no doubt about it. The composer made it clear to me at the first rehearsal!'

During the ensuing orchestral cheer I tried to hide my head under my chair. I am glad it happened, though, because at least I know the truth of the matter; a truth almost forgotten now. Some years later in Manchester we delivered the passage in that literal way for Giulini. He was surprised and delighted.

The *Nocturnes* had not been Monteux's only premiere, and certainly not his most famous. That distinction belongs to the notorious Parisian first night of Stravinsky's *Sacre*, when the audience rioted in protest. It is worth noting, in defence of the great man, that a friend of mine *who was there* insisted that it was not the music nor its performance which caused the riot but the incompetence of the dancers. I believe it, as would anyone who played for Monteux.

What fun he was, and what fun he had, too. A press conference remark of his is typical. Asked what his hobbies were he replied 'All my life I have had two hobbies; the model trains and the ladies. Now of course I am much too old ... for the model trains!'

Little wonder that he is remembered with such affection by those who played for him most; especially in the London Symphony, with which orchestra he found such a marvellous rapport late in his career. Hugo Maguire, who led for him there, summed their feelings up well: 'How we loved that man', he said. We did, Hugh; indeed we did.

CHAPTER 8

Change and Decay

The choice of chief conductor is the greatest challenge open to the management of a symphony orchestra: a rare opportunity for change and for exciting improvement, for a bold stroke. The possibility of catastrophic failure is equally clear. One is committed to a new personality, to new policies, to new methods and attitudes which cannot be reversed for some years. The orchestra is the creation, to some extent, of the last man. If it enjoyed him it will not readily discard his ideas. It is as well, perhaps, to consult the orchestra before choosing.

This principle was readily conceded by the management of the CBSO on Schwarz' departure. We were shown, during his last season, two likely candidates. One, though a good artist and conductor and an orchestra trainer of talent, had been a famous nuisance to our friends elsewhere. The orchestra voted, predictably, for the other.

This was what our manager had wished, expected, and planned, being quite sure that he knew what was best for us. In his place I hope I would have been equally sure and equally determined; but I hope that I would have been less transparent in my maneouvring and more successful in my choice.

The new man was Andrzej Panufnik, a recently arrived Polish musician of aristocratic background, a composer of great talent and a man of immense charm. He had been very successful in his homeland until falling foul of The Party. Now he had escaped via Switzerland, and looked for a foothold in the West.

This delightful and gifted man was able to settle, marry idyllically, and live out a long and successful composing life in England; but the Birmingham appointment was a setback for that orchestra and for music in Birmingham. I am glad, liking the man and admiring his music as I do, that his reputation survived.

Panufnik had been a successful conductor at home, we were told. We knew, and still know, little about Polish orchestras, but perhaps their conditions and standards were very different? The continental orchestras are given much more rehearsal time than we can afford. Maybe it's possible for a conductor to approach the rostrum less technically prepared there? Here we expect cast-iron certainty from the first downbeat. Panufnik's stick-technique was sadly far below that expected by the British orchestra. It speaks volumes for the natural charm of the man that the orchestra pulled him through several seasons, and that when he left there were still many besides myself who could remember with pleasure the man, his attitude to music and to the orchestra.

One would expect from a conductor-composer fidelity to other composers. Panufnik's approach to the music of others was astonishingly free. He was by temperament a romantic. To compare his natural style to his national music by invoking Chopin's *rubato* is perhaps trite, but so accurate as to be irresistible. The CBSO had been dedicated for years to the text delivered with the minimum of deliberate personal input. It was not easy to adjust to a chap who would elongate and accelerate apparently at his own whim. The first movement of his *Eroica* contained a memorable effect achieved in that way. It reminded one irresistably of a small train leaving a country station.

Panufnik was kind to me. Schwarz had encouraged my solo-aspirations with performances of the Haydn concerto and others. With Panufnik I gave the first modern performances of the Hummel, and the first broadcast too. Early music attracted him. He liked to begin programmes with Vivaldi or with early English music, progressing in chronological order through the evening. This sounds logical enough until we encounter the difficulty of following some classical or romantic giant, when anticlimax inevitably ensues. Such programme-building might sell seats today, when the public is readier for experiment, but in 1957 Birmingham knew what a symphony concert *looked like*. Our public began to melt. This is not unusual on a change of conductor. A new public may grow, and part of the old public return. Here neither happened.

It is to Panufnik's credit that he did not use the CBSO to promote his own works. I wish he had done so. It is virile stuff, strongly nationalistic, logically structured and marvellously scored; a delight to play and exciting to the ear. When it came, reluctantly in his second season, the early *Sinfonia Rustica* delighted us all, and audiences too.

There came a disastrous concert during International Geophysical Year, and associated with it, when we gave a programme of dance music, in chronological order of course, beginning with Haydn and ending with Bartok. The audience was pitifully sparse. In the band-room afterwards someone cruelly but wittily remarked that the CBSO had at least contributed its own non-magnetic pole. It was all such a pity, and such a waste.

In such a situation morale seeps away, and with it some degree of professional discipline and pride. We began to make fun of the silliness, as we felt it to be, of what we were doing; of the capricious performance of fanciful lists of music. Quite soon players began to leak away too. Few of the young Turks of the Schwarz regime were dedicated permanently to Birmingham. Their eyes were constantly looking sideways to London or Manchester. Now we began to look around in earnest.

My own first encounter with the metropolitan scene had taken place some years earlier. I'd been invited by Harry Blech to contribute my Haydn to a concert of the London Mozart Players, at that time our most celebrated exponents of the style. My appearance at the Royal Festival Hall had caused unpleasant ripples among the London trumpets. Blech told me after my performance that it had been necessary to pay solo fees to both the trumpets in the orchestra in order to secure their services for the evening. The old hands, survivors of the lean war years, were clinging to their places. New faces were not welcome. 'Getting in' would not be easy.

The crack, when it came, was in the LSO. The crack became a smash, and that orchestra was re-organised, repopulated, and improved beyond measure over a period of months. It seemed possible at one point that I might become first trumpet there, and I played some concerts and recordings in London, rather tightly fitted between CBSO commitments.

I spent the months of July and August '59 in a series of dashes up and down the brand-new M1 Motorway at the request of the London Symphony Orchestra in the hope of establishing myself there. That I failed to do so owed as much to the wear and tear of daily driving as to the presence of excellent competition; but those months were invaluable ones. The orchestra was stimulating company and the conductors notable.

The LSO has never given its direction entirely to its chief conductor.

Like the Vienna and Berlin orchestras, it believes that democracy encompasses musical direction; but from time to time it has appointed very famous chief conductors, and these are carefully consulted before any appointment is made or any artistic policy adopted. For this reason I was thoroughly exposed to Antal Dorati.

This eminent Hungarian had established a fine reputation in Mineapolis, where the orchestra had all but reached the first rank. His expectations in London were very high, and his musical and technical approach meticulously detailed. His ears were keen, unlike his eyes, which had already deteriorated to the point where scores were always memorised. With Dorati we recorded among other things a fine Tchaikowsky sixth.

I approached Dorati with the feeling of a skater on very thin ice. He'd already reacted badly to some of my colleagues. I was told of the famous day in the studio when, finding the trumpet talent inadequate, Dorati had demanded to know whether there was 'anyone in this country who can play the trumpet?'

There were lots, in fact; most wisely staying well clear of the current LSO turmoil. I was the rusher-in. Curiously, Dorati and I got on famously. I thought he did and said all the right things and my opinion seemed to be reciprocated. He went out of his way both then and later in Manchester to express his enjoyment of my work. But the tension in his LSO sessions was high: as much a product of the orchestra's situation as of the conductor's temperament.

Dorati, it seemed to me, contributed little to the music he conducted except exactitude. This rarely happens. Even when a conductor seeks clarity and precision obsessively, the personality usually emerges, and something of the man is given to the composer; but I never felt that my musical experience had been broadened by working with him. Technically, on the other hand, the gain was considerable. For him everything must be clear and every detail heard. This requires a first-rate orchestra and the LSO was already, though not completely overhauled, a new and exciting experience for me. For them too everything must work. They were a first-rate collection of performers and the pressure they exerted on one another, and on me, was huge.

The high point of their season was the visit of Leopold Stokowski. I'm glad I met Stokowski then, because my later experience of him was sad and very different. Stokey was an oddball among conductors and indeed among humanity. He was British, despite a lifelong determination to pretend otherwise. A graduate of the Royal College of Music he had, like many another, sought and found a career in the New World by adapting to its foibles. Among those until recently was an appearance of continental origin. With such a name it was not difficult to appear suitably exotic, and his protective colouring was so successful in the course of many years as to be difficult to abandon. Stokey spoke always in very restricted and heavily accented English and – as those placed close to him and involved in carrying him about town constantly complained – pretending a lesser knowledge of London than that of a two-day tourist. Whether or not it is really true that he asked, on passing the Palace of Westminster, what the 'big clock' was, will never be proven, but that we all believed it at the time showed the lengths to which he pursued his game.

A charlatan? Certainly not. Stokowski was one of the great conductors of his time and his influence on the development of the modern symphony orchestra, especially in America, was seminal. His instrument had been the organ and in a curious way his approach to the orchestra was that of a man playing it rather than leading it: an attitude many years in advance of its time. He was a fine transcriber of keyboard works for the orchestra, having made his own score of the *Pictures* of Moussorgsky, and his transcription of Bach's Toccata and Fugue in D Minor is justly famous through its inclusion in Disney's *Fantasia*, which he conducted. Colour was a preoccupation with him. He worked constantly to colour performance by balance and organisation; not, it must be emphasised, by rescoring.

His LSO programme was typical and marvellous. Beginning with the *Egmont* overture he followed with the Third Symphony of Brahms; then after the interval the *Concerto for Orchestra* by Bartok.

His rehearsal schedule was, for the times, extraordinary. He would not work more than once in each day, nor would he rehearse on the day of his concert. This is an admirable scheme, and one which can benefit performance enormously. It was hardly likely to be followed by the members of the LSO, who, like most members of the London profession, will fill every hour of the day with profitable industry if it offers. So Stokey's rehearsals were followed by rapid exits in all directions and to other orchestras.

In rehearsal he was no talker; just as well, in view of his speech pattern. He used his hands well and 'spoke' well with his face, so the attention of the orchestra was always completely focussed. His material was minutely edited. He was no trouble at all, and he got first-rate results in record time.

That he could be murderously hard on players was well known. The Stokey stories emanating from New York, Houston and, above all, Philadelphia have become legend. Naturally in this self-managing democracy there was no possibility of his inflicting serious damage on anyone — unless, possibly, it seemed to the directors, players all, that the conductor's criticism was justified ...

Yes, the atmosphere was tense. But he made no waves, and his reward was a superb concert. The Brahms, to one raised on Schwarz, was *personal*, perhaps, but nonetheless acceptable. The Bartok was almost insupportably exciting, every member of the orchestra giving five per cent more than he knew he could, and the finale's sense of growth to climax and collapse greater than in any performance I have since known. That music might have been composed for Stokowski to conduct.

I have particular cause to remember that finale because in it I came closer to disaster in performance than ever before or since. Trumpeters will not be surprised to read that at a certain point in it I resorted to a smaller instrument. Having rehearsed the passage that way I was naturally dependant on the machine for the notes. At the moment of putting it to my lips that evening I realised to my horror that *it was the wrong trumpet*. This was a moment, if ever there was, to try my orchestral technique to the limit. Adrenalin succeeds where science and industry fail. I transposed one of Bartok's least friendly passages into a new key, and escaped. My colleagues knew nothing of my fright. Curiously, however hard I've tried, I've never been able to play that passage in that key on purpose.

It was during that summer that I met Colin Davis again. Colin was very much a part of the LSO picture, as he has remained for most of his career. We played a Prom together, including a fine *Sinfonia da Requiem* of Britten. Colin was then in his thirtieth year and still the irresistably talented young Davis.

He has been, perhaps, the perfect example of a pattern once described from personal experience by Bruno Walter. According to Dr Walter, for the talented young conductor music has no difficulties and poses few questions. All is simple. Technique comes easily to sharp young reflexes; learning is quick when minds are young and receptive. There is an illusion of artistic certainty, not shared by elders and betters in the orchestra. The clever youngster is usually impatient, too, with orchestral limitations. He wants performance *now*. Friction is inevitable.

The orchestra is only too happy to find and encourage genuine young talent. There is so little of it about. What a pity it so often presents itself in the form of a pain in the neck! Fortunately as the musicians grows in experience his certainties are fewer. By the age of forty his life is full of questions and problems. Once so sure of himself, he is now certain of nothing. Now come the years of search, of doubt, of mistakes, of mismanagement, and of unconvincing performance. It is an unhappy time.

Then — Walter thought fifty the crucial age for this — the mist clears with the realisation that one is never definitively right, that technique is never perfect, and fine performance often a synthesis of quite likeable human imperfections; that there is room for opinion and time to change it, that the talented musician needs only to approach his work with educated sincerity to gain the respect of those around him. This is the time when his work blossoms, when all the tribulations of the middle years bear fruit; when he becomes the kind of conductor the orchestra welcomes.

All this we have seen happen to Colin. The results, in his sixties, are heart-warming, but in his thirties the experience of playing for him was very mixed. He was handsome, confident, indeed exuberant, over-using his substantial physique to a degree he would deplore today. He was also carelessly abrasive and hard to *like*. His talent was huge and unmistakable, or he could never have survived the irritation he gave to so many.

One had to enjoy the sheer physical impact of the man though; the vitality which he brought to music and to the orchestra. I remember his impatience with the LSO's rehearsal dynamic at the moment of the famous key-change in Ravel's *Bolero*. 'Come on, you lot', he shouted, 'I want a noise like a riot at a pop festival!' The noise was duly produced; but was it worth the effort at eleven am? Today's Colin would have left it for the concert, when he would have produced it simply by raising his arms for the first time in the piece. Oh dear, the enthusiastic ineptitude of the young conductor! And the orchestra has seen it so often. Still we suffer it. There is no other way to make a conductor. We have to knock off the roughnesses with a thousand small hammer-taps.

I was younger even than he was, so I found him more tolerable than did many of those around me; but I am glad to have seen the splendid end-product, so much later.

All this extra-mural activity was not approved by my employers in Birmingham. It is not good for orchestral morale that a prominent player is so obviously trying to escape. The thing spreads. The fit with the CBSO schedule, too, was occasionally more than tight. In the end it was argued, not unreasonably, that I might have been in the wrong concert hall at the wrong time. A polite resignation was proposed as the best solution. I declined this. The issue was not forced, but the atmosphere was unhappy. By this time Panufnik's tenure was at an end. Hugo Rignold, voted down by the orchestra at the first time of asking, was now imminently due to arrive and the prospect in Birmingham was much more hopeful. But once young feet begin to itch there is no cure but change. I was glad to be asked to audition for the Hallé Orchestra. I polished up my Haydn again and attended at the Civic Hall, Wolverhampton, where Barbirolli's orchestra was to play that evening.

* * *

Postscript

What happened at the LSO? The job went to a close contemporary of mine, a good friend and marvellous trumpeter who had been for some years principal trumpet in another regional orchestra. He satisfied London and its Symphony Orchestra utterly, but London did not suit *him*. The occasion of this discovery is one which has given good-natured merriment to his many friends and admirers ever since. He will not mind my recounting it, even if perhaps it has gained a little in the telling.

He went, one Sunday morning, to the BBC at Maida Vale to rehearse with his new friends for tomorrow evening's Prom concert. As a newcomer, carefully arriving very early, he found the studio ready but empty. He put his trumpet down on the first trumpet chair and went in search of tea. Two cups later, there being still no sign of the LSO, he enquired of the commissionaire and was told that the London Symphony Orchestra was not expected today.

Leaping into his car he drove to the obvious alternative, Morley College on the other side of the river. There was no sign of the LSO there either. Desperate now, he drove back to the only other Prom rehearsal venue he could imagine, the Duke's Hall at the Royal Academy of Music in Marylebone. Still no luck. Suddenly he realised that the LSO must be at the Albert Hall itself. Breathless but triumphant he arrived there one hour late for his rehearsal. Then he remembered that his instrument was in Studio One at Maida Vale ...

During the lunch interval my friend telephoned home. His work has been much enjoyed there ever since.

CHAPTER 9

Testing, Testing ...

If the Birmingham audition had been loaded in my favour, this second one was a fight against awful odds. In Birmingham I supplanted an aging player in an orchestra which had never heard fine trumpet playing. Here I was asking for the place left by a great trumpeter, under a conductor of world renown, with an awe-inspiring repertoire. The trial was commensurate.

JB entered with an entourage of seven or eight people. No democrat, he knew the value of good advice. From the far end of the room, furnished with a music-stand only – there was to be no pianist this time – I saw a very small man in a heavy overcoat despite the warm weather, his throat covered by a silk muffler, and a Verdi-type black hat on his head.* He and his group kept a distance. Only Willie Lang, the Hallé retiring first trumpet, approached. Willie I knew as a former solo cornet of the Black Dyke Band. Like me he had fallen into trumpet playing almost by accident, and with even less preparation. He was a brickie by trade, and a master-craftsman too. But he was a big lad, as they say in his native Yorkshire; a big aggressive trumpeter, and everything that I was not.

'Haydn, no doubt, lad?' he asked.

'Right, Willie' said I.

'When you're ready then. Give us a bit of the second. Then a bit of the third. What the Old Man is interested in is this', patting a pad of music as thick as the family Bible, 'so get yourself played in without selling the lot out, that's the best thing'.

I launched into unaccompanied Haydn, feeling as lonely as a small boy marooned on Ailsa Craig. I didn't get very far. It was time for the high jump.

The pad was opened. I played, during the next twenty minutes or so, a non-stop collection of the nastiest events ever collected together

---

*The famous hat was in fact the least Italian thing about him. He told me that he'd bought it at Dunn's, Piccadilly Circus.

to torment a player of my instrument: a trumpeter's nightmare. It became a battle of wits, not only to get the things played but to do that without running out of muscle. I could feel my friend silently cheering me on and hoping I could keep this up. We pressed on through Tchaikowsky, Beethoven, Mahler, Stravinsky, Bax, Ravel, the entire shooting-match without the smallest response from the other end of the room. There came a wonderful moment when we arrived at Delius' *Brigg Fair*, a famous minefield which 'looks nowt on paper', as Willie would have said. Here he hesitated.

'D'you fancy this one?' he asked.

'Not a lot, Willie' I replied. He turned over; a nice man, Bill Lang. We came to the end. At last JB approached.

'Very nice. Just one more thing. I wonder if you know this?' So saying he drew from his pocket the first trumpet part of the prelude to Wagner's *Parsifal*. This prelude is a very tall order at the beginning of the operatic evening at Covent Garden. It needs puff beyond belief. Ernest Hall once said laughingly that when he took his breath for the *Parsifal* prelude 'all the cigar smoke from the crush bar disappeared into the theatre!' As the final request at a long audition it represented either complete ignorance of the problems of the trumpeter, or sadism.

'Only on paper, Sir John' I replied, taking my life into my hands, 'It never seems to come up in the symphony orchestra.' His eyebrows rose. I could not know then, as I later came to know very well, that he often provoked auditioners. One needed temperamental resilience to work for him and he knew it.

'It comes up sometimes in MY orchestra,' was the reply. 'Play it from the beginning; the low passage first, then the high one.'

The low one is not low. The high one is stratospheric. I launched forth. I survived, to my own considerable surprise. But all was not over. He asked for it again, 'a little slower'. I did it again, telling myself that this was so unreasonable as to be funny — if it had been happening to someone else. Still he was not satisfied. 'Try it at this tempo' he suggested, beating the slowest eight-in-a-bar ever essayed by mortal man. So I did, escaping axphyxiation by a hairsbreadth. Now at last he seemed interested.

'You've been a pupil of my old friend Ernest', he said. 'How is he? Can he still play?' We were launched into five minutes of reflection on my teacher, his old LSO collegue of the twenties. And then, suddenly, 'Come along, let's play that again, and I'll conduct!'

So, one last attempt, with Barbirolli beating time, phrasing with his left hand, and croaking his personal *espressivo* accompaniment. My word, it was slow; slower than I have ever heard it done in performance. I made it, just.

'Thank you very much, young man', he said, 'we'll have to think about it, and you will hear from us shortly.'

Some time later, when I was safely established in the Hallé, my friend Terry Nagle, our marvellous first trombone throughout my stay, explained the JB audition system for brass players. JB knew nothing at all about the technique of the brass, but he *did* know that we tired unreasonably quickly in the context of his merciless rehearsals. So it was essential to him to discover whether we could stand the pace. If not, however fine the player he simply wouldn't do. So trumpeters went through the Wagner mill; horn players were required to play the second movement of Tchaikowsky's Fifth Symphony four times at least, and trombonists – Terry assured me with the wry smile of one who had suffered – four times through the infamous passage from Ravel's *Bolero*. Their physique nearly always cracked under this pressure. Alternatively they lost their composure and produced a tantrum. Either way they were unfit for JB's Hallé. 'We knew you were in', said my friend, 'when he started to conduct. When the old boy begins to conduct he's hooked.'

CHAPTER 10
Me, Elgar, and God

John Barbirolli gave up the New York Philharmonic in 1943 to take over the Hallé Orchestra. Even allowing for homesickness, and that he'd found the Toscanini legacy a mixed blessing, this says something about the immense prestige of the prewar Hallé.

That orchestra was no more. The old Hallé, with a handful of exceptions, had unexpectedly chosen to join the new BBC Orchestra. The new Chief Conductor of the Hallé must start almost from scratch. Any other man, that course still being open to him, might have taken the next boat back to the Big Apple. JB immediately set about auditioning players for the new Hallé. This was typical of the man, and fundamental to the character of the orchestra he founded. No orchestra has ever been more completely identified with one musician. He auditioned each player, choosing, in his own words, 'among the lame and the halt', because the fit and able were still at war. A creditable orchestra quickly emerged, and within months Barbirolli's Hallé was recognised by an astonished public as the best British orchestra of the day. JB had pulled a new Hallé 'out of the hat', the best of his many conjuring tricks.

There was nothing here of Beecham's famous 'find the ninety best players in the world and let them get on with the job'. The Hallé had no money for it, and there were in any case few fine players available at any price. JB's orchestra was drawn from many sources, some of them surprising. Their performance was less the product of talent and inspiration than of sweat, his and theirs.

It was also, in a marvellous way, the product of their unique social mix. Since talent pops up in all sorts of places, any symphony orchestra provides a wide variety of folk. I suppose it would be hard to find a wider assortment anywhere, other than in one of Her Majesty's prisons. Conventionally the mix is blended by shared experience and by the teaching institutions. Not so in the Hallé of 1943. These people had little in common except their enthusiasm for music, their determination to make a fine orchestra and total confidence in JB.

One more asset the early Hallé had in abundance: the north country habit of caring one for another. This remained, a unique quality, to the end of JB's time and after, and it made membership of the Hallé very special.

Among the loyal remnants of the old orchestra were remarkable talents. Arthur Lockwood, the aging first trumpet, was still among Britain's finest; Charles Collier, a survivor of Richter's Hallé, was a superb harpist. Pat Ryan was then and for many years after a marvellous lyric clarinetist. A disabled pensioner of the First World War, Paddy had been offered a job in Boston by Monteux, reaching the New York pierhead before turning and buying a return ticket. After one peep through the pier gate he had come to the conclusion – one which would surprise 'New York's Finest' but typical of Pat – that the USA was no place for an honest Irish boy. Of all that historic band Ryan was perhaps the jewel. It was typical of Hallé humour that this lovable and irrepressible Irish genius was known to us all as The Banshee.

The new Hallé included, for the time, a large proportion of women. An early programme listed 23, among them two horns, a double bass and the timpanist. A lady first trombone, Miss Maisie Ringham, was an early and sensational acquisition.

Very few of these people had previous experience of symphonic playing, or of full-time orchestral employment. They were, so to speak, a clean sheet. In that situation JB had been an inspired choice. He was a great teacher of the orchestra: perhaps the greatest of all teachers of string ensemble.

The regime with which he began still ruled when I joined, 17 years later. By that time the new Free Trade Hall had replaced the famous original, destroyed in the blitz, and the Hallé had returned from its temporary home among the circus elephants at Belle Vue. Preliminary rehearsals were held in a disused warehouse behind Central Station. It was a dismal place, the last one would have chosen as the birth-place for a symphony orchestra. There had been, I suppose, no room at the inn, and no money for the rent either.

JB's rehearsal days were *eleven hours long*, with the orchestra working in shifts. He would call the strings for three hours, the wind and brass next, then the whole orchestra in the evening. Between sessions he would 'crash out' on a camp bed. The next day the dose was repeated, with the wind and brass called for the early shift.

On the day of the concert he had the ritual three hours in the concert hall.

I have a vivid recollection of his appearance at my first rehearsal. He never entered the room until tuning had ceased and all was quiet. How very ill he looked. The tubby little Italian of my brass band concert ten years earlier had become a skeletal remnant, sunken-cheeked and pale; so pale that the eyes seemed to glow in contrast. At a glance any doctor would have diagnosed malnutrition. His voice, after an operation for throat cancer, was reduced to a croak. When he raised his hands to begin they shook.

I never remember seeing JB, in what were to be his last ten years, in a condition remotely resembling health. Where most conductors are scrupulously careful about their lifestyle, their schedule and their diet, jealously guarding their physique and their brains as irreplaceable tools, JB worked himself obsessively to destruction. We watched it happen, unable to help him; he would not help himself.

Perhaps this predicament, this all-consuming need to perform, was genetic and inevitable. He had been a hyperactive child; his parents made him a cellist because he would not stand still while practising the violin; but I have no doubt that the needs of the reformed Hallé provided the trigger. There had been pathetically little money. Audiences must pay. There must be as many concerts as possible. Coming from the USA, where public subsidy was unknown, JB faced that situation cheerfully. There had always been − and until the very end there always was − a teeming audience for the Hallé. All it need do was travel and play. In any case he distrusted subsidies, fearing that those who paid him to pipe might try to dictate the tunes. So from the very outset the Hallé had worked terribly hard for survival. Not for nothing was it called, in the early days, The Galley. The miracle is that so many fine players survived it, to become ornaments elsewhere, and that so many others lived and worked to happy old age *in* it. That JB lived out nearly thirty years of that regime is most remarkable of all.

He was surely the greatest workaholic of all time. Asked once what his idea of hell was, he replied immediately 'A quiet evening at home by myself'. He worked on every day he could, once telling me proudly that he would work every day *for the next three years*. Yes, even on Christmas day, in Tel Aviv. What would he conduct then? *'Messiah!'* I can hear his throaty chuckle still.

Even while travelling he worked. Once his car was involved in a collision, with a heated altercation between drivers. Immersed in a score, he noticed nothing. His first learning of scores was follow ed by intensive editing, especially of the string-writing. Each phrase and dynamic produced specific and meticulous technical instructions which he personally transferred to the first-desk parts before photocopying. This was a product of the early Hallé, when everything possible was done for string players. Hallé strings never attained to the metropolitan level of skill, player for player; but in JB's time, such was his expertise and his unremitting energy in conveying it, that this never showed.

Many other first-rate conductors have been first-rate orchestral string players, but no other, except perhaps Ormandy in Philadelphia, seems to have carried the search for effect through strings and bows to such lengths. JB was still able – and more than willing – even in the 'sixties to pick up a cello and demonstrate. This was relished by the orchestra and invariably rewarded with a cheer. When the demonstration went wrong of course the cheer was louder. He was not in the least put out. Order was quickly restored with a couple of raps of the stick on the desk and a reproachful and half-humorous 'Be quiet, children!'.

Basically his approach was to find the technical solution which would suit his weakest player and apply it to everyone. This might irritate the strong, but it worked. JB's strings were a model of unanimous clarity and at the formation of the Hallé certainly the best in the land. Nor was his technique merely a matter of getting it right and getting it together. He had a knack of changing the bowing and the string which could produce magically changed colour. To play the music was not enough for JB; he played the orchestra.

He saw drama in everything, and exploited the drama in music to the utmost. *Pianissimo*, obtained at the point of the bow, was hardly audible. *Fortissimo*, at the heel, could attain almost physical force. His gestures often related to bows rather than to beats, his stick being held across his body like a cello bow and the middle finger of his left hand vibrating on his lapel. A dead left hand was anathema to him. When he spotted one in rehearsal he would leap from the box, without stopping the playing, charge up to the offender and *vibrate under his nose*. That left hand was very eloquent; palm always open and demanding, it spoke a very personal language. The fingers were never separate and independent but the thumb, extraordinarily mobile, had a life of its own. Its top joint was capable of outward extension to a right angle, something I have never seen elsewhere. His eyes were everywhere.

'Get to the point! Point! Point!' was his constant call in soft passages. The Berlin Philharmonic, which loved him dearly and rewarded him with a one-take recording of Mahler's Ninth, called him *Spitze*.

Sometimes his gestures, formed by bowings, could be very entertaining. There is a point at the start of the first *allegro* of the *Fantastique* of Berlioz, involving extreme exchanges of dynamic and pizzicato interjections. This looked for all the world like a swimming instructor's demonstration of the breast-stroke. It was accurately imitated by the wind and brass, secure — as we imagined — behind our music stands, and this became ritual in rehearsal. One day when we forgot to do it he stopped and demanded that we 'pay attention!'. The passage was then repeated and we all joined in, to his immense satisfaction.

Yes, JB shared the orchestra's sense of humour, as he did every atom of its psychology. Concerning wind and brass, that was the limit of his knowledge. Strings were for him a highly disciplined instrument, the chief matter of the orchestra; wind and brass were colour. He looked to us for excitement, for flair, for personality. He seemed unaware of our need for the organised unanimity he brought to the strings. To me, as a new arrival, Hallé wind and brass, though often of virtuoso quality, seemed un-coordinated. I determined to bring to the job the skills I had learned from the Birmingham brass. I was lucky in my new colleagues; they were well aware of the need. We put a lot of time into the problem. We formed a first-rate brass ensemble, a freakish activity before Philip Jones & Co smashed the credibility barrier. Soon we created a new and interesting picture.

JB's reaction was mixed. He had enjoyed the unfettered virtuoso approach of the old firm. The grand gesture, the individualistic and even risky solo phrase, was the breath of life to him. Still he recognised our contribution, expressing puzzlement, after my first six months, to an intimate friend. 'The Hallé brass is better than it has ever been', he said, 'and I don't understand why that is. *All the good players have left*'.

There had indeed been a turnover of personnel that year, many fine players disappearing in the now traditional direction of the

[72]

BBC orchestra. One escapee observed soon afterwards that the 'Northern' was now no better, and the Hallé no worse for the changes. JB had created his second-generation Hallé, and his last.

It was a very different Hallé band from the first, which had worn itself to the uppers in the struggle for survival. I caught the dying of that situation in my first year there, when in five summer months we worked for only five days at home in Manchester. That, I was told, was a Hallé summer. Thankfully it never recurred. We had a new general manager, replacing one who had been resented by the orchestra as no manager before nor since, surely. The new man, though an accountant, was more civilised, and relaxed the pressure. There was, it seemed, just enough money to keep us solvent *and* sane

I found the new job a greater strain. Blowing the trumpet is a physical matter, and the environment in which we do it can make a great difference to the physical load. The Hallé was a bigger orchestra than the CBSO and here colour, excitement and drama were the basic diet. JB's strings provided for the wind a thrilling context but a formidable obstacle to audibility. We had to work hard to be heard; and Sir John demanded that we *were* heard. Our orchestra had, unsurprisingly, a transatlantic quality; a visiting American conductor once remarked that it was the only British orchestra with *steam*. Ernest Hall, who had known JB since they were youngsters together in the LSO, described him as 'merciless' to the brass. So he was; but then he was merciless to everyone else too, and to himself.

He said once that the secret of orchestral performance lay in unremitting rehearsal. Many experienced players would say that for the British orchestra at least it is not the only way, and not always the best; but for JB and his Hallé so it was. Nothing was kept back in rehearsal; he demanded the total effort all the time. The extra in performance was for him to extract. We ended his 11-hour days utterly whacked. In contrast he often seemed brighter, fitter, and happier at nine o'clock. It was as though the orchestra fed him.

Curiously his rehearsals, though intense, were almost light-hearted. There was an atmosphere of the family, of people who knew each other very well. Membership of the Hallé was not so much a professional as a personal commitment. Not for nothing did he call us *children*. He'd adopted us, and he expected filial loyalty in return.

Paternally, he had not the least objection to the kind of orchestral joke which destroys many conductors. He knew there was no vice in us. Once, when after a personal demonstration of cello technique a still, small, and very Lancastrian voice from the back of the orchestra commented *'Telegraphic address: Modesty, Manchester'*, Dad chuckled with everyone else.

He ran to extremes. 'Don't worry about overdoing it for me,' he said, 'Nobody ever managed that yet!' Once he asked our first oboe, after extending a Beethoven cadence far beyond any comfortable limit, how long that pause could really be. The player replied that what he needed was a colour-chart.

His gift for massive orchestral sound was really extraordinary, reinforced as it was by the ability to make people simply work hard. Reserve was useless; better far to get stuck in and die quickly. I remember a rehearsal of a Bruckner symphony where he prepared a massive wind and brass unison at great length, making progressively more and more sound. When he was satisfied that every decibel had been extracted he turned to the strings and said 'Now, that's not important – YOU'VE GOT THE TUNE!'. The orchestra was convulsed with laughter. For once he couldn't see the joke.

What a complex personality he was. Twenty years after his death old Hallé hands still speak of him with gratitude combined with protest, with disparagement and admiration, with affection and irritation; and always with different memories and impressions. He had the hide of a rhino, yet he was easily bruised by disloyalty or by the adverse response of a player he admired. He could react with black rage to technical failure, yet his personal sympathy for Hallé players in sickness or trouble was human and real. His demands on the orchestra en masse seemed often utterly callous yet he genuinely *cared* about each of us, our pressures, our families, and our doings. He visited players in hospital loaded with flowers and grapes. At Christmas there was a present for everyone, with a handshake for the boys and a kiss for the girls. The fact that ours were always cigarettes, smokers or not, and labelled 'British Airways Duty Free' was all part of the fun.

We remember him differently because he related personally to each one of us. If he could not reach a player, or if the player carefully excluded him, he was unhappy. It happened, sometimes. Musical antipathy must be the chief reason for such an exclusion, when it happens. What kind of musician, then, was JB, technique apart?

As the man, so it was with his music. He was a mass of contradictions, constantly taking one aback. The routine perception of the time, and one which has taken root, unfairly, with time and repetition by people who never worked with him, is that he was vulgar. Neville Cardus, who knew and admired him, once wrote that with JB there was always 'half an inch too much of astrakhan on collar and cuffs'. That's fair. The surprise was that the astrakham varied in inverse ratio to expectation. One might expect from him highly coloured Puccini, overstated Verdi, and sentimental Elgar. Rubbish! Yes, his *Butterfly* was emotionally overpowering. It overpowered by clear insight, by subtle and penetrating characterisation. It was understated – and devastating. I have heard nothing remotely comparable since. The Verdi Requiem, with JB, was an intimate act of faith rather than 'Verdi's best opera'. He overstated, often, and sometimes disastrously; for me he could destroy Brahms. But in so much of the repertoire he was a wonder. So often, since, I have experienced those pieces as catalogues of misunderstandings, of lost opportunities.

He could be good and bad in the same composer. His Tchaik 4 – and he loved the work – was poor; his Fifth and Sixth, which he played rarely and rehearsed much less, wonderful. In early Sibelius his preoccupation with the drama of the landscape often led him to forget its geology. Yet in the Fifth and Seventh Symphonies he was – and I write the words carefully – without equal. I remember a performance at the Helsinki Festival when the audience was simply *bombed* by the Fifth. There were, at its end, six or seven seconds of a silence so intense as I never expect to hear again, before the roar of the audience, leaping to its feet. Tauno Hanikainen, who had conducted the piece so often and knew the composer so well, said over supper that although it was late at night he would now go home and read the score again. 'After so long,' he said, 'an Italian conductor and a British orchestra have shown us the truth in this work.' Of all the many fine performances for which I thank JB I remember that concert as the summit of my symphonic experience.

His Elgar – now, there's a question! Fortunately the recordings exist, and will exist so long as does the gramophone in all its manifestations. Listen to his *Falstaff*, made in a single session in the old Kingsway Hall, using the time saved in making the Second Symphony, and after some years of neglect. That is incomparably the best recorded *Falstaff*. It was a glorious morning in the making.

The symphonies and the *Dream of Gerontius* I thought I knew well; perhaps too well. Elgar had been Birmingham's own composer. Now he was revealed to me for the first time. There is little point in comparing JB's performances, as critics do, with those of the admirable Boult, or the impeccable Sargent. JB played for people, and cared not a jot for cerebrators. Don't discuss JB's *Dream*; listen, if you can, with mind as open as his own. Wonder at the sincerity of his belief in Newman's poem, Elgar's music, and the faith they inseparately express. Others may have been more *correct* in their 'interpretation' of *Gerontius*. For JB it was not a matter of interpretation but of conviction, a conviction which made us all Catholics for an evening; an experience so intense, even in the recording studio, that members of the chorus were unable to sing when the prelude ended. Elgar would have loved it.

He was at his most lovably comic when rehearsing most intensely, and never more so than in the *Dream*. Jokes were 'out' on those days, when his personal faith combined with the work of a composer so close to him. The slightest levity could produce a bomb from the rostrum. One such incident produced an historic exchange of fire.

Someone had giggled, undeniably, while he was talking. He slapped down the stick on the score. 'I will not have you people laughing while I'm rehearsing this wonderful work', he croaked. 'It's an insult to me and an insult to Elgar'. Then, as his voice ebbed away with his temper, picking up the stick to resume, 'It's an insult to God, too.'

Came that still, small voice from the back of the room: 'In that order, naturally'.

Thank heaven no-one laughed.

JB was a cockney, and proud of it — a Londoner who'd spent his childhood holidays on Sussex beaches or on the pier at Southend; but he brought to his music a passionate commitment, inherited from his Venetian father, against which the British stiff upper lip had no defence. He believed in Elgar as a flesh-and-blood human being rather than as Master of the King's Music. Perhaps I can best illustrate this with the memory of an incident during the recording of the Second Symphony.

We had finished the slow movement and some of us accompanied JB, as he liked us to do, into the listening room for the playback. There came a moment when the sheer passion of a great string statement took us aback. It seemed as though for once JB really was over the top; that some bars had strayed in from *Cavalleria Rusticana*. Martin Milner and I exchanged worried glances. These were detected. When the music stopped JB came over to us, waving a bony finger under our noses. 'I know what you are thinking, you two,' he said with a grin, 'and you're wrong. All my life people have been telling me that Elgar was a respectable Edwardian gent. THAT'S ALL BALLS!' And off he toddled, chuckling happily, back to his beloved Hallé.

CHAPTER 11

Have Trumpet ...

Hallé travel reduced to a tolerable level at the time of my joining but, since we were good business for hirers and since we were never well enough subsidised, touring was much more important to us than to other orchestras of the time. The public's appetite for Barbirolli seemed insatiable. We never expected to see a thin house. When it happened JB's reaction was swift: 'If they don't want me here ...!' He would be seen no more in that place.

The season began with a tour. We would rehearse for perhaps three days and then set out on a round trip which began in Cheltenham. Then to Bristol and the South-West, turning back at Plymouth or even further afield, and often playing again in Cheltenham before returning. Financial considerations apart, this trip played the Hallé in for the season, musically and socially. The inevitable new intake, green from the Royal Academy, learned a great deal about the art of orchestral playing and many other equally important matters before the buses rumbled back home to Watson Street.

Most orchestras on the road play the shortest possible rehearsals. Not the Hallé. We worked for three hours each day, rehearsing not only this evening's music but huge chunks of the coming season. We would work at Mahler in Winchester Cathedral, for instance, before a concert containing Wagner, Delius and Elgar. It was killing work, but Manchester could be sure of highly polished stuff on the first night of the season as a result.

There were really three Hallé seasons. Concerts at Sheffield and Bradford, week by week, closely shadowed the home series. The Sheffield audience, including an enthusiastic contingent of young people who filled the platform behind us, was open, accepting, and fun-loving. The City Hall is a unique building, vast and ovoid, looking for all the world as a visiting Russian conductor wonderingly exclaimed like 'ein' cirkus!'. The famous stone lions which originally divided the orchestra neatly into two separate halves were removed during my time chiefly as a result of repeated caustic attacks by Beecham, but the place was still an acoustic trap. Guest conductors, fatally relaxed in the finale of a romantic symphony, sometimes found that unison had become canon or even fugato. I cannot remember a really fine concert played at Sheffield. Perhaps it was not possible in a hall where neither side of the orchestra could hear the other. But they loved us there, and we loved them too.

Bradford's St George's Hall is neither big nor marvellously beautiful, but it is a place where an orchestra can really play. The Philharmonic Society, as befitted so ancient an organisation – it is more than a century old now – had a mind of its own regarding programmes. JB's were carved in stone, naturally; but on other evenings Bradford would demand change. That we had played Dvorak in D minor perhaps five times in the previous week meant little to Bradford except, cannily, that we might be fed up with it by Friday. Bradford might typically demand instead the G major, at the cost of some hours of extra toil. The Bradford audience, too, was a hard nut to crack, with a rare level of criticism to satisfy. The difference between Bradford polite and Bradford delighted was very audible at 9.30. Bradford, I sometimes think, got the very best of the Hallé.

Among my happiest recollections of that town is that of a fish and chip restaurant of unparalleled quality, opposite the Alhambra Theatre, where the Hallé brass gathered for supper. One could eat memorable halibut, chips, with bread and butter and a cup of tea for three and sixpence there. We usually had two helpings each. Sheffield, alas, had no comparable delight to offer. To the orchestral nomad these things count.

The journeying to and from either city we turned into a sociable motor-rally. Hallé drivers were creative but not much admired by their insurers. In one year we had more than a score of accidents great and small. Martin Milner, our leader and a man of iron behind the wheel as with the violin, once wrote off a car and almost himself with it en route to Sheffield. After an afternoon in the infirmary he turned up, looking and no doubt feeling like a creation of Franken-stein, to play the solo violin in *Le Bourgeois Gentilhomme.* Very decently done it was too, for a man in utter agony.

Weather conditions over the Pennines were often alpine, and the route chosen crucial. Once, reaching the point of decision at Glossop, I found a sign informing me that 'The Snake pass is closed. Go via Hathersage'. This I duly attempted. Climbing determinedly on a road narrowing by the minute as the snow built up, I met a snow-plough coming down. He stopped, his blade inches from my radiator, and asked my destination. I told him. 'Well', he said, 'I wish you luck. But it's beaten me!' I arrived in time for the concert, by train.

Weather permitting, the orchestra gathered at various hostelries on the way home to analyse the damage done to our ensemble by this week's guest-conductor, and to discuss the means of repairing it tomorrow at Bradford or Sheffield as the case might be. On the following evening the discussion would be reopened at another pub a few miles away. The trick was to get the thing right before Manchester heard it on Sunday. We succeeded sometimes.

The people who conducted in JB's absences were rarely very distinguished. The exceptions, though, were occasionally wonderful. By what miracle we were granted ten days with Carlo Maria Giulini in 1968 I do not know, but I remember our General Manager telling a group of happy players that 'This is all for you. *We* don't need Giulini. *We* can fill the Free Trade Hall with George Weldon and a Tchaik night. So make the most of him while he's here.'

We needed no urging. For me, and for many others, Giulini's visit became a special time when all the right things happened and all the good influences came together.

His programmes were sensational in their demand on the Hallé brass. The *Pictures* of Moussorgsky, in Ravel's orchestration, figured in four concerts with Hindemith's *Concertmusic* for strings and brass. A second programme included Debussy's *Nocturnes* and the Second Symphony of Brahms.

We got ourselves into formidable shape for the great man. The brass did their homework together on the Hindemith, which was new to us. I did mine on the Moussorgsky. *Pictures* is a warhorse with most good orchestras. Visiting conductors so often ask for it that it is always part of the orchestral vernacular. But it is still difficult, especially for the first trumpet, who must open the piece unaccompanied.

Problem passages produce received solutions. We are taught those solutions by our professors. The opening of *Pictures* can be made safer (I can still hear Ernest Hall's exhortation 'Safety first, Bram! Conductors don't enjoy cracks!') by a deliberate, sprung attack. That was my approach, and that was what I intended to deliver for Giulini. But Italian visitors had often asked for the complete opposite: a risky *legato sostenuto* delivery which changed the nature of the prelude utterly. CMG, I thought, might be another. Some conductors might compromise. He might not. This worried me.

We had a good first morning with the Hindemith. He was obviously as pleased with our brass as we were with him, so during the lunch interval I decided to ask his advice about *Pictures* in case we were at odds. The result was one of the most fascinating conversations I have ever enjoyed with a musician. It went like this:

'Maestro' (he was the only conductor ever called by that name in the Hallé in my decade; it seemed immediately right) 'I wonder if you would talk to me about the Moussorgsky?'

'Of course. If you have a problem ...'

'Not really a problem ...'

A broad smile here. 'But you are spoiling your lunch break! Obviously there is a problem!'

'Well, the start of the piece. Some Italian conductors ask for a *legato* approach which is really trouble, you know ...'

'Yes, perhaps.'

My heart began to sink. 'It's so dangerous. It would be a terrible thing to spoil your concert with an accident at the beginning.'

'I am sure you will not do such a thing. Come, what is so dangerous?'

I explained that the risk in the octave leaps was doubled if I was deprived of my *deliberato* approach. He suggested that while the prelude might be *legato* the jumps could be attacked with deliberation. 'With such brass-playing here you can easily arrange that. It will not be a problem.'

He could see that I was not convinced. Opening the score he asked me to read the composer's initial instruction. It's long and complicated and ends with the words *senza allegrezza*.

'Tell me', said Giulini, 'what these two words mean in your language.'

I found this difficult.

'But it is simple. It means *without happiness*. These are the important words. Tell me, what is this prelude about?'

I told him what every A-level student knows: that it describes the man walking around the gallery, looking at the pictures.

'Yes. The question is – what kind of man? I think I know *your* man. He is beautifully dressed – a fine suit, silk tie with a pearl pin, nice haircut, shoes shining. He is the curator of the picture gallery and he is walking round, looking at the pictures and saying "What lucky people live here, that they have a clever man like me to choose their pictures." He is *pomposo*, your man!'

I had to admit that he had my man to a T.

'Now let me tell you about *my* man. Have you ever been to Milan?'

I had, indeed.

'But – on a wet Sunday? Milan is a bad place on Sunday in the rain. There is nowhere to go except Church. Well, my man is at Milan station on a wet Sunday and he has missed his train. There is no train for two hours. He is a poor man. His suit is poor, his raincoat is soaked, he has holes in his shoes. He looks across the street from the station, and he can see the art gallerie. He knows nothing about pictures, and cares nothing. But there is nothing else. So he crosses the street, with water in his shoes, and he goes in. Now he is looking at our pictures'.

Here the Maestro rose from his chair, turned up his collar, and walked round the room looking for all the world like a tramp with leaky shoes, bored out of his mind.

'Can you see my man?'

I could almost hear the water in his shoes.

'Well – if you will find that man for me I will paint the pictures which will make him an art lover for life!'

So I promised of course to play the most unhappy prelude to *Pictures* ever heard. I could do no less.

Came the concert. I waited for his signal to begin. He raised his hand. I raised my trumpet. He put down the stick, with an encouraging gesture which said 'When you are ready, my friend, begin!' Such wisdom, to know that difficulties are halved when we can choose our moment. I took my life into my hands and gave him exactly what he had asked. After two bars a graceful wave of the hands brought in the brass ensemble. What a master!

Four times we played that programme for Giulini. He made it all so easy. Later in the week we made a superb job of the *Nocturnes* too.

No-one who played for him during that visit will ever forget those concerts. For him, also, the Hallé seems to have provided something memorable. To JB the Maestro afterwards wrote of having been 'in a family', an atmosphere which he had never before felt in an orchestra. And before leaving he autographed my score of the Hindemith like this:

A Bram Gay

in grato ricordo per la sua preciosa collaborazione con profunda stima e viva simpatico umana.

C.M. Giulini Manchester. 14 Nov. 68.

CHAPTER 12
Two Titans
Second Interlude

Rudolf Kempe was a colossus. I first played for him in Birmingham, where he gave a marvellous and typical evening of Strauss, Mozart and Brahms. His unique qualities were much better shown to me later, at Covent Garden, but a story he told us during his Birmingham rehearsal deserves a place here.

He had arrived to rehearse Mozart in G Minor. We had mistakenly programmed the *Prague*. He would not change his programme, which began with *Don Juan* and ended with Brahms in D major. The librarian was summoned. While waiting, RK told us about a similar accident, much earlier in his career.

He had been in New York, resting between operas. Late one night his telephone rang. It was the Intendant of the Vienna State Opera, with a nightmare. In two days' time there was to be a gala opening of *Tosca* in Vienna, a great occasion with a new production. The conductor was sick. The occasion was much too important to give to a house conductor. The orchestra was asking for Kempe.

He dismissed the idea instantly. There was no Puccini in his repertoire. Even if there had been time to learn and rehearse, he was not the conductor for that piece. Vienna was a long way away. The thing was out of the question. He put down the telephone.

Two hours later the caller returned, even more worried. There was no comparable artist free. Kempe must please think again. Surely he must at least know the opera from his playing experience? And he must have heard it so many times ...?

Kempe was obdurate. What he did know of *Tosca* from his days in the orchestra was that like all Puccini it is a minefield, a work for the specialist, and absolutely not his business, especially not on one rehearsal. No, no, no!

Again, in an hour, came renewed pleadings, this time reinforced by the voice of the Vienna concertmaster. The House's reputation was at stake ... the orchestra had complete confidence ... there was a plane in three hours which could get him to Vienna via London in time for a long rehearsal with the orchestra and cast on the day of performance. The distinguished cast was pleading ...

In the end Kempe got up, telephoned for a score, drank some coffee and took a cab for the airport. Once aboard he settled down with the score and began to learn. He was a prodigious learner of scores, that man, but *Tosca* in a day was a tall order, even for him.

There was a fog at Heathrow, with a long delay. He arrived in Vienna much too late for any rehearsal at all. The limousine was waiting on the tarmac. Still reading his score he arrived at the Staatsoper one hour before the time of performance. The Intendant was so relieved, and so grateful. So would the Orchestra and the Company be, of course.

'But ... with no rehearsal, not even a piano run-through ... surely you don't expect ... the thing is impossible!

'Rudi', said his friend, 'If any man in the world can conduct his first *Boheme* without a rehearsal, you are that man!'

We asked him how it had gone. He said he honestly didn't know.

* * *

We could not know, when we met Bernard Haitink in Manchester, that we were watching the British debut of a conductor who would dominate the British scene during the last quarter of the century. We knew very little about him except that he was Dutch and had been given the conductorship of the Concertgebouw on the death of Van Beinum. Since he was still not yet thirty-five years old we naturally assumed that his appointment owed more to his nationality than to his talent. We were quickly and happily disillusioned.

We learned a great deal about him in the first ten minutes. In programming Stravinsky's *Rite* he had assumed that the Hallé, like every good orchestra in Europe, knew the work. This was a miscalculation. The Hallé under Barbirolli knew nothing of *The Rite*, having last played it twelve years earlier, and that very badly under an over-ambitious visitor. Many of us had never seen the work before. In fairness to the Hallé it must be said that the work was not much played in the UK then. It's expensive, and Manchester audiences were easily frightened. We looked forward to it with interest, but we thought young Bernard was on a hiding to nothing.

Haitink presented himself fresh, fit, happy, and altogether the right sort of chap with whom to spend a Hallé week. He said 'good morning' in nice English, and then 'We begin with Stravinsky, which of course we all know ...'

Martin Milner then acquainted him with his predicament. Haitink sat down abruptly on his stool, the colour ebbing from his face. There was a long silence. Then he collected himself, picked up the stick, and said 'Let's start at figure ...'

In that short time he had reorganised his day knowing, as we did not, that though the piece is very hairy indeed for half its length the rest is technically relatively simple; so simple that it is first-rate material with which to establish an understanding with a new orchestra.

These passages we rehearsed for an hour or more, generating the security of ensemble and the rhythmic vitality on which the piece depends. By this time we felt on pretty good terms with Stravinsky, and quite on top of half the work. It was all good fun, it seemed, and not a bit fearsome.

After the tea-break he suggested that we now play some other passages, very slowly. This we did, over and over again. The beat was clear and utterly secure. Haitink never dropped a stitch. The piece focussed itself, bar by bar, like a musical jigsaw. By one o'clock the *accelerando* had begun. At two-thirty we played *The Rite* from beginning to end without a mishap; not a performance yet, but a rehearsal miracle. The Hallé Orchestra, rarely a vehicle for twentieth-century music, had made friends with Stravinsky's monster. On the following evening, in the Free Trade Hall, it ate from our hands.

As in the case of Kempe, I was to learn very much more of Haitink in another place. For the moment let's give thanks again for the Dutch tradition founded by Mengelberg, passed by Van Beinum to this third great conductor, and demonstrated so clearly and so early in his career.

Why is it that the Dutch produce only one of these miracles at a time? Will another turn up to take his place? Apparently not, since the Concertgebouw looked to Italy for his replacement.

Let's leave Haitink to mature. But one remark, made by a Dutch player, is worth recording. The Concertgebouw board was in session, debating anxiously the succession to Van Beinum and terribly worried by Haitink's youth — he was then only twenty-eight. The matter was clinched by one disillusioned old hand, who said despairingly 'Oh, give the boy the job. He knows nothing, but *he is a conductor!*

Indeed he is. And he knows quite a lot, now.

CHAPTER 13
... Will Travel

Our Hallé first bassoon, Charles Cracknell, was a mountain of a man in whose hands the instrument was diminished to the size of a flute. He and I stood at the rail of a boat travelling up the Hardanger Fjord to an obscure Norwegian town where we were to play that evening. The day was radiant, the scene beautiful beyond description, and Charles was philosophically inclined. This was not unusual.

'Did you know', he asked, 'that the water here is more than seven hundred feet deep?'

This was news to me.

'What fun it would be', he went on, 'to pop one's *faggot* over the side and imagine it slowly sinking to the bottom ... glug, glug ...'

I suggested that the bassoon, being made of timber, might float.

'Yes', he sighed, 'there really is no getting rid of the thing! One is doomed, like the Flying Dutchman, to play it in every corner of the globe until doomsday. I don't know when the first concert on the moon will be, but I know who will be playing.'

From behind us came the famous croak. 'Yes, *mon petit basson*, AND IT WILL BE SOLD OUT, TOO!'

Most conductors are content to travel solo, enjoying the world's orchestras one by one. Not this one. His delight was to tour the Hallé, 'My great orchestra'. JB climbed the aircraft steps, orchestra in tow, with the enthusiasm of a scoutmaster going to a jamboree. On my first trip abroad with him and his band, sitting together in a very rough old Viscount (our charter firm went broke five days later, leaving us stranded in Cyprus), we talked of income tax. His Hallé salary, he was convinced, was worth less in hard cash than mine. Since his policy was to work for the Hallé for peanuts and collect the real income elsewhere, this may have been true. Suddenly he grabbed my sleeve and dragged me to the window. It was a cloudless day. 'Look!', he said, 'My native Venice!' Sure enough, there far below in the sun was the famous campanile.

His father, a Venetian cellist, had shared a desk with Toscanini in *Otello*, Verdi conducting. He'd married a lady from Arcachon, near Bordeaux, the home of the best oysters. They settled in Southampton Row, almost half-way between the opera and Bow Bells. Perhaps a child with such a background had only two options: he could be rootless, or at home everywhere. JB chose the second and it worked; a valuable trick in a trade where one must make friends quickly.

He had learned in New York that we were all in show business, like or lump it. That entailed matching one's concert to the audience. In the Royal Festival Hall, conducting Bruckner and receiving the medal of the Royal Philharmonic Society, he was the dignified servant of the muse. On tour he could be something much closer to John Philip Sousa.

His audience-appeal was immense. It was wonderful to see how, when the little figure came beetling into view, every face would instinctively break into a smile. Those gestures, often more choreographic than instructive, 'sold' the music wonderfully. He told me that he much preferred conducting the Hallé to any other orchestra because we understood him better. 'In other places I have to conduct like a policeman!'

A master at 'milking' the audience for applause, he rarely failed to achieve six curtain calls at the end of an evening. He had a marvellous way, when the applause was dying, of stopping just inside the stage entrance, where he would hold a brief conversation with anyone who happened to be about. The tail of his coat still being visible — on his best form he could even get it caught in the door — the audience was obliged to go on clapping.

If encouraged his encores could be extravagant to the point where the customers wanted to go home and couldn't. At the Dubrovnik Festival we gave a fine concert, ending with Brahms' second. This was an experienced audience and its delight was obvious. He responded with 30 minutes of Johann Strauss, including the *Zigeunerbaron* overture and *Tales*. Since the festival is played out of doors the audience almost literally waltzed away.

What a beautiful city Dubrovnik was then, and how I hope it is not all ruined now. JB marched us to the top of the walls one evening to see the sun go down on that lake of glowing pink tiles, with the Adriatic beyond. Next morning, out for a walk alone, he sat down at the foot of the wall-steps, taking off his hat in the sunshine and placing it on the ground at his feet. His dress, as often on informal occasions, was very shabby indeed, and he looked, as ever, quite ill. The local people dropped coppers into his hat. This he recounted to us later, without embarrassment, as evidence of the natural generosity of the Croat.

Few will forget our trip from the airport at Titograd to Dubrovnik, a day-long trek over mountainous roads in antique buses. At one point we crossed an inlet of the Adriatic by means of a terrifying ferry. Three barges had been lashed together with hawsers, and our boneshakers were driven on broadside. We were invited to alight and stand during the crossing. This we were glad to do since there seemed every likelihood that the vehicles might roll off. There was just room for a hundred people to stand around the perimeter. Halfway over, as we crossed the wake of a coaster plying up and down from Split, the whole mad contraption bucked and flexed, gaps opening everywhere. To round the day off our hotel announced, when we at last reeled in, that because of a mistake only two-thirds of our rooms could be made available 'until tomorrow'. We must sleep three-to-a-room. Protests from our management, who scented fraud and knew that 'tomorrow' might never come, proving ineffective, we sat down in the lounge and began to sing. The 'mistake' was quickly rectified.

Istanbul was a rare experience. We stayed at the Hilton, the first symphony orchestra ever to do so. We were meticulously catered for, down to the musak. At the moment of our arrival, by some miracle of Turkish-American technology, Beethoven began to play. Perhaps it stopped when we left for concerts; I don't know. What is certain is that the whole time we were in the building we were entertained, over and over, by the *Eroica* funeral march. Perhaps another orchestra would have remonstrated? The Hallé sense of humour was always a bit odd.

We visited, during my Hallé decade, 29 countries by my counting; some of them four times. We knew Switzerland very well. The great trek, though, was our six weeks in South America.

JB had done this circuit once before, with the Philharmonia. He knew the ground and became the courier *par excellence*. His health was now seriously deteriorating, though, and this was rough country for a man with a developing heart problem. In Mexico City, where we all suffered to some extent from the altitude, he was given oxygen between movements of the Walton Violin Concerto. This did not prevent him from showing us the pyramids next day. In Buenos Aires ie walked with us round the famous cemetery, the most ornate and expensive in the world, before our concert at the Teatro Colon.

The Colon is a vast theatre, the only first-rate opera house in South America, with a rich tradition of conducting and singing. We played before the proscenium, on the raised pit. It was something of a shock, passing through the curtains, to meet an interior rather like Covent Garden or La Scala, but as big as the Albert Hall, or so I remember it. Buenos Aires is a very Italian city, and we were warned that our audience would be hard to please, in the Italian operatic tradition. The theatre was sold out, and people were queueing outside the building for standing-places when we arrived, a whole day before the concert. This was rare, as symphony concerts were thought to be a second-rate pastime there; opera was the thing. But here was the Italian Maestro with a very Italianate Schubert C major. They loved him. They cheered and cheered. The friends we made — and what enormous steaks they fed us — in the local symphony orchestra could not remember such a reception for an orchestra in that theatre.

We played in Lima, Peru, after a whole day's flying over the Andes, gaining a new geographical perspective vertically. What we all wished was to visit Machu Picchu, a twenty-four-hour drive there and back. Four players not required in one concert made the trip, stopping three times during the long climb to re-tune their carburettor. Sadly, such treats are not for first trumpets.

Then to Santiago, where a British diplomat told a small Hallé supper party of the secure delights of serving in Chile where, he said, democracy was so stable because of the separation of the military and judiciary from the Government. In that way, unlike most of South America, it was just like home. That man will have found subsequent developments in Chile surprising, no doubt.

Our experience of the British diplomat abroad was very mixed. Greeting our presentation-line in turn, one such simply could not say the right thing. The brass, coming in together as always, fared especially badly. Terry Nagle suffered the push-me-off-the pavement joke. I was greeted as 'Little man, big noise, eh what?' and our tuba, bringing up the rear, feared the worst. A large but usually gentle man, a former steel worker from Rotherham, he took our Ambassador's hand firmly in his and announced in ringing Yorkshire tones 'My name's Roebuck.' The grip steadily increased, causing His Excellency's feet almost to rise from the floor as our friend continued, 'and I play t'tuuuuuuuuba!'

The man's subsequent career was very distinguished. We followed it with interest, and often wondered if he remembered that handshake.

Only once on that tour did we find anti-British feeling. At the start of a concert in Sao Paulo there was a demonstration by students which, despite creditable efforts by our friends to persuade us to the contrary, we recognised as anti-colonialist. JB responded with an Elgarian encore. Fortunately by that time the protesters were safely out of earshot. Perhaps, anyway, they would not have recognised *Land of Hope and Glory?*

Next morning some of us were finishing breakfast when JB entered, newspaper in hand, grinning broadly. We thought we were in for a lengthy translation of his reviews, but no. 'These people', he said, 'have a funny sense of humour. They are holding a national conference on birth-control ... *at a town called Concepcion!'*

CHAPTER 14

Goodbye, JB

It was all wonderful fun, but it was hard work and getting harder. In the end so many of JB's finest performances, quite impossible without him, were made almost in spite of him. As his condition worsened we had to fight for every concert. Killing work, it was killing the old man.

No other conductor, perhaps no other human being, would have struggled against those physical odds to the very end. There is a story that he was told to stop conducting because of the possibility of death on the box. His reported response, 'Rubbish! More people die in bed than conducting symphony orchestras!' would have been typical of his sense of humour. In any case, without his work he would have been dead in his own terms.

We had some near squeaks. A performance of Mahler's Second in York Minster went on unconducted for what seemed a lifetime as he blacked out, leaning on the score, and came round to resume. Terrifying. During a recording session in the Kingsway Hall – Delius' *Appalachia* was in progress – he fell from a high rostrum, unconscious. Before he could be rescued he was up again. 'Don't worry, children! I'm all right!' and on with the work. His determination was superhuman. It demanded a superhuman response from the orchestra.

At that time my solo work was becoming more important, but also more and more of an added load. As the Hallé never released us for other work, it was necessary to travel sometimes overnight to Glasgow, Cardiff or London to broadcast or televise a concerto, then back overnight for a Hallé trip. This was not good for the concerto, the Hallé concert, nor for me. But the Hallé situation was now so uncertain that it all had to be crammed in as insurance.

Uncertain? Yes. Few of us had confidence in the post-Barbirolli Hallé. In his time no other writ ran. He was, as the Indian proverb has it, the tall tree under which there is shade but no growth. The Hallé would go on; one would make a living at it. But the only justification for many of us in working there was the level of performance we achieved with JB. We had little confidence in Hallé management without him, and none in its ability to replace him. As in Birmingham, but for a very different reason, the leakage of players began.

Hallé-trained strings had no difficulty in finding jobs in London. JB's band had been a reservoir for the LSO, the BBC Symphony and Covent Garden for many years. The contacts were always alive. At his twenty-fifth anniversary concert, in a characteristic speech to the audience, Sir John remarked that on his visits to London he was always pleased to renew his acquaintance with so many famous players who had received their orchestral training in Manchester. 'Mind you', he added, 'most of them need a refresher course!'

It was not so easy for wind and brass players to leave the ship before its predicted grounding. There were fewer gaps for us, and the London profession defended itself well against hustlers and rustlers. We sat and waited and hoped.

For me the break came unexpectedly. I was telephoned one morning by the Orchestra Director at the Royal Opera House, who was looking urgently for a good trumpet to complete a tour in the north with the Royal Ballet's second eleven. I could not help him, but as the conversation ended I said wryly, 'On the other hand, if you need a dogsbody trumpet for the House orchestra I can supply a Hallé-trained one!'

The conversation developed. I learned later that my friend had conveyed it to Sir David Webster, his General Administrator, and was instantly told to hire me.

My friends thought me quite mad to give up a principal chair in the Hallé for a subsidiary position in the opera. They underestimated my fatigue. I knew that I could not keep up the Hallé pressure for 25 years more, until retirement. The prospect was not appealing anyway. Covent Garden seemed to be at least one answer; not the best, perhaps, but it was 'The bird in the hand'.

At the top of the staircase in the Hallé offices stands a large bust of Sir Charles Hallé. I remember feeling, as I passed it going down after my resignation, that I had first passed it going up only yesterday. Such, I suppose, was the effect of the pressure of work. A distinguished colleague, meeting me again on my arrival at Covent Garden, described his 20 years in the Hallé as 'a 20-year nightmare'. I was taken aback; he had been such a success and so much enjoyed.

This was the last response I had expected from him. On reflection I know what he meant.

*   *   *

Sir John died in the winter of 1969–70, some months after my leaving his orchestra. He had intended to conduct *Otello* at Covent Garden in the spring, but it was not to be. The news came with breakfast. He had spent the previous day rehearsing Brahms with the Philharmonia in preparation for a Japanese tour. He'd been in great form, and had gone to bed happy. After so long expectation, the news was somehow unbelievable.

Let's go back for a moment with JB to the very beginning of the new Hallé and before, and remember with him those dim and dusty days in the old warehouse when he auditioned his first band. This, as I remember, is what JB told the audience at the Free Trade Hall when he presented the Hallé medal to Oliver Bannister, his best find, the inimitable first flute who had joined at sixteen:

It was a depressing evening. It had been a depressing day, up there in the dust. Player after player, from nine in the morning to nine in the evening, and nothing to show for it. I'd had just about enough. The job seemed really impossible. I was ready to chuck it in and take the boat back to New York, I can tell you.

Then at nine o'clock the door opened and in came this little boy with a flute. Oh dear, I thought, children now! But we must be kind to the children. So I asked him his name. My name is Oliver Bannister sir, he said. Well, Oliver, I asked, what would you like to play for me? He replied that he would play whatever I liked; so I found the opening of L'Apres Midi and asked him to play that. He played, and as he played the sun came out.

Johnny, I said to myself, this is a sign. The thing can be done.

Well, it was done, but if Oliver had not come that evening things might have been very different. I might have gone away. You might not be sitting here now, enjoying this great orchestra. And let me tell you this. Oliver Bannister has been with me for twenty years, and every time he has played the sun has come out for me.

British music owes a great debt to JB. Its debt to the brave band who played with him is also considerable.

CHAPTER 15

The Enemy?

I left Manchester and the Hallé because I was terribly tired of the travel which seemed an essential part of the Hallé tradition, and because I was afraid of imminent artistic collapse there. The first reason had lost the Hallé many before me; but why, when the orchestra itself was so very strong at that time, did I fear the second? Would the loss of a conductor make such a difference?

I believed that it would and with hindsight I know that it did. Only players understand how one man in a team of a hundred can have such an effect. While I am en route for Covent Garden, then, let's look at conductors and conducting.

Players are hard on conductors. The hardest verdict I have ever heard was given to me, on entering the business, by a friend with two years' experience in the Royal Philharmonic: 'Conductors, with few exceptions, are the player's natural enemy. There are two kinds. On the one hand there are the great artists like Toscanini and Tommy. Their one wish is to help you to play, to enjoy music, and to be happy. All the others are bastards and all they do is bugger you about.'

This is an extreme view, but not an uncommon nor an unreasonable one, taken subjectively from a seat in the orchestra. The conductors we meet, day by day, are a decisive element in the quality of orchestral life. They fulfil the player or they frustrate him. They send him home happy to his wife and kids, feeling that all those years of grinding work at fiddle or flute have been worth while, or out to the pub to drown his resentment.

Toscanini and Tommy are of course dead, like all great men. Are there none left alive who are worth anything? Yes, of course there are; but they are few in comparison with the vast number of mediocrities who hopefully climb the rostrum steps every morning, stick in hand. If it were possible to institute a measurement of all the world's conductors, graduated from one to a hundred, with Karajan and Kleiber at 99 (perfection being out of the question; but is there any means of measuring Kleiber?), under the judgement of an orchestral consensus, very few would pass the 45% mark. Possibly as few as a hundred.

So, are so many conductors 'buggering us about?' No. They are honest professionals working hard at a nearly impossible art *and failing*. The few who wilfully abuse the orchestra — and there are a few, and some among the best conductors — do it for fun and through a mistaken idea of the psychology of the orchestra; there really are fools who believe that fear can produce performance. But the great horror of the mediocre conductor is that in his well-intentioned inadequate way he *bores* us. What can be worse, after a lifetime dedicated to music? Here is the source of a great resentment and many ulcers.

Is the art of the conductor then so difficult? The orchestra knows that it is; and that is why it suffers mediocrity so often and so patiently. Many of us could do the job badly, and this is the reason why *we must not do it*. Better by far to be a first-rate cellist or clarinettist, enjoyed by colleagues, audiences, and conductors, than to suffer as a boring conductor. Yes, suffer these must. They've aimed too near the sun and have fallen short and hard. The bruises which result are painful and permanent; and often, in the inevitable disclosure of psyche by the conductor to the orchestra, depressingly obvious.

Difficult then: perhaps the most difficult of all the performing arts. Can the job be defined? A treasured old dictionary, much quoted in bandrooms, has it that a conductor is 'an object or thing which conducts'. The Oxford is more generous, with: 'The director of an orchestra or chorus, who indicates to the performers the rhythm, expression, etc., of the music by motions of the baton or the hands'. Well, what is so difficult about that? We've all 'got rhythm', and the signals by which it is conveyed to the orchestra are quite simple; an international semaphore system which can be taught quite quickly to anyone but a motor-moron. The orchestra, too, seems perfectly well aware of the rhythm and of every other aspect of the music. The naive audience may wonder whether the conductor is necessary at all except to start the piece. The impression given by von Karajan, for instance, to such an audience was probably that he emoted in response to the Berlin Philharmonic rather than that he created performance through it; a beautiful and satisfying illusion born of transcendental technique.

That wizard once demonstrated to a master-class how minutely calculated that technique really was, using a climactic moment of Bruckner in rehearsal. He brought in each section of the orchestra, in turn, untidily before the others *though perfect in ensemble within itself.* A matter of perhaps a fifth of a second each, but ruinous. Next time he produced the complete ensemble, tight as a nut, without any change in his gestures visible to the audience. This was all the more remarkable because it is quite difficult to persuade the Berlin Philharmonic to play untidily, however inept the direction.

How was it done? Is conducting on that scale simply a God-given talent? To some extent yes; but von K had applied to his natural gift a phenomenal intelligence and decades of hard work. His technical skills became instinctive, so that in the end he seemed to conduct music simply by living through it; but they *were* skills nevertheless, and skills he had devised and taught to himself. Von Karajan was, I think, the first of the modern conductors. Before him the orchestra was a group to be commanded; now it has become, for the best of his successors, an instrument to be played.

Few can do it, but as time goes by the craft of conducting, rather than its mystique, is more and more recognised. It is also more necessary as orchestras become more demanding. Today's highly professional players will not accept amateur direction, however 'gifted'. They demand skills at least as great as their own, and why not? A conductor must lead from the front, literally, and to be one step ahead of the band – in itself no easy feat – is not enough.

How is a conductor made? The British player, perhaps the greatest cynic in these islands, will reply instantly 'By luck and a hard neck!' That reply does great injustice to some very hard-working and dedicated people; but there is no evidence of a British conducting 'school' to compare with those of Leningrad, Milan, or Vienna. It is no accident that these places produced Roszdesvensky, Muti, Abbado, and Mravinsky.

Opportunity is important. Countries in which no large town is complete without its orchestra, and no city without its opera house, naturally breed more conductors. There is no job to compare with that of repetiteur, teaching and accompanying voices in an opera house as a training-ground for the aspiring Toscanini. Some time ago a famous German conductor was asked how he got his first job. His reply went something like this: 'Like every other conductor, of course,

I replied to an advertisement for music staff in a very small and very poor opera house and I got the job.'

Intrigued, his interviewer pressed for details. How exactly did one 'get the job?'

'In the routine way. I queued up with many others. Eventually I was shown into the presence of the Music Director and the Intendant. On the piano were two scores; orchestra scores of course, not piano scores. I was asked to choose one, open wherever I liked, play and sing. The scores were *Walkure* and *Wozzeck*. I am a baritone, as you can hear. Who would volunteer to sing *Wozzeck*? I chose Wagner, turned to Wotan's Farewell, played and sang. I suppose I did it better than the others. I got the job'.

That young man, a newly finished student, could play the piano fluently at sight from the orchestra score. He could sing. He knew the two works. He knew where to find the *Farewell*, perhaps the only immediately singable baritone passage in *Walkure* for the amateur. In a land where until recently there were only two opera houses, such a background is rare. Small wonder, then, that we produce so few important conductors. When we do produce them — and happily we do — they rarely have these practical skills.

Klemperer, who came up by that traditional route, insisted also that the conductor must compose, however badly. Without that skill, he asked, how could the conductor understand the problems of the composer?

So! A difficult job. What then is the minimal demand of the orchestra? Where do we draw the line?

First the conductor must be able to 'drive the car'; to control the basic ensemble. Given an experienced orchestra he should be able to give a safe, conventional performance of, say, the *New World* or of the Eighth of Beethoven, or *Scheherazade*; one in which nothing will go seriously wrong. That is the basic requirement; that he should be as competent to control the notes as we are to play them. That's where professionalism begins.

The music itself is 'his business'. We hope always for some appreciation of the composer's intention, for musical conscience, but these are not essential to us. Only an utter barbarian on the box causes musicians to down tools in artistic protest. We know that the audience will not blame us for his misconceptions. We know too that at the end of the concert we can scrub the slate clean and hope for better luck tomorrow. Stick-incompetence, on the other hand, raises our hackles very quickly because it handicaps us.

We very much admire the man who can deliver performance through the hands alone. Some are so talented in this way as to render words nearly unnecessary. They save a vast amount of time and make lots of friends. Seiji Ozawa, rehearsing at Covent Garden, observed that to be Japanese, with very little English, was a very lucky thing because 'Mouth is greatest enemy of conductor'. He was right. Beyond this basic level technical control is not enough. Standing as he does between the composer and the audience the conductor has an equal responsibility to both. He should bring to the music something important from his own study, his own experience, and his own personality. It may be argued that what is needed is the score, pure and simple, untouched by a second mind. Bunkum! In that case the computer would rule. Ninety other minds, perhaps, will have their effect, and he must co-ordinate and discipline their input. But it is vital that the conductor's personal contribution should be of a cultured and sensitive mind; one in tune with the composer, his period, and his problems.

It is not difficult to be musical in the abstract. It is not difficult either to become technically, *physically* proficient. But technique inhibits musicianship, as musicianship can inhibit technique. This conflict can be crucial. Every gesture may affect the sound. The conductor cannot move a muscle without causing something audible to happen. Every reflex in ninety minds and bodies is tuned to respond to his. Our primitive semaphore now becomes a matter of intricate and subtle body-language.

The strings are perhaps the most receptive, the most vulnerable to physical suggestion. They make their sounds by arm-movements, and their response to the conductor's arms and hands is instinctive and immediate. They need gestures which, while not sacrificing for a moment the precise direction needed by the whole orchestra, will produce the appropriate texture of sound. This can be very different in Stravinsky and Elgar, in Brahms and Britten. It is by physical gesture, inescapably the expression of the personality, that the greater conductors make their own very personal sound. That unique quality, often expressed through many different orchestras, is one of the factors which make the great interpreter. It is as personal as the singer's voice.

[99]

The orchestra would add to all these one qualification more. Ideally the conductor should learn his repertoire from the inside, in the orchestra; as a string player, preferably, but as a player anyway. There he will see enough bad conducting to learn how not to do it. Most important of all he will come to understand us.

We are his instrument: the most complicated instrument of all.

CHAPTER 16

A Leap in the Dark

At the end of Solti's 'Golden Decade' the reputation of the Orchestra of the Royal Opera House stood very high. I heard it in its own theatre for the first time before I joined, in a performance of *Peter Grimes* under Colin Davis. I thought it a good opera band, though hardly justifying the critical raving which then prevailed; 'corruscating brilliance' was among the descriptions used in the press.

On sitting down for the first time to play with the orchestra I quickly realised that there was a great deal wrong with it. While there were, and I trust always will be, players of world class at Covent Garden, there was then a serious lack of quality among the rank and file of strings, and what talent existed was very much less well organised than in the Hallé.

The orchestra was the Hallé in inverse: basically a roughish string band liberally decorated with glorious talent among its principals. Solti's stunning performances were obtained by long and repetitive rehearsals of an elite selection of players. There was a 'Music Director's Orchestra' within the larger body. When he was not about selection was less careful, rehearsal was much shorter, conducting often poor, and playing consequently less meticulous. Not to put too fine a point on it, I was very disappointed indeed. Had I been offered a transfer back to Manchester at the end of my first two weeks I would have jumped at it.

To add to my depression, because Solti worked only with known qualities I was not included in his pieces for a long time. Instead I was given an extended course in the art of the theatre orchestra based largely on routine 'revived' opera under rather dull conductors, liberally mixed with ballet under the vigorous direction of John Lanchbery.

The theatre really is a different job. It is impossible to realise how different without experiencing it. Some changes the player expects and accepts on leaving the platform for the pit. Others come as a shock. The most devastating in its musical implications is the impossibility of hearing the orchestra in the way to which one has been accustomed.

However the pit orchestra is seated – and hardly a week goes by without some new, inspired, and doomed experiment in seating – the ensemble is never truly heard by those playing in it. Some pits are better than others in this respect, naturally; but the orchestra, conditioned by the concert platform, insists that there are no good ones, only bad ones and impossible ones. At Covent Garden those on the extremes of the pit have the biggest problem. Not only can the heavy brass – the trumpets, trombones and tuba – of the Covent Garden Orchestra not see the wind and horns; they cannot hear them except when they are resting, when it matters least. Contact between cellos and basses is nearly as difficult. Even firsts and seconds, at extremes, are inaudible to each other.

It goes without saying that on a flat floor we can see nothing except the conductor on his rostrum and the player in front; so the ensemble is much more directly in the hands of the conductor than in the symphony orchestra. The approach of the 'big chamber group', the symphonic ideal, is out of the question in the pit. There is no hope for the conductor who likes the orchestra to find its own attack.

New arrivals on the Covent Garden rostrum are often appalled by its problems. Sometimes they try to solve them by re-seating; this is silly. We've been looking for a solution since 1943 and *everything* has been tried. We very much admired the response of Zubin Mehta, who on his first viewing of the pit said 'Well, it looks all wrong to me but they are used to it; and there are a hundred of them and only one of me!'

Mechanical precision we can achieve mechanically. Given an articulate beat we can play on it, all together. But ensemble is only the beginning. What of tuning? What of balance? What of blend between parts? all these matters need ears. At Covent Garden they need radar too. One develops radar then! But when, at the end of *Tristan* or *Götterdämmerung*, the final wind chords sat in tune, I marvelled and gave thanks for dedication and concentration; I also prayed for the day when something might be done about the problem in the way of restructuring of the pit. Unfortunately that may not be enough. The acoustic of the theatre itself, in relation to the orchestra in the pit, is the real problem.

The repertoire of the theatre is new to the symphonic player. This, with the subsidised canteen and the season ticket to the same station each day, is among the job's attractions, but it can pose problems even for the experienced. Naturally we play quite a lot of opera and ballet on the concert platform, but suites from *Nutcracker, Firebird* and *Petrouchka* are small preparation for the live monsters themselves. Those ladies and gentlemen, dancers and singers, who perform over our heads are a new factor and a potent one. They have minds and problems of their own and they are not always under the control of the conductor — or not to the extent he and we might wish. That is another reason why the theatre orchestra must have clear, confident, and flexible direction. It cannot be sure from moment to moment what will happen.

Mind you, the first-rate opera orchestra has a first-rate awareness of its own, and this sometimes operates independently of the conductor. As one of my colleagues told me very early — and it has proved more than true — if they drop a ball into the pit we can usually chuck it back directly without waiting for the umpire. And when the umpire himself drops a ball the orchestra usually knows what to do with that, too. Many conductors have had cause to be grateful for this.

In much of the repertoire the orchestra is amazingly on top of the work, to the astonishment of the new player. The hard fact is that some operas, and especially the Italian repertoire, are unplayable at international level without an experienced band, however good the conductor and however long the rehearsal. Puccini demands second-to-second flexibility within a structure of amazing complexity. If the player must stop to think the entry is gone.

I discovered this on my first morning, in *La Boheme* with Edward Downes. The brass contribution to the first act consists largely of one figure, an interjection in various keys:

There were no voices present. Here was a jigsaw with crucial missing pieces. Not once did I succeed in getting that figure played, while those around me knocked the entries in with the effortless unanimity of a machine. The Garden orchestra can almost *sing* those pieces; (they would say 'What d'you mean, *almost?*'). My friends found my predicament great fun. They'd seen it all before. One was kind enough to tell me that he'd had the same experience on first meeting that opera except that he'd been sight-reading it in performance and got the figure in *once*. Yes, it was in the wrong place.

Ballet poses special problems, all the more irritating to the musician because since ballet cannot be heard (except under the stage, where the effect is that of a herd of small rhythmic elephants) and the orchestra cannot see it, the reasons for its difficulties are not clear. The better the dancer, in the purely technical sense, the more likely it is that we find ourselves playing Tchaikowsky – especially Tchaikowsky – at strange and variable speeds. The famous *Rose Adagio* from *The Sleeping Beauty* is in every sense a classic illustration. In that marvellous piece the Prima Ballerina must turn, *en pointe*, completely round, very slowly, steadying herself only momentarily on the fingertips of her changing partners. The finer the dancer the slower the turn. Makarova was magnificent at this point; the lady seemed able to stay up there until morning. The audience loved it. We all admired it. But what of the music? It was destroyed. Just as well, perhaps, that no-one seemed to be listening to it, through the thunderous applause. Poor Tchaikowsky! Still, he worked with the ballet, and he was used to all this.

Then again it is tragically true that many choreographers set music which cannot be danced, or so it seems from the outcome, without distortion. Why this should be, when the ballet repertoire teems with musical masterpieces, who can say? Of course ballet needs renewal through music, but why choose those works which don't work? If they speak to the choreographer so strongly that he must set them, then why not set them well and musically? Why bend *Das Lied von der Erde*? Why play Tchaikowsky's *Serenade for Strings* (yes, that man has really suffered!) with the movements out of order? There will never be mutual respect between pit and stage while these things go unchecked.

The great balletic achievements of my time at Covent Garden came when Bernard Haitink, with a fine sense of responsibility for all the House's music, conducted the *Romeo and Juliet* of Prokofiev and an evening of Stravinsky: *Firebird, Scènes de Ballet* and the *Rite*. Then, some years later, Ravel's *Daphnis*. These are works in which he is at his wonderful best, and they are scores written for the ballet; scores which need not bend. The playing was superb. The dancers were inspired by it. This surely is the way ballet should be. But these things were deep in a very cloudy crystal ball when I played my first *Beauty* in 1969, and of all the depressions in our weekly task then, none compared with the prospect of two *Swan Lakes* on Saturday. We played ballet very badly then. It was not always our fault. The improvement has been wonderful to hear, though slow to come.

A different job? A different world! And, with Solti's leaving, one due for upheaval. The arrival of a new music director is always a traumatic time. Colin Davis was knocking at the door.

CHAPTER 17

An end ...

We wondered about Colin Davis. On the whole, orchestral opinion held that he would be more trouble 'off the box' than Solti had been, since his stay at the BBC had not produced a better orchestra nor a happier one. On the box we certainly expected less of him than of Solti. True, he was a theatrical by instinct and his natural talent, backed by a developed technique, was formidable; but the Chelsea Opera Group and Sadler's Wells were not to be compared with the Solti operatic background. And Solti was, well, Solti. We hoped, we doubted, and we waited.

Early posterity judges Colin's mark on Covent Garden to have been less successful than Solti's. Posterity, though, is famously liable to superficial conclusions in the short term. Ours is a business in which it pays to advertise, and among Colin's likeable idiosyncrasies is a distaste for personal promotion and publicity. Solti knows the value of both. This difference has had its effect on public perception. Colin's contribution cannot be assessed without a clear picture of the situation he inherited. I was not in that picture until the very end, but some aspects of it are clear.

Solti had joined a House of great name and prestige but of no very great current reputation: an undeniable advantage for a mark-maker. Covent Garden, however glorious its history may appear on record-sleeves, was a young institution. The prewar Garden was a seasonal affair, very dependent on the energy and bank-balance of Sir Thomas Beecham. It employed the LSO and the LPO − each orchestra in turn as TB gained or lost control over it − and played those pieces Tommy thought London needed. Our operatic debt to Beecham cannot be over-estimated. The least we can say of him is that he constantly reminded us over a long lifetime of the shame of having no national opera company of our own. Without his persistence and largesse we might well have none still; but the establishment of a permanent opera company at Covent Garden was beyond even him. It was done without him, at the same time as the setting up of the new regional symphony orchestras.

David Webster, the General Administrator appointed with miraculous serendipity by the Arts Council, worked wonders on a shoestring but that shoestring didn't extend to a great Music Director. Karl Rankl, the first incumbent, was a man of great experience but little charisma. Webster, recognising the need for that quality, tried in turn to secure Erich Kleiber and John Barbirolli – who used the offer to pressure Manchester for more money for the Hallé. Eventually Webster engaged Rafael Kubelik.

It is irresistibly tempting to speculate about what might have been had Walter Legge – very much in evidence in the debates of the time – been in control rather than Webster. Legge's adverse opinion of artistic standards at Covent Garden in its early days is no secret. His own solution, as demonstrated at the Philharmonia, was vastly more imaginative and successful at least in the orchestral sense. Could von Karajan and the Philharmonia have been secured for the Opera? Perhaps. Could the Opera have paid for so exciting an approach? Certainly not on the budget then offered. But would EMI have helped the Opera, as it helped the Philharmonia, with a mammoth recording commitment? Possibly. What a wonderful package that might have been, and how operatic standards here would have been advanced. Where then was the rub? Making a hypothetical objection to a perhaps fanciful idea, I would say that this solution would have placed the future of British opera in the hands of the directors of a recording company, unthinkable in principle; and with hindsight, remembering the severance of the EMI-Philharmonia connection and the chaos into which that wonderful orchestra was then plunged, perhaps Covent Garden had a narrow escape.

In any case Kubelik was a bold appointment, a musician and conductor of world stature. He believed in operatic ensemble and strove for a truly national opera company. Those who played for him at Covent Garden remember him with affection and admiration, amounting almost to defence. Something was lacking: a certain sense of the theatre perhaps? A warm and understanding human being he is, but no extrovert. The theatre is a place for showmen.

Curiously, the great success during the pre-Solti period was one who seemed quite removed from show business. In performance Rudolf Kempe, like Haitink today, seemed absorbed in the music and the orchestra to an extent which almost excluded audiences, making any suggestion of show ridiculous. For those who watched, rather than listened, very little was projected backwards. These are musicians' conductors. Kempe would have been the perfect Covent Garden appointment, his achievement even greater than Solti's. Why? Because he was a great trainer of the orchestra, having learned the job from the inside and in a fine school at Leipzig; he was as fine a natural musician, with considerable operatic background; his performances in the House, particularly in the Solti repertoire − the Strauss pieces and the *Ring* − were superior in the opinion of most who played with both men; and because he would have given Covent Garden everything he had to give, without reserve. The orchestra would have been saved years of development. Kempe would have built it, though at a cost, probably, to the security of many who worked in it; Solti did not.

To measure the rate of orchestral improvement by the number of changes made within the band would be facile and silly; but it is significant that during Solti's ten years only one change was made in the orchestra *at his insistence*, while all his recordings but two − and the two were not among his greatest successes − were made elsewhere. To go into the recording studio with an orchestra is the conductor's vote of confidence. To fail to do so with one's own orchestra is an unmistakeable statement of opinion as to its quality.

I wonder whether Solti could have improved the orchestra had he really tried. His standards are immensely high − none higher − but the means of obtaining them, in matters of pure orchestral technique, are beyond him. A brilliant mind, he must know this. Fine orchestras have been supplied ready-made to him for many years. Had he imposed internal change on the Garden orchestra he might well have made mistakes.

The business might have made him unpopular, what's more, and this would not have suited him. He is certainly not the cold-hearted egomaniac of his public presentation, the famous 'screaming skull', 'the only conductor who can go into a revolving door behind you and come out in front'. No, here is a man with a heart, a warm human being who, when colleagues measure up to his high standards, responds in the most positive way. Let's not forget, either, that his life had been hard, though finally lucky as only the enormously talented and hardworking deserve, and that he may have suffered the inadequate simply for humanitarian reasons. Solti was not an axe-man at Covent Garden, even where the wood was obviously dead. Kempe, I think, would have been merciless.

Merciless? The word will raise the eyebrows of players brought up in today's world, where orchestral management has become civilised. Not only structures but attitudes were different in the 'fifties and 'sixties. Today's Garden orchestra thinks of itself as permanently employed and attached to the House, but at the outset the House contract was a seasonal one, players being engaged from September to July and remaining essentially part of the great London freelance market. They did not depend on re-engagement, nor did the House depend, as it so much depends today, on their return after the holiday. Lines were kept open, other work was maintained and non-renewal of the contract in the following season was not the professional and personal disaster it has since become. This produced a certain toughness on both sides; a player too often late for rehearsal would easily disappear in July, while a manager giving unwarranted trouble to a more valuable player would find that he'd lost him — and sometimes before the expiration of the contract too.

Morris Smith, who built the first orchestra for Webster, has left an unenviable reputation among players who have forgotten the climate and ethos in which he lived and worked not merely as a manager but as a player himself. I met Morris; he tried in vain to give me a place at the Garden in 1955, uselessly against the wish of Kubelik, who saw that I was not ready. I cannot say that I liked Smith. I think that he might well have exploited the flexibility given to him by conditions at the Garden to an extent which players found it hard to forgive. But he was, I suspect, no worse and no better in his treatment of players than were his contemporaries. The speed with which weakness was purged in the early Philharmonia, for instance, is legendary.

As John Tooley once observed, it was very much easier to manage the Garden Orchestra in the 'fifties than in the 'eighties. If the Musicians' Union and the better organisation of the players have been partly responsible for the change, the employer-employee relationship in modern society has also had its due effect, as has industrial law.

The orchestra left to Solti by Kubelik was at least a good one, then, kept up to scratch by strong management. A recording made just before Solti's appointment, a pot-pourri called *Solti at the Opera*, is the work of a far better orchestra than the one I joined ten years later. So there had been no urgent need for overhaul. Solti's failure, whether deliberate or not, was to relax the supervision of the orchestra and to reduce its self-esteem by constant championship of others in the recording studio.

Still, who could have resisted the Vienna Philharmonic? Who would have argued with the Decca mandarins the virtues of the Covent Garden orchestra against it? Solti's choice was simply a hard-headed artistic and commercial one, owing nothing to his middle-European background nor to a personal sympathy with the Viennese. The opposite, in fact, must have been true. The Philharmoniker, it is well known, enjoys most those conductors who disturb it least, and Solti is a wonderful disturber of preconceived ideas in the orchestra. He is Hungarian, which hardly helped. He is a Jew, and that certainly did not. They worked together because he knew they were the ideal orchestra for him at that time and because they knew he was good business. Both were proved right. But in London it will always be argued that much of his Vienna recorded repertoire, including that wonderful *Ring*, was learned at Covent Garden. From a seat in the orchestra it counted against him and always will. All the more remarkable then is the affection in which Solti is still held at the Garden. While he contributed little to the development of the orchestra *as an instrument*, nor to the standing of the players within the House, no conductor is more welcome in that pit today. This speaks not only for the performance he brings but for the quality of the man.

Now he was leaving, and the orchestra regretted it. They recognised his achievement; and like every orchestra they very much preferred 'the devil they knew'.

CHAPTER 18
... and a beginning

Colin Davis came to us at exactly the right time in his career. The worst, the middle period, was over. He'd had an indifferent time at the BBC with the Symphony Orchestra, an orchestra temperamentally unsuited to his enthusiastic approach to music, tennis, or whatever else he takes up. Colin is a vigorous human being. He likes life to be fun. The BBC takes itself very seriously. The canteen atmosphere is very unlike that at Covent Garden.

He'd made mistakes there, of course: what chief conductor does not? There had been change without impressive improvement, and that is never enjoyed by orchestras nor by those who run them. In any case, Colin is that rare bird among British conductors, one happier in the theatre than on the platform. He will readily point out that the opera theatre is the most exciting toy in the world. 'Wonderful pictures ... those voices ... these terrific scores! What more can a man ask? Much more exciting than the symphony orchestra!' Once, in our early days together, in a fit of nostalgia I told him that I would swap the complete output of Verdi for the finale of Brahms' fourth. Laughing, he chased me out of the room. He came up through opera, first attracting notice with the Chelsea Opera Group, and then exploding upon the public when called to deputise for the ailing Klemperer at the Festival Hall. He'd served his apprenticeship at Sadler's Wells. A rare bird, Colin; a conductor who takes operatic obstacles and complications in his stride with a smile, knowing that they often contribute, in a strange way, to the performance. The production of opera, like a second marriage, is a triumph of optimism over experience.

Early on he showed signs of his old impatience, of the bull-at-gate Colin. The orchestra needed change. There were sad things in it. At the end of his first season he gave instructions for the dismissal of a handful of players. The orchestra reacted firmly, though in a very different way from today's established reflex. Nowadays there would be protracted domestic discussion within the House, followed by union negotiation. In those days the Musicians' Union had not the muscle for such things, so the orchestra flexed its own. Its tactic was simple. A complete section of the orchestra resigned, headed by its distinguished principal. The players were reinstated.

The lesson was not lost on either side. The orchestra, having saved the necks of some inadequate players simply for the sake of putting an early brake on the Music Director, began to consider more reasonable means of resolving that problem in future. The Music Director and the house began to consider constructively how artistic standards were to be raised without constant conflict with valuable players.

This was the first warning to Administration at the Garden that a completely new approach to orchestra management would soon be needed. The Webster-Smith autocracy, to which any kind of consultation with the orchestra would have been anathema, had gone. John Tooley was tomorrow's man. He and Colin began to cast about for help. They had no intention of fighting a good orchestra, packed with admirable old friends, for ten years; but they would not suffer stagnation either.

Musically things went well. Colin opened with his inimitable Berlioz, the complete *Trojans*, beautifully produced, marvellously sung, conducted and played. A triumph. We recorded it too. There were endless sessions in the studio, earning lots of extra money for a grateful orchestra and chorus. Our *Trojans* was an award-winner, and not only from record companies. The prize from the City of Paris decorates the office wall still. The *Légion d'Honneur* decorates Colin.

This marked the start of a wonderful series of recordings. Whether we were the best orchestra available to Colin and the Philips company I don't know. I doubt it. But with him it was very much a matter of 'love me, love my dog'. Utterly loyal to his orchestra and to Covent Garden, Colin brought all his opera recordings to us during his years in the job. We rewarded him with some splendid things. There was a prizewinning *Così* in 1975, all the more gratifying because Solti had also recorded that opera in that year. There was a superb *Clemenza* to follow, and many more.

Once encouraged, others followed suit. There was a *Fanciulla* with Mehta, Domingo singing; a *Luisa Miller*, with Maazel. John Pritchard made *L'Elisir d'Amore*. These things are habit-forming. Success brings more of the same. We made Richard Rodney Bennett's wonderful film score for *Murder on the Orient Express*, with Charles Taylor, our redoubtable leader for 29 years, contributing an authentic fiddle in an Istanbul tea-shop. We began to feel like a good orchestra.

In the house Colin was wonderfully supported by Helga Schmidt, our Viennese Artistic Administrator: a lady of fine judgement and apparently unlimited acquaintance among operatic high-flyers. Helga delivered a catalogue of conductors such as the Solti period had never seen. Kempe, who had rarely appeared during the *golden decade*; Abbado, Muti, Maazel, Rozdesvensky, and eventually the unobtainable Kleiber.

Such people would do wonders for the orchestra and the House. They have a predictable knack, however, of demonstrating an orchestra's weaknesses. The trick was not simply to produce these names once, but to bring them back for more.

The orchestra was in need of overhaul, without doubt. And now Colin was working with the practical Tooley. John knew that orchestra building at the Garden would be a slow job, not to be approached with an axe and suddenly, but carefully and progressively. The orchestra is a tree in which some wood is always growing and some dying. Orchestral development is not a matter of dramatic gestures but of small, simple and unnoticed adjustments, day by day.

For this long haul these two would need a new attitude in the orchestra office. They began to look around for the right man. They looked, first of all, in the orchestra itself; a solution with which the members would certainly have agreed, however debatable the final choice.

That's where I came in and where my trumpet went out.

CHAPTER 19
Dogsbody

From star turn on the concert platform to dogsbody in the pit, the adjustment had been quite difficult. I soon discovered that keeping my form up would not be easy without the pressure of concert-exposure every day and a brass section of my own to lead. Occasionally I was given something important to play but in general my work was obscure. I was by no means a perfect low trumpet, and to be a first trumpet *occasionally* is difficult. For the second time in my career I found myself in a job which a wiser manager would not have given to me. On the other hand, I had space to relax, sit back, and take stock; a good idea, after 20 intensive years.

It helped that our principal trumpet was a fine artist and a wonderful colleague. Harry Dilley had been at Covent Garden since the late 'forties. The most remarkable trumpeter with whom I've been privileged to work, he was kindness itself. We had a lot of background in common, from the Salvation Army up through the Guards. He seemed glad to have me, probably because his other trumpets were so much younger. In his sixties, Harry played like a man of twenty-five, a trumpeter's trumpeter with a unique place in the London profession. A modest and retiring man, he could have been famous, but the comparative anonymity of the opera pit suited him. Even the admiration of his colleagues embarrassed Harry a little. We played wonderful repertoire together, his astonishing performance a compensation for the fun I was missing.

Sometimes there was enough to keep us both occupied. The operas of Strauss, for instance, are a revelation to the symphonic musician, conditioned to believe that the orchestral poems are difficult. I think it would be easier to play all the tone poems in one evening than *Die Frau Ohne Schatten* once. I was not admitted to the *Ring* yet, but there was *Tristan*, and *Tannhäuser*, and *Parsifal*, which had given Barbirolli such fun at my expense. Dilley dealt with all these things with ease. I was able to learn and admire, while counting bars rest by the thousand. Solti, a great admirer, described Harry Dilley to me much later as 'A first-class player, by any standard, anywhere in the world'.

What a fascinating artist, musician and human being Sir Georg Solti is. I had met his musical attitudes once long before, in Birmingham, though in a very different personality. Here again is the Toscanini tradition, powered by a million-volt generator; electricity on two legs. Such energy! Solti could power Battersea. We used to say that the lights burned brighter when he came through the stage door.

He has the distinguishing mark of the really first-rate conductor, the steamroller mentality, the inability to make u-turns. He has learned and prepared; he knows where he is going and how he will get there, and debate only demonstrates that he has done his homework best. It is remarkable how uncomplicated life in the pit becomes when he is about. There are no latecomers; even British Rail seems to be under his control. Seating problems are much reduced − there is always room for the most fractious violinist to play. Enquiries about misprints, bowing conferences among violas, are few. Life becomes a matter of keeping up with the quicksilver brain behind the penetrating eyes. Even in his generous rehearsal schedules there is not a moment to spare, it seems; everything depends on the next 30 seconds. Solti waits for nothing.

He is not a classic stick-technician. In matters of ensemble this is not very important because his knack of making the sound at precisely the right point in time renders the attack predictable. Listeners would do well, I think, not to watch him because his gestures, aimed at complete rhythmic accuracy, can be distracting; but there is nothing wrong with the sounds. Solti knows our theatre, none better; and he takes more care with the balance of sound in it than any other conductor. Typically he does not ask for opinion, trusting no judgement but his own. When the purely orchestral work is done and the voices appear with the production he will often hand over the stick to the assisting music-staff for fifteen minutes while he stands in the stalls, the most problematic space, listening. That is very wise. Ours is not a helpful House.

He supervises for himself detail which almost every conductor might leave to others. His casts are personally chosen down to the last small part; in *Rosenkavalier*, where the three orphans make the briefest of appearances in the first act, he will audition even these for himself.

His near-obsession with rhythm can be problematic for singers. To one distinguished soprano, an old friend and impervious to insult, he once called over the orchestra 'My dear, you are dragging again! You are the biggest dragger in the business! Do not drag for me!'

He has total command of the score itself, learned no doubt at the keyboard. He is proud of his pianism, once reminding us all in a TV conversation that if he had not become a *great* conductor he would have been a *great* pianist. Conceit? It is no more than the truth.

On his early return as a guest during the Davis period he showed concern at what he felt to be a deteriorated orchestra; there had been a loss of form on his departure and repair took time. As things improved he came to approve and enjoy. In his eighties he has become a father-figure we can enjoy in return. Conventionally one might say that he has mellowed, but this is not a word I would apply to Solti. It implies a softening, and Solti is no softy. If the surface manner is softening it reveals, I think, the man who was always there: warm, enthusiastic, enjoying his music, the world and all the folks around him. Now he permits himself to show it — a little.

In rehearsal he keeps alive the famous joking feuds with the old orchestra; and to the exchanges of wit — which he takes care never to win — with his first trombone, Harold Nash, and his first horn, the irrepressible Tony Tunstall, he brings memorable new gags of his own. A loose attack in the wind will produce 'Come come, my dears! This hire-purchase business will not do!' And to a string department in some technical difficulty 'My dears you are SCHVIM-MING! DO NOT SCHVIM!!'

He understands brass and wind technique even less than Barbirolli did, if that is possible. In the recording studio, when a recurrent brass mishap threatened the completion of a *Don Carlos* session, he repeatedly gave the least useful instruction to the trombones: 'Attack the note! Come, come, attack the note!' A rapidly deteriorating situation was resolved by Nash with a response which deserves immortality: 'Yes, Mr Solti, we are attacking the note. But the note is defending itself!'

The resulting roar of laughter produced a perfect 'take' next time. Solti's performances owe much to tension, but tension can be a dangerous enemy.

The subtlety of Solti's relationship with the Covent Garden orchestra was shown to us once again in the '91–92 season, when a disastrous dispute between orchestra and House ran away with the time he needed to rehearse a new production of *Boccanegra*. Sir Georg demands and gets lavish orchestral time, but when the dust settled only one three-hour session remained of the four he had planned. That he was still with us, awaiting events, was a tribute to the tact of our Opera Director, Paul Findlay, for whom Solti has the warmest regard. Entering the pit Solti said to a very tense orchestra 'Well, Covent Garden has a problem. We have three hours in which to solve it. This is only possible because I have your goodwill.' The resulting rehearsal miracle and the performances which followed showed beyond doubt that he was right.

In my early days in the opera orchestra I met Rudolf Kempe again. His *Elektra* was a revelation in both music and technique. I had seen something of the technique long before, but exercised at a lower level. There would have been little point in unleashing that giant engine in preparing for a single symphony concert in Birmingham, where the orchestra might well have cracked under the shock. He could be an awesome, an intimidating, figure on the box. It took a tough and very experienced orchestra to cope with him.

There is a story about *Elektra*, of a general rehearsal where Karl Böhm, conducting, asked Strauss what more he could do to improve his performance, and was told that there was nothing; the score was perfect, and a matter entirely between the composer and the orchestra. Nothing that he nor any other conductor could do would have the slightest effect upon it. This sounds very silly, and of course it is not the whole truth, because a bad conductor can wreck anything. But there is a certain truth in it. *Elektra* is a wonderful piece of writing for the orchestra, with the kind of rhythmic impulse which makes for a self-sufficient momentum; and it is so very difficult in every single part of the orchestra that the orchestra develops a knack of getting its collective head down and playing regardless. Unless it is actually disturbed, it will play the work. Colin Davis, after a performance he conducted in an emergency, once remarked that in a sense it was only necessary to arrange a big punch with the opening *Agamemnon*! and keep out of trouble until the last one; in between the thing ran on lines like a train.

Kempe brought to *Elektra* his unique talent for orchestral balance. This the orchestra, busy with its notes, rarely manages for itself despite Strauss' detailed instructions. *Elektra* is so intricate a score, and the orchestra so vast, that apart from note-getting – and a good orchestra looks after its own notes – *Elektra* rehearsals are chiefly a matter of balance adjustment. This can involve endless discussion and masses of pencilled notes, both self-defeating because the score is, as the composer observed, perfectly engineered. Kempe supervised and adjusted balance from bar to bar throughout the piece *with his hands*.

His stick-technique was exemplary and original. Basic matters of ensemble were generally contained in a very small area, in front of his body, and for most of the time occupied only one hand. The left was free, and usually hung limply at his left side, waiting to give entries when needed but above all to control the dynamic of the orchestra, collectively and individually. To achieve this he needed our eyes. Nothing was easier for him. We never took our eyes from the man for a second. He was a very big man, a commanding presence. His own eyes were everywhere, uncomfortably so because he really did seem to be coldly, analytically and pitilessly evaluating everything.

Very few conductors, only the very best of the best, have the ability to hear exactly what the orchestra is producing. Most conduct imaginary performances, caught up in their own activity and totally dependent on what they have organised in rehearsal. But Kempe heard everything, and he had the technique to control what was happening from second to second throughout the longest work. The means looked beautifully simple. If he wished less of a voice or an instrument the left hand would come up, in front of his body, palm vertical and facing the problem. By some magic of his own eyes it was always clear, in a pit of a hundred people, exactly which of us was to give way. This gesture was usually hidden from the audience. But if he needed more of a voice, then the left hand would come up like a whip and the index finger would land – that is how it felt! – on the end of one's nose. His arms, once extended, seemed ten feet long.

In Strauss, balance is vital. There is such potential for congestion; so many interesting notes, usually overplayed because no player enjoys inaudible virtuosity. Yet only the perfectly calculated balance can work. Kempe delivered that perfection.

He had another unique talent, and one which I cannot explain. I saw it in Birmingham with Mozart, in Manchester with Brahms, and – my goodness – I saw it at Covent Garden in Strauss. He could convey tempo without moving a muscle, standing stone-still but vibrating with some inner tension for perhaps ten seconds before starting the work. Then it would begin, under perfect control. Perhaps the tempo was predictable simply because it was right? I don't know; but he was the only conductor I ever met who did not always depend, in the conventional way, on the preparatory beat for secure tempo.

I cannot say that I *enjoyed* playing for Kempe. He was just too much, too intimidating a presence. Enjoyment was for the audience. One would have loved him for some sign of weakness. It never came. He would have been, as I have suggested, a very great Music Director at Covent Garden, but he would have kept the Orchestra Director very busy, I think.

But — such performances!

At this time, during Solti's last season, Giulini appeared; not in the theatre, alas, but to record *Don Carlos* for EMI. We were invited to make that recording during the rehearsals for a Solti *Ring*. It made for an interesting month. Day after day, three hours at Covent Garden, then a fast journey to Walthamstow where the Maestro would be waiting, with his cast, for six hours of Verdi. The contrast between two styles, two approaches to music, and two conducting personalities could hardly have been better illustrated. With Solti three hours of excitement, steam, concentration, and stress. Within 15 minutes of beginning with Giulini all was lyricism, sunshine, and relaxed warmth. Not that relaxation meant an inferior level of music-making, but a different world in which to live and to express ourselves.

Giulini noticed me early in the series, and asked what I was doing at Covent Garden. I explained as best I could. His response was typical. 'You are wrong', he said. 'Your place is in Manchester, looking after that fine orchestra with the wonderful tradition of the family. It needs you now more than ever.'

That is a fine recording, with Montserrat Caballé a miraculous Elisabetta. Giulini, thanking us for our work at the end of the long haul, observed that 'not once had we to repeat any passage for the orchestra.' Nor, we replied, for him either.

We were not to see the great man again for more than a decade. And I was never to play for him again.

CHAPTER 20
Out and About

Only once during my first five years at the Royal Opera was my previous experience as a first trumpet put to serious and urgent use. It happened at the premiere of Tippett's opera *The Knot Garden*. I was not in this piece and had heard nothing of it in rehearsal. I'd previously played only two works of Tippett, the Second Piano Concerto and the Concerto for Orchestra. *The Knot Garden*, according to the canteen buzz, was fearsome for all concerned and especially for the trumpet. I was quite happy not to be involved in Colin's three weeks of intensive and enthusiastic preparation. Then, two hours before the curtain, I was telephoned and asked to come in. Harry Dilley was 'down' with influenza; someone must play. Had I realised that I was entitled to decline I might well have done so, but no-one had read the small print to me, so I fell for it.

The opera is scored for small wind and brass. I examined the part with emotions verging on panic. It seemed an appallingly rough ride. All one could do was to read like mad and play for dear life. This I did, aided by impeccable direction from Colin and by a constant feed of information from my colleagues, who counted bars, shouted cues, nudged for entries when I seemed to be at risk, and generally did everything but blow my trumpet. A good time was had by all, as the saying goes, except me. I cherish notes from the conductor and composer thanking me for 'an astonishing display of technique and professionalism.' But I'm sure I lost ten pounds and gained ten years that evening. Three months later, listening to Harry record the piece, I could not believe I'd survived it. Well, perhaps I had been for one evening worth my salary to the Royal Opera.

Such freak occurrences apart I had to look to the freelance market for excitement and of course for extra income. Freelance work came slowly at first. The Garden gave us so little time, and its schedule was so inflexible, that many lollipops had to be declined. This is still the situation today and a great irritation it is to the members of the orchestra, but there is no cure without damage to the House's work.

On those rare occasions when the diary permitted it was marvellous to meet the London Philharmonic and to renew my acquaintance with the LSO.

As I had discovered much earlier in my career, the work which would come my way, as a newcomer, was usually that too boring for important players or too dangerous for the others. I preferred the latter variety, and very much valued my days in the LPO. There I met Bernard Haitink again. His principal trumpet, Gordon Webb – one of the most remarkable players London has ever heard, and a great loss when he disappeared homewards to New Zealand – admired my work and kept me busy bumping. 'Bumping' is the term used to describe the practice of reinforcing and resting principal players in strenuous performances by the use of a second player on the same part. Horns have always done this, and it's become a commonplace in London in recent years among trumpets too. I find it hard to imagine two personalities less similar than Gordon and myself, nor two musicians closer in taste. We got on famously.

I have yet to experience a better working atmosphere than in the London Philharmonic during the years of Bernard Haitink's conductorship. The quality of the playing was marvellous, individually and collectively, yet it was achieved without the knife-edge of professional insecurity which has so often accompanied high standards in London. In the 'seventies the members of the LPO played their hearts out for their orchestra. They *believed* in it. It was a superb band in which to play, and first-rate company. I believe, and most people who played there at that time will agree, that this happy situation stemmed from its chief conductor. The orchestra reflected the man.

Haitink was recording his second Mahler cycle, the first having been made much earlier with the Concertgebouw. Having completed the Third Symphony he was currently giving it at the Festival Hall. The solo trumpet who had recorded the famous offstage solo in that work was no longer available. I was asked to play it.

Gordon warned me that 'The Boss' was tricky in Mahler. It would be best if I had a conversation with him well in advance. I was produced for Haitink's inspection at Maida Vale, where the LPO was recording for the BBC. We were introduced. He eyed me curiously. 'Surely we have met before, somewhere ...?' I reminded him of *The Rite* in Manchester. Recognition dawned with a smile, then 'Have you played this work for JB?'

I had; and a fine old putting through the mill it had been, too.

'I'm sorry to have put you to this quite unnecessary trouble. There is no need for us to talk about it. Let's meet on the day of the concert'.

Could any greater compliment he paid by one conductor to another? I did not tell Haitink that in the impecunious Hallé I had been obliged to play not only the offstage solo but the entire symphony too.

In the LPO I met Stokowski again, much changed. In old age then, eccentric had become the grotesque. We were recording Tchaikowsky's *Capriccio Italien*, which is tricky at any time and really frightening given the likelihood of fun and games with Stokey. The nice thing about being a freelance on these occasions is that one's job is not on the line. This permits a certain relaxation not available to regular members of the orchestra, and this often works in the performer's favour.

Stokey was now very difficult; always looking for trouble, making it when he couldn't find it, and striking attitudes in his fractured English. My passage arrived; I knocked it out in a neck-or-nothing, muck-or-nettles way. Like unreliable dogs, difficult passages bite oftener when we approach them tentatively. The trick came off nicely. Stokey stopped and made observations to the strings; nothing to me. Then he asked for the passage again. I recognised an old ploy. When a difficult passage goes well the first time it is usually possible to make it go wrong if we do it often enough. When it goes wrong, teach the player how to do it. This game is a great waste of time and if — as happens all too often — the victim has nothing in reserve, it can make real trouble. If that is what Stokey wanted it was not his day. I played that passage six times before he gave up. My friends found this hugely entertaining. Their feet shuffled constantly in the traditional way.

Others were not so lucky. Small crises followed each other in rapid succession, then the big one. The playbacks were relayed into the studio during Stokowski's sessions, so that everyone could listen and learn. This is a sound idea, but it is inevitable that during listening time someone will escape to the loo, or to telephone home, to put ten bob on the three-thirty, or just for a smoke. True to form, one first violinist vanished. On his return the great chief turned at the door of the wigwam and addressed the criminal in awful tones.

'YOU! Why you go? I not go! Listen! Concertmaster not go; orkester not go. All stay, listen! Not listen, not get better. You have wife, children? (He did not wait for the reply.) Not get better, wife, children, starve! Orkester not get better, ALL children starve!'

At this point the trombones rose as one from their seats and left the room. Trombonists are like that. Stokey wound himself up for another explosion. Rodney Friend, a leader in more senses than one, defused it. 'Maestro, perhaps it is time now for the intermission ...?' We were quite sure that nothing recorded in that memorable but terrifying week would ever reach the catalogues. The *Caprice* I think did not. There was a *Nutcracker Suite* with a march of such extreme tempo that we would have laughed any other conductor out of the room. It's still in the shops; nuts but no cracker, as we all agreed at the time. What a pity that such an artist should end so badly. Was he, at the end, deliberately silly? I was not there when, during a Mahler recording with another orchestra, he asked of the leader 'Who wrote this music ...?'

All this was great fun; the sort of thing which improves the life of the pit-musician vastly. There was then, and always had been, a tendency among members of the Garden Orchestra to regard the job as a safe base on which to build a stimulating and interesting freelance connection. To say that we did our best work outside and 'did what we could' for the Garden is perhaps to press the point too hard, but there was a certain truth in it. It was an attractive life and I was happy enough. Then our Orchestra Director resigned, and almost by accident I found myelf in a 'hot seat' of new design.

CHAPTER 21

The Electric Chair

It's a unique job, Orchestra Director at Covent Garden: a high-wire act. One is Blondin over Niagara. On one bank stands the orchestra; on the other the General Director and Administration. We communicate by inadequate semaphore, misunderstood with equal ease at either end of the wire. Unlike Blondin, one is not permitted to walk more than a yard or two in either direction. The legs get very tired at times. People have been known to fall.

The working week runs to 168 hours, since sleep is something which comes between telephone calls and waking nightmares, usually relating to imaginary sins of omission which might wreck tomorrow's performance. Living in the Fens, a sixty-minute trip away from 'the smoke', provides two hours each day in which 'they' can't get at me. I need them.

Why did I do it? Someone must, no doubt, and the job is very much envied, mainly by folks who haven't the smallest idea what it's about. There is no other like it even in the other great opera houses, where orchestra management is often a province of Heads of Music Staff or some other appendage of the Music Director. Covent Garden has always taken orchestra management seriously.

It's a very different job now from the one I took on in 1974. Utterly out of date in its attitude to the orchestra, with little sense of inevitable change in the profession, the House and the orchestra office had for years faced the rising tide of democracy like Canute on the beach.

Covent Garden, at any level, distrusts change; understandably so, because its structure is so intricate that the smallest adjustment risks unpredictable repercussions. This is an opera and ballet factory, and anyone of experience in international opera or ballet will say that it's the most competent they have ever met. At Covent Garden the schedule is not merely an optimistic theory, as in so many other places. It really works, to the amazement of visiting singers, dancers, and conductors. That schedule is carefully built on a sound basis of

Above: *Carlo Maria Giulini*

Above right: *Carlos Kleiber*

Right: *Bernard Haitink*

Sir John Barbirolli

Sir Thomas Beecham

Rudolf Kempe

Rudolf Schwarz

Riccardo Muti

Sir Adrian Boult

Sir Colin Davis

Claudio Abbado

Right: *The author in his Army days.*

Below: *The author (left) and Jonathan Summers in a 1979 production of 'Don Pasquale', at Covent Garden.*

custom and practice in every part of the house, not least in the orchestra. The changes which I saw as necessary and urgent on my appointment were for this and for many other reasons to be approached with care.

I had much to learn from my two immediate predecessors. Excellent people and good managers, they pursued two opposite paths; each eminently reasonable, each a dead end.

After the twenty-eight-year regime of Morris Smith major change was inevitable. So much of what he did had been disliked by the orchestra that the next man was inevitably in for a rough time. The orchestra's unspoken objective was simple. Smith's replacement was not to be allowed to build a situation as powerful as his had been.

His successor, John Murphy, had been a Liverpool and then a Hallé manager, equally admired in either place. A natural choice for the Liverpudlian General Administrator David Webster, he was much easier to manipulate than Smith, especially by experienced metropolitan players in their theatrical element where he was finding his feet. Inside the administration, too, he met problems. Had he instituted gradual change by means of existing methods he might have fared better; but he was a 'new broom' man who underestimated both the efficiency of the machine he inherited and its resistance to change. Struggling, he made many small mistakes. When I arrived, a year and a half later, I was astonished to discover how low was his stock. A delightfully honest and open man, he had gained the nickname *Macchiavelli*.

The orchestra can be as cruel as schoolboys. The pressures created around my old friend were enormous. This good manager and thoroughly nice man, trying hard to please everyone, pleased none. It was said of him, and I think with justice, that our orchestra was probably the only one in the United Kingdom which he could not have successfully managed. Happily he was able to find a home with the Bournemouth Symphony, where he was, as in Liverpool and Manchester, a great success.

He was followed by Bernard Harman, one of our timpanists, an old soldier and an old Covent Garden hand. Bernard knew his environment thoroughly. He trod on no toes and relied upon the structure in which he had served for many years. The bandroom relaxed, having demonstrated its distrust of change, but there was in the air a new expectation that the job should now move positively;

that the orchestra ought to be motivated and its energy harnessed in the interest of the job and all those in it. This was very much the opinion of the new Music Director. Obviously attitudes must change if the orchestra was to be improved and the best talent gained and retained. The old subservience to an autocracy was, even at the time of my joining, no longer acceptable at Covent Garden. A holding operation was not the answer. Management must move and improve. There were risks to be weighed, taken or avoided. It was no job for Harman, and he left for a professorship. Once again the House was looking around for an Orchestra Director.

Nine members of the orchestra applied for the job, with eighty outsiders. Having talked often to my friends about it, I know that their motivation was the right one; they saw that Covent Garden held the possibility of a fine orchestra and a happy job and that both must come together or not at all. They feared the House would make a mistaken appointment and they dreaded the years of boredom a mistake might bring. Each offered himself in an effort to avert this. I was the last to do so, nearly missing the boat.

It was a spur-of-the-moment thing, a chance remark in passing to Sir John Tooley. Until he asked me whether I was serious I didn't know whether I was or not. I told him so. He suggested that I think about it for a week. If I was serious I might write and tell him what I thought I had to offer the House.

I pondered whether I wished to go on trumpeting for twenty years more. I wondered whether the orchestra would have me; not that they would be asked, but goodwill would be vital. I looked again at the orchestra: overworked, underpaid, anonymous, under-appreciated, atrociously accommodated, and for much of the time bored. So much fine talent wasted. I decided to do what I could. The first thing was to get the job. Was I up to it? JT and Colin must decide.

I wrote a letter. The next day Colin cornered me in the pit and said 'Look, John is taking you seriously. I hope you are serious.' I told him that I was. 'One thing worries me', he said, 'and that is that I can't be responsible for your giving up playing. If you do you will be as miserable as hell. Unless you promise to keep in practice and play a little I can't encourage this.'

That seemed reasonable. For the whole of my life I'd hardly known what it was to leave home without a trumpet-case. Keeping in practice seemed the most natural requirement in the world. I promised.

My discussion with JT was entertaining. In reply to his first question, 'Tell me how you will improve the playing for the ballet', I light-heartedly suggested that he might change all the repertoire, send the dancers to music-appreciation classes, and sack the entire conducting staff. This went down pretty badly. 'If you are saying the thing is impossible then this conversation is going to be very short' was his response. But I insisted that the problem was one for the House to solve, not for the orchestra or its management alone.

We talked all round the job, in ever-increasing circles. Eventually he suggested that I go away for another week and think again. I could come back if I was still certain I wished to press on. In the meantime he would talk to others.

A week later we had a very brief meeting. After two minutes he picked up the phone and spoke to the Orchestra Manager, Honor Thackrah. 'Bram Gay is to have the run of the office for one week at times when the orchestra is out of the house. He is to be shown everything except the salary list. You two must talk the whole situation out thoroughly and see what you can make of it.' Putting the phone down he observed that the orchestra salary list was the most inflammable piece of paper in the house and that he didn't want me to get my fingers burned until and unless it became necessary.

Honor is a remarkable lady; when she retired, long after, laden with good wishes and decorated by The Queen, I described her as among the most remarkable people ever involved in arts administration in the United Kingdom. Even then, 17 years earlier, she was the doyenne of British orchestra management, having joined in the 'forties as Morris Smith's secretary. Honor had been offered the senior position twice already. Since her first care was always for her home, she preferred her own desk which released her, as a rule, at 5.30; but never before making sure that the evening was safe, sound, and within the possibility of management by any person of half-intelligence. Honor overlooked nothing. It was typical of her attention to detail that her last visit before leaving for home each evening was to the conductors' room, to make sure it had been properly cleaned for this evening's visitor; not her responsibility but, since it was her opera house and the visitor her visitor, just good manners.

There was nothing Honor did not know about the opera orchestra and its repertoire, and her knowledge of the London freelance profession was encyclopaedic. Most of those in it had been at Covent

Garden at some time or other and Honor had seen them both in and out. She knew from long experience the reaction one might expect from our own orchestra in any situation. The other source of problems, the conductor list, she knew equally well. Honor was not surprised at my arrival; since a good relationship with the Orchestra Manager was an essential of the job, she'd been consulted very early. I knew very well that there would be no hope of success unless this marvellous lady and I saw eye to eye, and my research was aimed entirely at the question: could I see the job Honor's way? If not, I must not take it on.

We talked endlessly about the problem. Obviously, since Honor had helped to build the status quo she was not much interested in change, especially as such change as she had so far seen had been all bad. I think she found my determination to develop the orchestra disturbing. 'No-one comes to Covent Garden to hear the orchestra', she told me. 'We accompany singers and dancers and we don't expect to be noticed'. This was exactly the state of affairs I was pledged to end. Nothing would satisfy me until our orchestra challenged the big four at the Festival Hall. I wonder, had I known that seventeen years would elapse before a Music Director would take us on that short but significant trip over Waterloo Bridge, would I have taken the job? One thing is certain: to suggest such a thing to Honor in 1974 would have been to rule myself out. My friend would have referred me back to John Tooley with a recommendation for a lunatic asylum rather than the orchestra office.

On one thing we were agreed: democracy, inconvenient to managers though it might be, was here to stay. We responded differently to it in that Honor thought it an unfortunate fact of modern life, while my own naive assessment was more hopeful. We both believed that the orchestra looked for positive management, nothing being less appreciated downstairs than inertia; and we also knew that the current round of pay negotiations with the Musicians' Union would be crucial to the success of any incoming Orchestra Director.

Those talks were an annual nightmare. Because Covent Garden has never enough money, there are no good years for them; just bad ones and dreadful ones, with the consequences of mismanagement too dire to contemplate. They are led by the House's Director of Administration, and in that period they were conducted jointly with those of English National Opera under the chairmanship of the Association of British Orchestras. I thought it a very bad idea that someone outside the House should negotiate the conditions under which my orchestra was employed and create the climate in which I must manage. I feared that under such a system the needs of the Royal Opera House might be set aside in favour of those of the other company and of the symphony orchestras, who are not famous for their encouragement of opera orchestras. I was determined anyway that coming into the job in the late spring, when this steamy pot was already bubbling, I must not be handicapped by the work of anyone else; so when my week with Honor was up I included among my recommendations to John Tooley one that this year's claim for a better basic wage should be met in full. That claim was, in my opinion, in or out of management, entirely fair.

Before we met again John and Colin had decided that I was to be given my chance. Honor had decided for them, certainly. In retrospect I find her choice surprising. We were temperamental and methodical opposites – how Virgo managed to produce two such contrasts is one for the astrologers to explain – and I can only suppose that she found me less worrying than the other possibilities. Certainly she thought me manageable, and events proved her right. I was adroitly managed through the seventeen years to come, as a cabinet minister is managed by a first-rate permanent secretary who has forgotten more of the job than the bright-eyed boy in the big chair can ever learn. Time and again, faced with Honor's adverse advice, I reconsidered with benefit to all concerned; and the ideas which got through the fine mesh of her mind never failed.

John listened carefully to my ideas. His eyebrows rose at my demand for more money for the orchestra. A virtuoso of the encouraging non-committal, he somehow persuaded me to set it aside. Subsequently he delivered in full, not in order to give me a flying start, but because my assessment was correct.

My appointment was to begin on May day 1974. It was announced to the orchestra on a day when I was not called. I crept into the House to hear John say that 'The new Orchestra Director is to be Bram Gay.'

There was a silence. The thing had been well concealed. And then in the hush a voice in the violas asked ... 'Who?'

Well, it is a big orchestra, I'd been with it for only five years, and he *was* a viola player.

* * *

A few days later a message arrived from my friend John Murphy, on tour with his Bournemouth Symphony. The job, said John, was wonderful; he'd loved it and he knew I would do well. But I must not forget that the office chair was wired for electricity and that the current came on without notice.

I promised myself always to wear rubber shoes.

CHAPTER 22
Sitting Comfortably?

My friends in the brass were cheered at the arrival of another brass player in my seat, the preponderance of trumpeters and trombonists among orchestra managers and chairmen of self-managing orchestras being in a curious way a matter of unspoken pride to us all. I explain this phenomenon as a demonstration of the solo-playing temperament of brass players. A trumpet can't hide; neither can a manager.

The orchestra received my appointment kindly. They were surprised by it, my profile to date having been very low. My colleagues gave me a long honeymoon in which to get my act together, and I still feel a special bond with those members of the orchestra who were there before me and who, to a man, gave me very great encouragement at that time. The received wisdom is that a manager is never loved and cannot manage if that's his priority; far better that the orchestra should dislike him than that they dislike one another. Hugh Maguire, that wise leprechaun who led the orchestra for some years, put the problem into focus for me: 'To annoy only one of us every two weeks would be an achievement in your job, and you must by now have got round the band several times; so there is at least a sizeable minority, after so many years, which would be happy to see you go. Just cheer yourself up with the thought that if they really hated you they could see you off in a month. And you are still here!'

The acid test, perhaps, lies in the number of orchestra members with whom the manager feels welcome at a canteen table. When welcoming new players to the orchestra I invariably told them that the Orchestra of the Royal Opera House contained the most civilised collection of musicians anywhere on earth, and that I know this because after so many years they were still kind to me.

I found, though, that during the period of union negotiations for the coming season I must keep a tactful distance. The late and great Sir David Webster had a neat and tidy way with the Musicians' Union. He would invite the Branch Secretary to his office, shake his hand and say 'So good of you to come. You will be pleased to know that we propose to offer further employment to your members in the coming season. The rates of pay are contained in this envelope!' With that the poor chap would be ushered out.

I found that things had changed. My first leader at the table was a man of wide experience and background but of such marvellously good nature that he instinctively wished to concede anything he possibly could without producing apoplexy among the ROH Board. Some of what he wished to concede would have produced the same result in his Orchestra Director, so internal relations on our side were often more strained than across the table.

The union side at that time was led by a rare character, a socialist of great and sincere conviction who had fought Franco with the International Brigade. Since he was not a musician he had little idea of our business except for a generalised impression that players must be protected from conductors and managers, fascists all. His opening remark at our first meeting was to ask that his objection to my red shirt, an obvious provocation, be minuted. I responded by offering to take the offending garment off, conditional on his removing his blue trousers. We got on famously thereafter. He offered advice from time to time over canteen tea, advice which told me more about him than about the union. A thirty-year member, I needed little help there.

It was all a matter, he said, of the size of the gun. When contemplating a confrontation with the union I ought to ask myself 'Is their gun bigger, or is mine? That is the only thing which counts, because if theirs is bigger I cannot win. Regardless of any principle, they will pull the trigger.' This advice was offered in a true spirit of friendliness to a new manager, in the hope that it would save me many sleepless nights.

There was a memorable exchange, too, during negotiations, when I mentioned the word 'right'. He asked whether I meant a legal right or a moral one. I replied that I had the former in mind. 'Oh ... that's all right then. For a moment I thought you were talking about a moral one. We're not interested in those!'

Since we had already decided to make a settlement on the basis of the figure he demanded, we were in a position to enjoy this chap — for a time. Light-years removed from the attitudes of his members, his negotiating tactics provided more fun than fret. His most famous declaration is still quoted far beyond the confines of my office: 'We will erode every prerogative of management,' he said, 'leaving only that of providing the money!' We replied that if the union would only accept the last, we would happily concede all the others.

Attitudes like these cut little ice, serving only to demonstrate the intellectual gap which separated players and union officials at that time; a gap which has since been well closed. One union official, though, gave me serious cause for thought concerning the Royal Opera House and its historic attitudes towards players. He had been a trumpeter too, and a fine one, in the BBC's Northern Dance Orchestra. We knew each other well, and I approached our first conversation in this new relationship with a certain confidence. He ushered me into his office with all the old easy charm, gave me a cup of tea and said 'We are old friends, Bram?'

I agreed that we were, and expressed the hope that this might long continue.

'Well', he replied, 'let's just get one thing clear. You represent the worst employer in the business. I represent the poor bastards you are screwing.'

There was, then, work to be done. There must be substantial change of a kind the orchestra could unmistakably see and feel, if the House and the Orchestra were ever to make friends. The union pressed for change too. The ideas fired at me across the negotiating table were far in advance – if the word may be used to describe a rapid descent into anarchy – of any urged on other managers. I asked the reason and was told frankly that a general fighting a battle looked always for the weakest point to attack; the Royal Opera House was in chaos, managerially speaking, and therefore it was the obvious place to force through radical change.

I looked for the most vociferous of the claims made by the MU on behalf of my friends, and discovered that what was demanded was 'a decisive voice in the choice of players for the Orchestra.' For them this was the big plum. Well, since I'd always doubted the wisdom of a free hand for Music Directors in these choices this seemed an eminently reasonable concession to make.

We spent many weeks debating the system by which new players were to be chosen. I thought the whole thing very simple, but having discovered that I liked the idea the other side quickly discovered endless potential vice in it. Our discussions resulted in a complicated agreement which has ever since provided much bandroom debate. Very few mistakes have been made in selection, though the process can be almost ludicrously slow. It grows slower too, as the orchestra's standards rise; but I would back the judgement of an orchestra panel against that of a solo music director any day. There will be trouble, perhaps, should Covent Garden one day enlist a music director to whom the idea of choice by committee, with the risk of his being over-ruled, is unacceptable. I shall have retired by then, thankfully.

This was to be the only fundamental change made in the managing of our orchestra for many years. It paid dividends in the quality and motivation of players. It has also created a vast amount of work for them. This they discharge with a degree of conscientiousness which puts some of the symphonic democracies to shame.

Artistically there was a long long way to go. Listening now to the Giulini *Don Carlos* recording of 1970 I find it musically satisfying but lacking in basic orchestral resource. Hearing again Colin's *Cosi* of four years later, marvellous Mozart though it is, I know that this is not playing Covent Garden would accept from us today. I did not know, then, how far the orchestra could be developed. I had no horizon; just a determination to go the whole hog, *totus porcus*.

There would never be enough money. Motivation and organisation must provide. I had seen this principle succeed in Manchester, but it would be harder to bring off in London. I did not see Colin Davis as a Barbirolli, prepared to work almost non-stop with one orchestra around the year and do his own gardening. Our orchestra must build itself.

One change was essential. Principal players must be present at every rehearsal and performance. This may seem obvious, but since the job began it had been customary for the next-best player in each section to lead several calls each week; customary and necessary, because there were too many calls for any one player. So we'd adopted, tacitly and of necessity, two levels of performance. The first team had always been present for Solti, while lesser mortals often made do with the second. There was in a sense a 'music director's orchestra', a special collection of people. This was hard on the others, but under our budgetary restraints inescapable. My solution was to enlist a second team of equal principals.

My 'equal' was not to be a word only. These players would play for the same level of conductor, in the same repertoire, and for the same money. This was the first time of asking the House for substantial new spending on the orchestra. I bent the figures into all manner of fraud and almost managed to convince myself that the thing would finance itself. This fooled no-one, but John Tooley pretended to believe me and paid up.

The next artistic leap was shamed upon me by John Pritchard, a conductor loved at the Garden as everywhere else. JP came to us with Donizetti, for which I scheduled the routine orchestral treatment. During the rehearsal period there would be some rotation of players at the back of each string department. This we did simply to save money. Players incurring overtime were taken out and their friends put in. This system had an advantage for members of the orchestra who could, if they wished, rotate for themselves and escape to other work or for a quiet evening off. Rotation was simply a deputy system of half-rehearsed players from within, and it saved five per cent of my budget. The catch was that the conductor must work with an orchestra which was not entirely rehearsed.

JP came to me on his fourth day and asked me 'Who on earth are these strange people at the back of the strings?' Hardly a new boy at the ROH, he knew very well what was happening, and he'd decided to make a stand on behalf of visiting conductors. I reminded him of the system, barely keeping a straight face. He asked me whether I treated the Music Director's repertoire in this way. I readily admitted that I did not.

'Bram', he said, 'are you telling me that Colin's pieces are more important than mine?'

I replied that I was only doing what we had always done with Donizetti, a composer we all knew rather well, and with visiting conductors.

'Well', said JP in that sweet and reasonable way of his, 'just telephone all those people I worked with for the first three days and invite them back tomorrow. Don't tell me they won't come, or that you can't afford them, or any of that nonsense. Just arrange for me to have absolutely the same orchestra from now until the end of my stay. *Otherwise I will never come here again.*'

Among that delightful man's many talents was one for being charming and utterly firm at the same time. We telephoned the originals and they came.

He was right of course. Looking carefully at the list of conductors Miss Schmidt had promised, I realised that in future the orchestra would have to be 'locked in' for each work. I conveyed this expensive idea to JT, who demanded that I cost it precisely. He hated the result but he found the money. We became the first of the world's great opera orchestras to guarantee to conductors that from the first rehearsal to the last performance there would be an unchanged orchestra.

We are famous for this today, but at first visiting maestros would not believe it, especially those of long experience in Europe, where opera orchestras, after the first night of the opera, can be *ad hoc.* Karl Böhm simply would not take my promise seriously. 'Mr Gay', said he, 'I've been in this business a long time and I've heard every possible excuse of orchestra managers. What you are telling me is not true. Nowhere in the world can this happen. I ask only to be prepared for the worst. You pull my leg. Let us talk about what will really happen.'

I repeated my promise. I offered to buy him a bottle of cognac if he should find a change in his orchestra. Immediately he became cagey. What would I want from him if I succeeded? I asked only for the stick with which he would conduct *Figaro* and he readily agreed. An economical man, Dr Böhm; in the event he gave me a broken one. It hangs in a frame on the wall of the Orchestra office still, nicely autographed, with many others won in the same way.

One other major advantage I needed: I must have numbers in the pit. Twelve first violins, the routine Garden ration, would never be enough in that unhelpful acoustic. Now I was talking about real money, and the door was firmly closed. It did not open until we proved our point in Milan two years later.

That event set a deadline against which I was required to produce a certain level of orchestral improvement. I spent a lot of time listening, assessing our strengths and our weaknesses, the latter far outweighing the former. I remember a performance of *Otello* when the first act brought to mind a famous remark of a distinguished critic of the 'thirties who compared the ensemble of the London Symphony Orchestra to an anthill. Here, I told myself, was an anthill of my very own.

We'd lost many people since Solti's departure; not necessarily the best of our talent, and in some cases well lost, but there was no sense of the team now. To some extent this was due to anno domini; our leader, the splendid Charles Taylor, was at the age when most people retire from business, and Anthony Pini, our celebrated principal cellist, was in his middle seventies. Let no-one say that these two were past playing; but they were not the men to begin a process of reconstruction and still less to see Colin through a long tenure. Charles was ready to retire, and characteristically did so when it was most convenient for the House. Pini was less helpful; his was the case used by the orchestra to show me, as they had shown my predecessor, that the carefree axe would not be permitted. They put up a splendid fight. Admiring him, as did every other player who worked with him, I remember those days as among my least happy of all. Remarkably – and it was in a way a measure of the man – he and I remained on good personal terms to the very end. He was an old hand, old enough to recognise the difference between a professional judgement and a personal one. His protest was that of experience against two professional infants, as he saw us, Davis and Gay.

I had always known, of course, that the orchestra would fight tooth-and-nail a Music Director who aimed at improvement through rapid replacement of players. Colin had a reputation for this, fairly or unfairly, and they were determined to teach him better manners. Already, before my arrival, they had reduced him to near-despair regarding improvement of the orchestra. Now he expected a better band quite soon.

I could only advise 'softly-softly'. This must have sounded like outright cowardice, coming from a chap selected – I suppose – for his apparent energy and artistic ambition; but since politics, and especially orchestral politics, is the art of the possible, I had no intention of sinking my Music Director under a burden of impossibilities. I suggested that there were many small things we could all do together to improve matters, and that even one small improvement each week would work wonders. I placed great faith in the judgement of the orchestra itself. No-one comes into our business to play badly, nor to work with bad players. The faults must be exposed as handicaps to us all. Then, when the orchestra was ready, we would push at the open door. Many weaknesses would go without formal effort on our part, 'embarrassed' out. Change was not a matter for an axe once a month but for sandpaper every day.

This is a slow policy; one which works best when the conducting is best. Capable players flourish under fine conductors while weak ones wilt under the pressure. A terrible fact this, but inescapable, that many people come into orchestras determined to play well and sure they can do so, only to discover that they are just not up to it. The wise find jobs where they can contribute at their own level. That was part of our plan at Covent Garden when the long sequence of great conductors began, early in Colin's reign. It is time to look at one of the greatest of these.

CHAPTER 23
The 'Little' CK

'In this business', as Barbirolli once sagely observed, 'only fools use superlatives. Someone will do it better tomorrow morning.' This is true. Yet I and a happy few others have met a superlative in the sense that we find the idea of a 'better' conductor than Carlos Kleiber inconceivable. On the orchestra's scale of one to a hundred, with the 'good' conductors starting at fifty-five and the 'real' ones — the Abbados, the Mutis, the Haitinks, the Davises and the Levines in the nineties, this man is off the top of the scale with the needle spinning wildly and the orchestra cheering like mad.

Until the younger Kleiber exploded on the Royal Opera House in the late 'seventies I had heard of only one Kleiber. 'Dr Kleiber', as the House has always called him, first implanted in the minds of those in charge at Covent Garden the principle that first-rate opera begins with a first-rate orchestra. This he did during the tenure of Karl Rankl, while preparing *Der Rosenkavalier* and *Wozzeck*; memorable performances which impelled the House to offer him the post of Music Director. Alas, he declined it.

He was a super conductor and musician and a kind man, much liked by the orchestra. Few visiting conductors have left so happy and lasting a memory. It remains even today, 40 years on, when so few of that orchestra still play. When, some years ago, a lesser man asked us to change some of Erich Kleiber's pencilled instructions in the *Wozzeck* material there was outraged protest from the orchestra. Here then was one of those really great conductors, like Toscanini, Walter, and Furtwängler, for whom I arrived too late. I was in time to meet his son; a compensation for which I am truly grateful.

Carlos arrived with *Rosenkavalier*, on the sudden death of Josef Krips. All kinds of cautionary bells were sounded before he appeared. He was, we were told, the finest-balanced of temperaments, liable to disappear in the direction of Heathrow, never to reappear, if upset. We are inured of course to the routine threat of 'Unless ... I go home!' This is a tactic of the fourth-rate and it cuts no ice at Covent

[139]

Garden. But here apparently was one who would not threaten, but simply go, leaving us all to reason why.

CK has never walked away from the Royal Opera, nor given the least sign of so doing. If it has happened in other places I suspect that the gesture was deserved. Kleiber works at an extraordinary level of musical, technical, and intellectual creativity, placing orchestra, singers, producers, managers and even technical staff under immense pressure. He accepts the same pressure for himself; failure on the part of any one of us, consequently, is potentially explosive. The ROH rises to occasions like this. Even the stage crew recognises the difference between a conductor and A Conductor. The challenge is taken up; the level of endeavour rockets. There is nothing organised nor deliberate about this, nor of intimidation; simply a unanimous effort to make the best of a rare event. If in some other place the team has failed to do that then yes, CK might have walked out. Routine attitudes cannot produce his performance. He is not a routine artist.

A rare event his visit really is. By choice he conducts very little, and in the same way his repertoire is small. This is certainly not a matter of musical or technical limitation. His early career in German opera houses hauled him through a vast repertoire, and no-one who has worked for him doubts his ability to conduct any of it now at the drop of a hat. It is not a matter of choice for those who engage him either. A producer for one of the great recording companies once despairingly told me that they would be glad to record with CK 'absolutely anything he would like to record, starting tomorrow if he wishes it.' There is probably no other conductor of whom that is true. Opera intendants and managers of symphony orchestras feel the same way. As for their orchestras — well, if there is one conductor alive for whom they would play without money, this is he.

Kleiber is very much at home in England, and genuinely enjoys being here. Educated at a school for children of British and American diplomats in Buenos Aires, where the family took refuge during the war, his command of the language is awesome. Better still, he understands the psychology of the British in a way achieved by no other German conductor of my experience. At best, these laugh at our jokes with difficulty. Kleiber makes them; we laugh with him. His British background is astonishingly broad. The works of Sullivan are old friends of his, having been learned at school, and once, putting a tentative head around his door before *Elektra* (there are evenings when, like every other conductor and human being, he is better left to himself) I was received in broad Scots:

> Scots wha' hae wi' Wallace bled!
> Scots wham Bruce has oft-times led
> Welcome to y're gory bed
> Or to victorie!

Happily, having served in a Scots regiment, I knew that tonight was Burns Nicht. Optimistically I began the *Ode to a Mouse* which, to his delight, I could not finish. And this from a man who must conduct Strauss in 30 minutes' time.

There are few important musicians who, having made room in their heads for so much music, find space for so much else. And it is because of this, I think, that Kleiber's music-making is such a delight. Shaw's advice, that the mind ought not to be filled up with unnecessary junk like an attic, does not apply when the attic is unlimited. The artist can use everything he can absorb, if he has the capacity for storing it and for finding it, intuitively, at exactly the right moment.

Kleiber conducts rarely but studies endlessly. His *Otello* begins where Verdi began; with Shakespeare. No score can satisfy him but a facsimile of Verdi's own; a window into the mind of the composer which the impersonal print cannot provide. He treasures Weber's original *Freischütz*, inherited from his father, and his Dresden recording of that opera is surely one of the great musical achievements of the gramophone.

It is said that his preparation for the New Year's Day concert in Vienna took three months of study, with careful reference back to the work of the masters of the style, Clemens Krauss (whom he calls 'the BIG CK') especially. *Three months of Strauss waltzes!* And why not? If the pieces had not been worth so much why would Kleiber play them?

This approach so often produces the nit-picking bore, the man who counts every leaf on every tree but is blind to the wood; but with Kleiber the broad view, the sweep of the work, the fine sense of proportion with which relative climaxes are scaled, all benefit from the lucid presentation of the composer's detail. Exact engineering rather than inspired performance? Are the two mutually exclusive? No, this huge intellect is not the master of the artist but his servant.

It would be presumptuous to suggest the reason why Kleiber conducts so little and so rarely, but I have often wondered whether perhaps it lies in the impossibility, in his own terms, of doing it well. His reaction after each performance may be one of complete disappointment. The more we know, the less we enjoy, sometimes. Perhaps it is a miracle that Kleiber still conducts at all — that he does not limit himself to the perfect enjoyment of music suggested by Newman to those who looked for the perfect *Ring*: that produced in silence by a solitary reading of the score. If so, it is a happy miracle.

He is without doubt the most difficult artist to book. Rudolf Bing, in his autobiography, told us that Kleiber never writes letters. This is not true; but perhaps letters from opera and concert managers, relating to dates and occasions, may gather dust indefinitely. Happy the opera house where Kleiber has friends.

Conductors who appear rarely must surely find technique difficult. Not this one, apparently. Years of youthful experience seem to have provided him with infallible reflexes. Most conductors are obliged to choose, from bar to bar, between clear time-beating and expressive direction of phrase. With Kleiber the two are complementary. The *phrase* is conducted, all the time. Yet within the phrase is impeccable direction. Sometimes within a great sweep of line there comes the merest crisp 'click' — perhaps with the little finger of the baton hand — which is observed only by the one player who must punctuate at that point; seen because Kleiber has collected for the gesture *his eye alone*. This combination of 'safe driving' and musical communication makes him such a reliable conductor. He can deliver superb performance on minimal rehearsal when needs must. As he once said, 'There are two ways to rehearse — three hours or three months. We can play it tonight if we have to.' In fact, as a leaper-into-the-breach in emergencies he has no equal. The man can play the orchestra like a piano.

On his first morning at Covent Garden Kleiber rehearsed the *Rosenkavalier* prelude for almost three hours: an extraordinary feat considering that the music takes about a minute and a half and that the orchestra knew it rather well before he began. The opera would have taken a year to rehearse at that rate. But during the next five days the whole work was complete. Once an understanding was reached all else followed of itself.

Most great conductors need time for this. So much depends upon the first 20 minutes; the period of mutual sounding-out, the maestro often much more nervous than the players. At this point Kleiber can be disconcerting. There is about him a nervous anxiety not for himself but for the piece. He is happier only when he finds in the orchestra people who will share that responsibility and are prepared to drive themselves to their wits' end to discharge it with him. Even then, working with him must always be an electric experience. The orchestra is never relaxed. The better the work goes the greater the tension because the more fragile the creation.

Conventionally this is no way to play anything, and especially opera. The evening is long and all opera is booby-trapped for conductors and players. Such an approach from any other conductor would be destructive. The orchestra might rebel, or its concentration might break. In Kleiber's case neither seems possible. An evening with him is one of the great lifetime opportunities for self-realisation through performance; not exhausting but liberating. It is something for which we have been waiting and working all our lives. Our only regret, after five or six performances, is that there cannot be five or six more. That is impossible; we have been electrified, but the man must recharge his batteries.

Nor does his search for perfection end with the last rehearsal. He will scan the score again before each performance, reminding himself of the things which he must improve this evening. New advice is tendered to members of the orchestra on small postcards, hand-written and distributed personally among the music-stands. Once this habit is discovered there is naturally a tendency to go early into the pit each evening in the hope of collecting one of these personal treasures. My Kleibergram was culled from a performance of *Elektra*.

Unlike the elder Kleiber the son may be, but he has learned much from the great Doctor and not all of it simply musical. Erich Kleiber once told David Webster at Covent Garden that if there were no problems in today's schedule he must make some. Kleiber problems come in many varieties. The old man used to inspect the House each evening and would call House Management if he found a dirty ash-tray in the crush bar. Ash-trays, we were given to understand, were part of Kleiber's performance. Carlos can be upset, in the same way, by an unswept green-room floor, and quite unmoved by the excuse that two other conductors have used the room earlier in the day.

In rehearsal, too, when things seem just a little too cosy, he can create a highly effective panic. One memorable morning – enjoyable to that point — he suddenly exploded with wrath at the quality of our *Otello* storm. 'This lightning! It looks like a man fiddling with an electric light-bulb! And do you call this thunder? You live in England and you don't know what a thunderstorm is?'

When I went afterwards to invite him to choose a better storm I found him in high good humour. 'I hope I was not *too far* over the top this morning. But it seemed to need something ...!' Who else would balance the loss of rehearsal time against the gain in adrenalin?

We value our Kleibergrams as evidence that we played for this unique man. He values equally all the cards which come back *to him from the orchestra.* He will not share them, but he did once reveal that ours were more polite than those of the Wiener Staatsoper. I am glad.

CHAPTER 24
Italian Epic

In the spring of 1976 La Scala brought to London revelatory performances of *Boccanegra, Cenerentola,* and the Verdi Requiem. We took to Milan our *Grimes, La Clemenza di Tito,* and *Benvenuto Cellini.*

Opera companies are too expensive to tour. This is one of the attractions of the game for any escapee from the symphony orchestra. The Royal Opera had travelled only twice previously: to what was then Rhodesia to celebrate that country's centenary, and to Berlin and Munich in the 1969–70 season.

This was my first tour in management. I knew from watching Hallé management that the thing was not easy; but the huge burden of travelling the whole outfit, more than three hundred in all, was shouldered by Opera-Company Management, leaving us to run our orchestra much as we do at home. Since the Covent Garden machine is accustomed to touring the Royal Ballet on a global scale, it coped with an opera tour to Milan with the ease of a commuter-trip from Croydon to Charing Cross. There were no hitches; no memorable catastrophes. This has been nearly true of every such expedition since.

My worry was that our people, so splendidly self-disciplined at home, might kick over the traces abroad. Symphony orchestras sometimes do, and not only British ones.

Some idea of what the British orchestra on tour can do at its worst – and of course its worst is not typical – was given to me much later by a visiting conductor. His had been a rough trip, with many minor mishaps in travel and accommodation: a common experience in the 'sixties and 'seventies in eastern Europe and by no means always to be laid at the door of orchestra management. The orchestra had become increasingly resentful, and had taken to the liquid cure. Before the final concert my friend was told that half of the orchestra was unwell, though some of the unwell would necessarily play. Otherwise no concert.

How did it go?

'It occurred to me during the overture,' he said wryly, 'that I might have been better off with the other half.'

Colin had suffered in this way too, and his fears were no secret. But whether because of the efficiency of our planning or the natural good manners of Gardeners, the Orchestra and the Company behaved in Milan with the same relaxed good order as in London. This made possible very distinguished performance indeed; just as well, since the Milanese under Abbado set London afire in our absence.

The Scala visit came at exactly the right time for the orchestra. Having lost considerable ground on Solti's departure we had turned the tide. The work was far from complete but the upward trend was well established. The challenge was timely and welcome.

The Scala is a fascinating theatre. While it has neither the grandeur of the old Paris Opera, where the foyer alone would make an admirable set for the second-act finale of *Aida*, nor the intimacy of Covent Garden, it is the House where so much operatic history was made. Verdi and Toscanini conducted there; ultimate operatic standards are in its stones. We were under no illusions as to what was required of us.

We were surprised to find so much of the building itself in a dilapidated state at that time. Every second mirror in that House — and it is lavishly furnished with mirrors — seemed to need resilvering. The plush and the carpet were plentiful but worn. More directly disturbing to us was the loose floor in the pit and the unreliability of the pit electrics. I spent half my Milan time, so it seemed to me, crawling between players on a dusty floor, wobbling light-plugs to get a glim.

Otherwise that pit was a luxury. With more space than we had ever been allowed at home, even for the *Ring*, we were able to play with symphonic strings for the first time. At first, though, there were problems. Having arranged our luxurious orchestra Covent Garden fashion in the pit we found that nothing worked, acoustically. Despite its wonderful size, this pit like all pits was 'a character'. How to humour it? Eventually we found the secret. The firsts must sit in front of the conductor, the seconds on his left. The bass seating must move, and the wind. It was all very odd, but we did it. A revelation! For the first time we could hear each other as well as on a concert-platform. The orchestra settled down to play with a will.

Of the three operas on tour, *Benvenuto Cellini* was a rarity, never since seen at home, and revived for Milan no doubt because Colin's

Berlioz was thought to be essential. *Les Troyens* would have been a better idea but since Jon Vickers was essential to *Grimes*, and we had no other Aeneas, that was impossible. As matters turned out, and to the surprise of most of us, we had a great success with *Cellini*, the orchestra turning in work of remarkable quality and the chorus responding with glorious precision and energy.

My most vivid recollection of that opening night is the reception given to the overture. I played fifth trumpet in *Cellini*. Fifth trumpet escapes after the overture, much envied by his friends. It was easy to leave the pit during the applause. To my surprise, after going down to the bandroom, stowing my trumpet, dressing for the street, and walking to the stage door — a matter of four or five minutes in all — I could hear the applause still. Wonderful! That applause was Colin's, the orchestra's, and *mine*. Nothing to do with opera. Everything to do with orchestral quality.

Colin was announced in the press next day as 'The man who invented Berlioz'. This will have embarrassed him if he read it; Colin never reads a review. But he is one of very few conductors who make sense of that composer. One critic, praising the Company, said that what made this evening so special was not the cast, which was neither better nor worse than a Scala cast, nor the production, which was really old and tired and in no way interesting. No, it was the Music Director, his orchestra and his chorus which were remarkable, and London should be proud of such a team.

This was the evening when the tide turned for the Covent Garden Orchestra. Having heard the result of a full-sized orchestra in a good pit our Board became orchestral enthusiasts. We were promised the Wagner pit at home every night, at the cost of a row of seats, and a budget for bigger strings. At last I was allowed to think that some people at least would come to Covent Garden to hear the orchestra. I was right. Today the opera orchestra is no longer a second-class body at which the symphonic big four look down a collective nose. At Covent Garden the sounds from the pit are worthy of any concert-hall in the land.

We had fun with the Scala administration. Having left a complete stage band in London to help them with *Boccanegra*, and trumpets for their Requiem, we were promised in return four mandolins for *Cellini*. Our band duly arrived; not so their mandolins. At each of three rehearsals the promise was renewed in vain. At the fourth

Colin applied a rare remedy. Putting down the stick he asked us not to be disturbed, please, by the following uncharacteristic scene. He then turned to the House and shouted abuse into the darkness for two minutes, with threats of imminent departure of the entire Royal Opera. Within five minutes four players arrived. Even La Scala, it seems, can behave like a comic-opera Italian theatre.

The pit floor, too, continued to provide problems. Colin was a great jumper-up-and-down in those days and nothing energised him more than Berlioz. Though without an ounce of fat he is a very big chap. The result was a continuous small earthquake which made it quite difficult for the brass to keep mouthpieces on faces. We complained to no avail. Eventually our first trombone, a man of considerable wit much practised at the expense of music directors, suggested that if Colin would not stand still we would nail him to the floor, adding that this would be easy because 'conductors all have holes in their feet.' At this our friend reduced his physical output a little; but in the *Cellini* finale he still looked likely to qualify for the next Olympics. I don't know when I've seen a conductor enjoy himself more.

Grimes was as great a success in Milan as in London. A shoestring production, using many of the costumes from a previous one, it contained a classic cast of natural dramatic choices for the roles. Jon Vickers' Peter has been heavily criticised by purists, but it was dramatically superb. The man got so much inside Grimes that on this tour and later in Japan we found ourselves occasionally addressing him as 'Peter'. Three Covent Garden recordings now exist, Ben's, Colin's, and Bernard Haitink's. We can choose for ourselves. I would not be without any. Davis, with Vickers and Heather Harper – as always wonderful and impeccably accurate – Geraint Evans, Tom Allen and that marvellous ensemble did a great deal for the piece and for the composer, one of whom we were all very proud indeed. We have so often been accused, as the international houses inevitably are, of rent-a-cast production. Here was ensemble opera at the highest level. The Milanese loved it.

The mad scene, played in a black-out, leaving Vickers alone for several minutes with no orchestral support, was simply terrifying. How could a man get so close to madness without becoming unhinged? These were moments of awful tension in the theatre, narrowly escaping disaster on the first night in Milan through a catastrophe in the pit. One of our cellists, having suffered for several days with a stomach upset, passed out in the dark. He fell forward over his cello, with dire consequences for the instrument, and collapsed with a crash on the floor. The poor man was deep at the back of the pit, close to the timpani. We had the tricky job of extricating him from that crowded place in total darkness, without wrecking the scene. Fortunately our friend came round quickly. We still smile together about that evening, but at the time it was very un-funny indeed.

Our Mozart fared a shade less well. John Pritchard, as fine a Mozartian as we will ever see, was not at home with that work. Perhaps Colin's *Clemenza*, a very different performance, had been too recent, or perhaps the opera itself was not JP's best Mozart. Perhaps, again, Italy has a special taste in that composer? I often suspect so. The piece was beautifully delivered, in a wonderful production of which we were very proud and which had been rapturously received at home; but we felt it had not come off as had the other two works.

Between operas we were royally entertained. I saw Venice for the first time and the Teatro Fenice, a blue-and-gold jewel-box, surely the most perfect theatre imaginable for Mozart. They were working at *Rheingold*, which could not possibly succeed there, where the pit is hardly big enough to contain Wagner's strings, let alone the attendant wind and brass. They showed us their production, done entirely by back-projected film. The whole epic was run through scenically for us in fifteen minutes and it had cost, they told us, only £15,000. Among the entranced orchestra and chorus the atmosphere was pregnant with suggestions that Covent Garden had something to learn here.

On the way back, after a lunch which demonstrated the potency of the local wine — we were provided with a bottle each and many of us unsuspectingly drank it — we visited the Verdi house at Busetto. Verdi enthusiasts as we are, we'd been finding Milan's nearly-religious adulation of the composer more than a bit trying. The name of *Il Maestro* was rarely mentioned at La Scala except in hushed tones. We had already developed our own antidote, translating him into the English 'Joe Green', but here in his own house the atmosphere was of a visit to the shrine of San Giuseppi. This roused one of our number to polite protest. As we left the building he asked for silence because

'I have something of very great importance to say. In a word: MOZART!' There was a round of enthusiastic applause. I hope our generous hosts were not offended. In any case, 'twas their wine that did it.

CHAPTER 25

The Man at the Top

To be Music Director at Covent Garden is the ultimate honour British music can bestow upon a conductor. Colin Davis achieved it at an age when it was still possible for him to go on to other great things both as Music Director abroad and as a distinguished tourist. His has been a story-book success.

He was always operatic by instinct. He sings well (the orchestra sometimes good-humouredly wishes he would shut up) and he married a singer, which must have helped. He learned the operatic ropes with the Chelsea Opera Group and the symphonic ones with the BBC Scottish Orchestra before Klemperer's illness gave him the big 'break'. He was Music Director at Sadler's Wells, and Chief Conductor of the BBC Symphony Orchestra. No British conductor could have had a better training than this, short of immersion in the continental operatic scene as a repetiteur. That was never possible for Colin; he is not a good pianist.

Opera will always be Colin's first love, I believe. He has nearly always seemed more at home in the pit than on the platform. A natural Music Director for Covent Garden, then? Well, what is this job? What goes on in the room at the top of that antique lift near the stage door?

For every occupant the job is different. The man makes the job, and the job makes or breaks the man. It's a team job, carried on for much of the year without the physical presence of the captain, who must ensure that his presence is always felt and that his policies and attitudes are always remembered. He must be prepared for the mid-night telephone call asking emergency advice; for the reminder of *Götterdämmerung* when he is deeply into Mahler's Ninth in Berlin. We in turn must be ready for the call from Tokyo, half-way through our Sunday roast, demanding details of a rehearsal schedule.

The work takes up perhaps half the conductor's time but very much more of his mind. Since it is for his commitment that he is paid rather than for his performances, his remuneration is comparatively modest, and subject to increase only when he performs. If it suits him to be in London at the expense of better-paid work abroad, then he may conduct often at Covent Garden. If not then he can take on two or three new productions, keeping tabs for the rest of the year on his musical establishment with days in his office when it suits him. Either way his musical and personal style must be imprinted on the House which, like its public, will hold him personally responsible for all matters musical, and — justly or unjustly — for much else.

He is top man on a sizeable pyramid. There is a music staff of repetiteurs, managed by the Head of Music Staff. While Chorus Director and Orchestra Director will report directly to him, every player and every singer will expect his personal interest. The choice of repertoire — not only his own but that of every visitor — is in his gift. It is impossible for any one man to pull all these strings together, because in repertoire and scheduling so much depends on availabilities of artists and other conductors. The demands of the people who sell Covent Garden's tickets are not to be neglected either. It's not surprising, then, that so many decisions are made by a concensus of his colleagues or that those who finalise repertoire, conducting, casting, and scheduling work on the opposite side of Floral Street. Still, the responsibility is his and his influence can and should be paramount. The first requirement, then, is that he must build a good team and learn to manage it. To be a conductor is not enough; he must become Managing Director of an Opera Factory too. Small wonder that in some continental Houses the Music Director becomes Intendant, collaring all the work and accepting all the responsibility. A colossal task, it may seem simpler than delegation; but at Covent Garden, where the ballet is of equal importance and where the chief executive must spend most of his days with the begging-bowl, that solution is impossible.

Since Colin is dedicated to his home and family he was very much the domestic boss. He lived with us and he knew every face in the building and every quirk of the establishment. By no means the establishment's man, he knew that when all else failed it was possible, even in John Tooley's civilised and rational organisation, to achieve his end by a show of temperament; but the Great Conductor pose was quite foreign to him. In others he seems to find it pretentious and to varying degrees comic. Covent Garden is a very informal organisation, and that suited him. No-one there called him 'Sir Colin'; he stood on no ceremony, impatient of status, of routines and systems, when they got in the way of the work. Had anyone called him *Maestro* he would probably have suspected it was because his name had been forgotten. Understanding the problems of the player and of the manager, he conceded to the frustrations of neither.

I discovered the practical Colin very quickly. Before rehearsal one morning he telephoned to say that the pit had not been cleaned. I gave him the reason; a cleaner was sick and no-one was available to do the work. Colin asked me to come down. At the pit door he offered me the choice of two brooms. He'd sent the orchestra to the canteen, and the pit staff were already moving chairs. He and I swept the floor. The message was clear. This was typical of the man.

What of the conductor? Conductors are measured by their weaknesses, often, and this is especially true of Music Directors, who are expected to put up a first-rate show all round the repertory and, being human, never do. Conventionally the British do not conduct Italian opera easily, Puccini and earlier Verdi especially, though they often do well with *Otello* and *Falstaff*. It is the rum-ti-tum Verdi which beats them; those repetitive rhythms and clichés which are in Milan an act of faith. Colin was not at his best in that repertory. His recorded Italians are an uneven collection, though his *Tosca* is really fine. It is to his credit that he tried and kept trying; it is very easy indeed for a Music Director to opt out; to confine himself to party pieces.

Did Colin have party pieces? Not in the opera house anyway; there is so little performable operatic Berlioz, and only one opera of Stravinsky, the two composers who made him famous. True, his *Cellini*, his *Troyens* and his *Rake* were among his very best things; but leaving aside his achievement in twentieth-century opera it was in Mozart that he excelled.

There was a magic time at Covent Garden when we played Mozart each night for three weeks; *Figaro, Così* and *Giovanni*, all with Colin. A marathon. Yet he found time and energy to conduct the wind serenades in the Covent Garden Piazza at lunchtime too. He could live on Mozart, I think. 'However bad the day', he once told me, 'it can always be put right by thirty-two bars of *Così*. When I'm an old man and can please myself I will conduct nothing else but Mozart. Mozart is the only *real* composer. All the others are amateurs, more or less.' Then 'So many orchestras play Mozart on their knees. Very dangerous. It's an ideal position for getting a kick in the pants.'

Once in a television interview he was asked what it was that made Mozart unique. His reply was memorable: 'He was one of only two human beings who made no mistakes: Mozart and Jesus Christ.'

There is nothing celebral nor stylised about Colin's Mozart, nor about anything else he conducts. For him, as for Beecham, music is first and foremost 'a matter of making a beautiful sound'. His Mozart *sings*. He was lucky, perhaps, in some of the artists with whom he played it at Covent Garden. Te Kanawa's Countess, one of the great operatic events of the century, would not have been possible without Colin's faith in the young singer, nor without the musical understanding they built together. The young Kiri brought him natural musicality, the quality with which he works best. If some more experienced singers like Colin less that may be because of his dislike for the routine, the 'yet-another' performance. For him the next is always special; perhaps, too, knowing quite a lot about their art, he's a hard man to persuade in a vocal argument. Singers prefer conductable conductors.

Colin worked hard, within Covent Garden's precarious budget, for twentieth-century opera. He was a tireless advocate of Tippett, playing and recording a marvellous *Midsummer Marriage* and giving premieres of *The Knot Garden* and *The Icebreak*. The Orchestra loved the first of these. Sensing our increasing resistance as the works grew more and more abstract, he pressed harder, supplying a libretto of *Icebreak* to everyone in the pit. This ploy was not a success because we found the words even less intelligible than the music; but his committed advocacy produced a fine performance, regardless.

His *Wozzeck*, again, was marvellous, and the premiere of the complete *Lulu* was among the great achievements of his reign. His *Peter Grimes* was masterly, inextricably caught up though it will always be with the critical argument over Jon Vickers' Peter, very different from Pears' original.

All this, taken with the meat of the repertoire from *Carmen* to *The Ring*, is impossible to reconcile with the persistent critical view of Davis as a lucky hangover from the days of British amateurism. It represents a very different picture: of a hard-working learner of scores with a fine vocal and choral technique and a firm grasp of the problems of the stage. It also required, as a first measure, a mastery of the orchestra far beyond the ordinary. An opera music-director indeed.

In his early days Colin's technique was very physical. The young Davis will have given little pleasure to his teacher, the arch-economist

Boult. There was no helping this. He had to work it out. With Colin, music is a matter of self-expression, and he had an excess of energy to express. Covent Garden saw the refinement of his technique from the exuberant to the economic. It enjoyed both, and the learning curve too.

His hands are superb, among the best in the game. No-one notices this, nor should they. The stick is a means to an end, not a spectacle. He learned — not too late — the science of the gesture, the use of the hands to produce sound, and like the best of the best he has combined the science with his own instinct. The result is a flexible, personal communication with the orchestra. He talks little at rehearsal. It was fascinating to watch his first half-hour, returning in later seasons. He would plough on uncomplaining through 20 minutes of indifferent work, only stopping when the orchestra began to play well. Then he'd return to 'the top' and do it again. This time vintage Davis would result. Occasionally, rarely, he'll stop and talk, but once the language is understood there is little need. An opera conductor through and through, he conducts the complete ensemble. Once he advised a young visiting conductor, coming with *Zauberflöte*, to hold no purely orchestral rehearsal at all, but to call the cast from the start. Naturally he expected the orchestra and singers, with his built-in Mozart, to teach the young man, and teach they did. But underlying that suggestion was a very important principle: opera is a unity. Hard, then, to discount Colin 'on the box'. What of the managing director of the opera factory?

For me he was an ideal colleague, knowing well the quagmire in which orchestra management walks and the way which his own attitudes could sustain or drown us. Never once did we feel ourselves undermined by him. Never did he show the fatal, comfortable weakness for 'sucking up' to the orchestra, yet he steered a fair and open course between management and managed. It came naturally to him. He'd been a player, and he enjoys players as few conductors genuinely do, I think; can the matador genuinely like the bull? The matador knows with fearful certainty that his bull is not only stronger but smarter. It can always finish him. Colin, as we all knew before he arrived, had been given a roughish ride by players in orchestras here and there. Yet he trusted the Covent Garden orchestra and it trusted him back. The results were always fine, and sometimes wonderful.

His 'wobblies' were rare, always calculated, and never at the expense of a player. Colin was always the reasonable man. This entails conceding to inadequacies sometimes. Logically there are two alternatives when a player fails: one can fire the man or put up with him. While firing is and must always be an option, none of us being better than his last performance, it cannot be a routine solution or a player would leave every orchestra every day, leaving no-one to be fired except the conductor. The decision requires fine judgement, and in any civilised environment that decision must carry the judgement of the orchestra. The attitude attributed to Sargent, that 'security is the enemy of orchestral standards', is rubbish. The player needs security, security to make a mistake, because without a mistake one can make nothing. Risks must be taken, necks must be stuck out. Colin knew that. He took risks and made music like a player, which is what, after all, he is.

The history of the orchestra in his time is one of building, of patient and painstaking improvement of a band he found in a poorish way and which he handed to his successor in a state of readiness for even greater things. Part of his success lay in his willingness to entrust some of that work to the orchestra itself and part in the continuous encouragement he supplied, year upon year, most significantly by the rich recordings he brought to them. He left an orchestra and a House much improved for his stay, and in the pit he left many friends.

CHAPTER 26
JT

The author of a recent book about conductors described the atmosphere of the Royal Opera House in John Tooley's time as 'cosy'. To one looking in vain for the chaos of Paris or the politics of Vienna this may have seemed fair; but no-one who worked in the House at that time would have so described it.

It was above all a practical place. JT knew the House and everyone in it, Nibelheim to Valhalla, every detail of the way it worked and the way the team ran it. He knew our qualities and our limitations to an inch and he got the best possible results from each of us.

JT is 'a gentleman' of the natural sort which are seldom made, rarely born, and much valued by close colleagues. He had the knack of employing as associates people who would instinctively behave in every situation as he himself would. Attitudes breed quickly in a tightly run team, and Covent Garden became a very personal statement of John's attitudes to art and life.

His attitude to our art was simply expressed. 'Excellence', he said, 'is what this place is all about. If we fail to provide it we have no right to take the money.'

He could be infuriating. In a quandary, with the whole room waiting for a decision, he might well say 'Let's come back to that, shall we?' This meant simply that he understood that a judgement of Solomon was expected of him; that he was not Solomon and therefore not in a position to deliver, and that we would do well to go away and beat each other over the head with the problem and not come back until we'd cracked it.

Again, he might forcefully say, in response to a situation he really hated, that 'The answer to that question is *no!*' when we all knew that a positive would be forced from him within hours. We knew what he meant; that he deplored and resented the inevitable and would expect us to avoid a recurrence.

He was a good delegator in that he never seemed to look over one's shoulder, and a clever one in that he knew how the work was going without looking. We respected him for knowing our jobs as he knew his own. If any manager in the House had died overnight, JT could have picked up the threads personally next morning.

He had, it was often said, a cushion-quality, the tendency to display the impression of the last chap who'd sat on him. It was an impression only; no-one sat on John Tooley. His habit of making encouraging noises in response to a good argument sometimes created a mistaken impression of agreement, but he knew most if not all of the arguments in advance. If hearing them rehearsed was sometimes something of a bore for him he never showed it. He steered his own course in the end.

Sadly, many of his qualities were fully appreciated only by those immediately around him. The House on the whole thought him parsimonious because he resisted its financial demands whether at the level of wage-claims or departmental budgeting, but no-one who knows the financial predicament of the Royal Opera House could doubt the wisdom of that resistance. The idea of 'spending one's way out of trouble' was foreign to JT; he didn't spend what he couldn't earn. He also understood, as does everyone who has seen the results produced in highly subsidised Houses abroad, that money is no substitute for talent, ideas and good management. Faced with a miserly nation he became an internationally-acclaimed virtuoso at the extraction of blood from stones. If some of us felt from time to time that it was our blood and from our stones, that was the name of the game. It still is, and I suppose ever shall be, in the UK.

He succeeded his chief, Sir David Webster. He must have been a great backup for DW; the ideal chap to trail that tough character around the House, dispensing balm where needed — rather often, probably. Perhaps it was this conditioning which made him so un-failingly nice to us all? If so it worked surprisingly well. Heads of departments understood that it was for them to apply the pressure. Bruised people could always appeal to JT and the oil would be poured as bountifully as ever. He was invariably accessible and this kept him constantly in touch with the House. His grapevine was better than any of ours. He never missed an opportunity to talk with what industry calls the shop floor; in the street, on the tube, or in a corridor, his daily interchange provided him with frank opinions on the state of the House and the performance of his lieutenants.

Living in a matchbox flat around the corner enabled him to collect his mail before most of us had finished breakfast at home (at Covent

Garden, where the day is inexorably geared to the 7.30 deadline, administration inclines to a ten o'clock start and a 7.30-if-you-are-very-lucky exit) and then to start work over breakfast. He would often, before that, walk around the innards of the place, giving 'good morning' by name to those passed en route. New faces were spotted and their names solicited and remembered; not only those of players, dancers, or choristers but of cleaners too. His eyes were everywhere. He knew every piece of scuffed wallpaper, how long it had been there and what it would cost to replace.

His was a full day, but whenever there was a gap in his diary he would walk across Floral Street to inspect whatever was going on, a constant presence with always a word of constructive comment about what he saw or what he had seen or heard last evening. A fine piece of playing from a player would be rewarded with a kind word over the pit rail. A query about who that oboist had been who deputised in last evening's emergency, and why we had not done better, was the sort of thing my office expected of him. It was extraordinary, too, how often his popping-up in the theatre coincided with the kind of crisis he was so well equipped to defuse: the hysterical diva, the conductor with one foot in the Heathrow taxi, or the indignant tenor could always depend on him for the right word and a timely solution to the problem. His timing was as impeccable as his sources of information.

His criticism, always forthright, somehow remained kind. Summoned to the presence to account for a bad evening, I must have looked too crestfallen to kick. 'Bram', he said sorrowfully, 'last evening was ... not one of our best, was it?'

Disaster in performance could produce an instant rocket. A finger would tap a shoulder and I would be beckoned into the crush bar to explain. I well remember a *Boccanegra* when a trumpet fanfare did not materialise, leaving an embarrassing hiatus.

'What happened?'

From my Grand Tier seat how could I know?'

'Well, find out, please. I'll be here waiting'.

I spent a tricky ten minutes downstairs listening to a tale of missed tannoy-calls, sleeping trumpeters and distracted orchestra management, returning with very little to offer, and certainly no opinion about the responsibility for the disaster. JT, on the other hand, had one.

'Everything, absolutely everything which happens down there is your responsibility. If the trumpet doesn't blow, that's down to you. Remember that.'

Braced up perhaps by the hock of two intervals, I was brave enough to point out that if everything down there was my responsibility then surely everything of mine was his too.

Smiling, he was a move ahead of my game. 'Ah, but I can fire you, and you can't fire me ...'

The crush bar was the scene of much of JT's best work, accommodating the best-laid plots and advice for which his office day had left no time. We could generally find him there after the overture, drinking very sparingly – an attack of hepatitis had deprived him of the pleasures of alcohol – and we queued for a few words. If he was not 'in' then he was almost certainly 'in' somewhere else: in Hamburg, Vienna, Paris, Berlin, or Munich perhaps. It was a commonplace for him to say during an afternoon meeting: 'This must be over by four; I have a plane to catch', but his presence in the House by breakfast time next day was certain. As Beecham told Neville Cardus, surprised at finding him in London rather than in Stockholm, 'I have been to Stockholm; I had no intention of emigrating there.' JT saw little of these towns except their operas and their airports.

He lived for the place as no-one has done since, and few before him. Webster's weekends had been sacrosanct; it was said that he would not be disturbed before Monday if the House burned down on Saturday. Tooley gave Covent Garden a 24-hour day and a seven-day week for decades.

John was the best off-the-cuff speaker I have ever heard; as the House's front man, personally responsible for most of its public relations, he had a lot of practice. He was a wizard; and his spells were not prepared at length nor at leisure – of which he had none. A few minutes in a taxi, between his desk and a formal lunch, was all he needed to prepare himself. What a parliamentarian he would have made! The material flowed in an unhesitating and beautifully-spoken stream; never forced, never boring. Only once did he tire us, and that was at a formal lecture in Los Angeles for which he had prepared a lecture on the history and development of the Royal Opera House. He was best, as the first Lord Liverpool described his own similar talent, 'upon the un-pinioned wing'.

His conversation was as polished as his public utterance; he polished everything. Even his signature unfailingly required a good old-fashioned fountain-pen.

The critics gave him hell. It may be fairly admitted that after the departure of Helga Schmidt as Artistic Administrator the Tooley-Davis regime did less well in casting and production than formerly, but the press has been less than fair to the achievement of either. This attitude was and is part of the Covent Garden picture, and one to which we are all inured. As a flagship the House attracts the fire. What we never discover is why the fire? Are we the enemy? Why was the public perception of Covent Garden in Tooley's time so very far from the truth? Was this the result of poor public relations, of neglect of 'The image'? Hardly. I think it is because a great deal of hard work was invested by powerful people in that cause. A very famous musician, the head of one of our most famous teaching institutions, once described the House to me as 'The artistic equivalent of Fleet Street before commonsense arrived there', an opinion so ridiculous that I was left speechless. Yet this has been for many years the popular view of Covent Garden.

Credit has never been given to John Tooley and his Music Director for the immense work done for British music and for modern opera. The first-ever complete *Lulu* — a wonderful production marvellously conducted by Colin — the operas of Peter Maxwell Davis, of Tippett, of John Taverner, of Stockhausen and Berio, all were given masterly premieres, beautifully produced, conducted, sung and played. This is carefully forgotten by Tooley's detractors. That such things were ever undertaken by an establishment so starved for money is a miracle; one envisioned in faith, sustained by conviction and created by masterly penny-pinched organisation.

That organisation is a Tooley achievement and it is the best anywhere. Visiting conductors and artists are astonished at the accuracy and consistency which we take for granted. The atmosphere in which we work, too, fascinates visitors. All are agreed that there is simply nowhere on earth like Covent Garden in which to sing, dance, conduct, produce or premiere a work. They feel they are with friends. Like any healthy family, the House confines its internal spats to domestic circles and occasions. It embarrasses no outsider. And all this it achieves in a building inadequate and ill-equipped for anything but the crudest of productions, on an annual budget which would not finance the Paris Opera for six months.

This is JT's legacy. When asked what he considered his best achievement at Covent Garden, he replied that 'It is still there.'

It is a pity that as time went on the public assessment of his work, as created by the press and believed by many of those who knew no more of Covent Garden than they read there, so unfairly declined. In the House, and in the other great opera houses of the world, people knew better. Among those who know and understand most his reputation was, and remains, enormous. It is utterly deserved.

CHAPTER 27
Baedeker Opera

One must keep aware of available talent against the rainy day, and colleagues sometimes ask a second opinion on a conductor; so a perquisite of the Orchestra Director's job is an occasional opportunity to travel and listen to other orchestras and the companies for which they play.

This can be a mixed blessing, an artistic lucky dip. While the possibility of hearing really bad playing or singing in the UK today is slight, the quality of operatic production is much less reliable. I think with a shudder of an *Oberon* involving an Ayatollah and a Reagan lookalike; and of a *Giovanni* where the Don, instead of being dragged resisting off to Hell, begged admittance at its door. I was with him in spirit; I would have accepted any exit from that production.

The Floral Street fare reduces most feasts to a comparative Naafi-break. We play better, sing better, conduct better, and whatever the press pretends we generally produce better than our friends in the other British theatres. So we must; excellence *is* the name of our game. But Leeds, Cardiff, Glasgow, and English National Opera provide memorable opera too.

ENO (the initials are invariably pronounced as a word at Covent Garden, like the name of the famous fruit salts) is ever the hound at our heels, our national habit of favouring the underdog being nowhere more in evidence than in press and public appraisal. The ENO orchestra has improved beyond measure in recent years because Peter Jonas as General Manager understood, as Lord Harewood before him seemed not to do, that the orchestra is the bedrock of operatic performance, and that a good orchestra was possible at the Coliseum as everywhere else. It is a pity that this policy came so late; too late, for instance, to provide Reginald Goodall with the orchestra he deserved for his ENO Wagner. Today that orchestra would be provided, without doubt, and today's orchestra costs little more, in relative terms, than it did in Goodall's time.

What can one say about Goodall? What a puzzle! Must one accept the verdict of a conductor-friend, that Reggie was neither a good conductor nor a bad one but simply did not conduct at all? There is more than a grain of truth in this. Goodall's hands were much less useful in terms of ensemble than was the leader with the violin. Is this what really happened in Reggie's performances? Perhaps Reggie rehearsed and the leader led? I offer the suggestion with some reservation because I was never aware in his performances of leadership at all. On the other hand, we performed the pieces; there was tempo and there was, if not accurate ensemble, *musical* unity. His performance belonged not to him alone, but to everyone involved.

The Royal Opera House has been criticised for not having given Goodall the rostrum more frequently. All kinds of motives have been imputed to General Directors and Music Directors by Goodall devotees, but the reasons for the House's apparent neglect of this artist are clear, surely? How could the Wagner of Solti and Goodall co-exist? On the one hand, energy, tension, precise articulation; on the other, leisure, expanse, reflection, and scale? The Music Director is entitled to stamp his personality on his House, and nowhere is it more crucially expressed than in the *Ring*. Solti and Goodall were incompatible in the repertoire which meant most to them. Thank God London heard them both.

Why did Goodall accept so cheerfully a life of seclusion and the role of coach? Perhaps it was because his standards were too high for any but the great international opera houses, and because his approach was one which no international house could afford. They simply have not time to build an opera, least of all a Wagner opera, bar by bar and phrase by phrase over a period of three months for four or five audiences to hear. Who can pay for this? Who can plan it? Only a lightly-loaded house, prepared to repeat other repertoire without rehearsal for many weeks while Reggie monopolised the orchestra and the singers. Even the bass trumpet, preparing with Goodall, was given a rehearsal with the conductor alone. That lucky man must have learned more Wagner in those three hours than in an orchestral lifetime. But at Covent Garden the orchestra must be conducted, not indoctrinated. Nor was the ROH alone in despairing of Goodall. Why was he not heard at Bayreuth? There had been no comparable Wagner there since Knappertsbusch, the Bayreuth orchestra's ideal, once described to me as 'Goodall with a clear beat'.

I spent happy hours with Reggie in the Covent Garden stalls, listening to Haitink's Wagner and warming myself at his praise. Our orchestra had no greater fan than Reggie. The impossibility of applying himself to it was simply a fact of his life, and remembering the astonishing quality of his performances elsewhere it is inconceivable that he felt frustrated by it.

The wisdom of Solti's isolation from Goodall was illustrated, much later, when Colin Davis took the opposite course, trying at first to approach Wagner from Reggie's perspective and failing. When the best Davis *Ring* comes, Goodall will have contributed to it but it will bear little resemblance to his own.

Orchestral reaction to Reggie was predictable. Those at ENO and Welsh National Opera who had the benefit of his teaching remember his rehearsals and performances as career-peaks. The Garden orchestra admired Reggie too, but since it could not play for him it preferred not to try. I played in his last performance there, a *Fidelio* of superb musical intention bedevilled by a complete lack of ensemble and rhythmic bite, the drama undermined by the lack of cohesion in the pit. Certainly on that occasion Reggie did not 'conduct'. I played *Parsifal* with him, and *Walkure* too as part of a cycle in the Davis series. This was the worst possible way to use Goodall. We could not play the work, as had his other orchestras, like a huge chamber group thoroughly prepared. We needed clear direction, and there was none. We waited for each other throughout an endless evening, and the result was simply untidy. The vassals cheered but they were wrong; the finest of musical intentions loses its way if not adequately conveyed. Still I am glad to have played for Reggie, and still more glad to have talked with him: a privilege which has been valued by the greatest of visiting conductors.

I remember his *Tristan* at ENO: a wonderful evening marred only by an over-generous orchestral sound and by a silly production. I think of Reggie's words to me, watching *Parsifal* at the Garden: 'I don't worry too much about production. I think the last time I enjoyed a Wagner production was Wieland Wagner's *Ring* at Bayreuth. Since then I've tried not to look.' Perhaps he would have agreed with Newman's idea of the perfect performance: one enjoyed in silence, at home by the fire with the score.

The regional opera companies, all created since I came into opera, are a marvellous new contribution to the artistic life of the nation.

Scottish and Welsh National Opera were at first seasonal, employing the regional orchestras. My own first foray into opera was at Llandudno, in the Odeon cinema, with Welsh National and the CBSO. I remember little of it except our failure to come to terms with *Tosca* (which I now find very unsurprising) and the fact that the diva really did bounce back from her trampoline. Yes, I saw it!

Scottish Opera was better organised, through the hard work of Alexander Gibson, an old Sadler's Wells man. Scotland played the *Ring* with his Scottish National Orchestra before it had its own opera orchestra, and the opera company grew from that start.

Opera North was a brave and imaginative idea of Lord Harewood's, starting as the Leeds Branch of the Coliseum and quickly growing into independence, neatly coinciding with Harewood's 'retirement' to Yorkshire. Life without an opera house would have been intolerable for that man, to whom British opera owes almost as much as to Webster.

Each company in turn needed a brand-new orchestra. Welsh had the neatest solution, absconding with most of the orchestra of our touring ballet company, and on that foundation building a fine opera orchestra which has thrived under positive and ambitious music directors. It is still, to my ears, the most mature of the three regional competitors.

In Scotland and Yorkshire orchestras were formed from scratch. What opportunities, and how well they were seized! The great advantage of the 'new band' in the regions is that it harnesses the energy of the young and ambitious player. Lack of experience weighs little against enthusiasm when proper time is available for rehearsal. Strings in Leeds and Cardiff have been known to give up days of their rest-periods to quartets and to preparing difficult new works together.

The downside of regional opera lies in the small theatres which limit the size of productions and orchestras. Small string bodies demand of the wind and brass unnatural restraint which can result in a kind of permanent *mezzoforte*. Welsh National, under Sir Charles Mackerras, defied this situation, and played Strauss' *Salome*, for instance, in theatres from which huge chunks of the stalls were 'untimely ripp'd' to make room for the orchestra. Viewed from the circle, unfortunately, the orchestra became the show; a pretty good show, I must say. What is most wonderful is today's public acceptance of British opera. Where 50 years back we had so few orchestras, we have now not only orchestras but opera houses. The gramophone and the BBC have played a great part in all this. So has enlightened government. Enlightened? Well, there is at least a glimmer! The happy day when every town of moderate population has its own symphony orchestra and opera house is still a pipe-dream, but no more so than was today's situation when I played my Haydn for Rudolf Schwarz.

In Europe that is the natural state of affairs. It was a humbling experience, arriving in a small town in the Black Forest, to find a thriving opera company, its orchestra also playing for ballet and in symphony concerts, its audience attending with the regularity the British give only to football, and all on a municipal budget smaller than that of Bolton. To find that the local Toscanini, enthusiastically adopted by the local people, was a Scot and that among his principal singers were several products of the Royal Northern College of Music gave further food for thought. It's good that our artists can find work and experience in these places, but how much better if that employment were to be had at home! It would do no great harm, either, to British orchestras. Europe is liberally sprinkled with British players, singers and conductors. Most would come home if they could. Part of our job at Covent Garden is to spot the best and bring them home at the appropriate time. Sometimes we score, sometimes we're too late. Donald Runnicles leapt, as Music Director, from modest Freiburg to glamorous San Francisco without putting down at Heathrow. So much the worse for us.

I have a vivid memory of hearing Carlo Rizzi for the first time, in an obscure theatre near Genoa (no place for a weekend visit, incidentally, and if you ask why a weekend for one performance I would point out that the mad economics of airlines dictate that if we step aboard a plane on Friday we cannot afford to step out again until Sunday) with a bad orchestra, an uneven cast and an undisciplined chorus, making unfailing musical sense of obscure Rossini. Without third-rate foreign opera of that kind such artists could not be provided for Covent Garden. What skinflint parasites we are, and of what native riches we deprive ourselves.

Those occasions represent one end of the European rainbow. The great opera festivals lie at the other. These are rarely business occasions for me, but my job has provided a facility denied to so many – the tickets. Armed with these promising bits of paper I like to head eastward at the start of my summer break, arriving a day or two later at

Salzburg or Bayreuth. In a good year, both; it very much depends on the Salzburg conducting because without a friend in the pit I cannot hope for a seat.

I'm a hillman and I love Austria. Above Kitzbühl, for me every glen is the Wolf's and every brook Beethoven's. Waking in the Tyrol, how better to end the day than with Mozart and the Vienna Philharmonic in his birthplace?

That orchestra is a disarming presence to which, like every other musician, I lift my critical hat − before putting it back on again, simple acceptance having been conditioned out of me. No orchestra plays Mozart as they do. The secret, we're told, is in the intonation. 'We are not better than everyone else', the players say, 'but we tune more carefully'. This theory is congenial, but there is more to it, surely. They are not only the oldest symphony orchestra but the one least interfered with, and their tradition of resistance to technical advice is famous. The highest praise offered to one great maestro by the Vienna was that he 'hardly disturbed us'. Are they then unteachable? No; they are as interested in ideas as any orchestra but they prefer to express them in their own language. The best-appreciated conductors there are those who offer themselves for Viennese translation. The results speak, or rather sing, for themselves. Only madmen complain.

Salzburg, Mozart and the Philharmoniker taken together offer an ideal basis for comparison between conductors. It is possible to hear on successive evenings a breathtaking *Zauberflöte*, for instance, and an infuriating *Giovanni*. Even that orchestra cannot save a conductor to whom Mozart does not speak, and it is sadly true that among the world's greatest are some who ought not to be let loose on this composer. He is too simple for them, needing no help, no translation and no ethnic, authentic approach. Mozart just *is*. All a musician need do is make friends with him. This is not so hard. One should simply walk up, look him in the eye, hold out a hand and say 'How are you, my friend?' and all will be well. Why so many crawl up to him on their knees I can't imagine. Remembering the man's sense of humour this is not only silly but dangerous. He will so often respond with a kick in the pants and go off laughing. Equally silly is the conductor who tries to 'command' Mozart. The composer takes his music home, leaving only the notes. The best for which an audience can hope is that the conductor and orchestra will not be noticed at all and that we will be left with our marvellous friend.

To invert one of Colin's remarks, it is true that however wonderful the day it may be ruined by a bad *Figaro*, and Salzburg can provide this too. Money cannot guarantee the result, least of all in opera. I have heard bad Mozart in Salzburg and splendid Mozart in Cardiff. But, *Zauberflöte* in Salzburg with Solti! That was an evening to remember.

Salzburg is a tourist trap for the hiker and the Festival enthusiast, each at his level. The Grosse Festspielhaus audience is, surely, the most spectacular in the world, the foyer a gallery of high fashion. We must not assume that these folks do not enjoy music, that they come simply to dress and be seen and to prove that they can afford Salzburg. There is no reason why the rich cannot enjoy music. But the taste displayed is often less than Mozartian, and one must wonder!

For a display of taste in the opera foyer Paris is incomparable. The interval promenade up and down those vast marble staircases is a theatre in itself, and to attend there without very careful attention to one's dress is to risk spoiling the evening for a thousand others. How sad that the new Bastille Opera is not in tune with this essential of Parisian life. A 'people's opera', perhaps; but ought not a people's opera house to remember the people's aspirations? The old house, now that has style. What a good thing it is still used. Those who deride Covent Garden as elitist ought to visit the Palais Garnier and see a real elite.

Bayreuth dresses well, but this is the dressing of people doing justice to a unique occasion in their lives. That is what Bayreuth is for thousands of German music-lovers each year, the lucky minority who achieve a seat. Once after a *Meistersinger* there I met a Hamburg couple, schoolteachers, who had applied each year since their marriage – 25 years. Now they had succeeded, and had cancelled their holiday to drive from Hamburg for one performance. I felt so deeply for them that had my seat for *Lohengrin* the next day been mine to give away I would have done so.

Bayreuth is a unique experience, one which deserves a chapter to itself.

CHAPTER 28

The Outsider

Each great composer, though trapped in his period, speaks a personal language; while Mozart superficially resembled Haydn, Handel, Bach, Elgar, Richard Strauss, they are for the musician unmistakeable voices.

Wagner's musical individuality is of a special order. Try as we may to relate him to his contemporaries, he will not belong. The man himself hardly belonged: a bad egg who exploited every friend, knowing no loyalty except to his own talent, a talent so enormous that he succeeded despite a lifetime of monstrous behaviour. He took the wife of his friend and champion, with what result? 'To the composer of *Tristan*', said the wronged husband, 'one forgives everything!' It is a remarkable fact that musicians, a cynical lot on the whole, have never doubted the sincerity of von Bülow's response.

What are we to make of a man who proposed a new art-form, involving the ultimate fusion of all the arts, for which he would write the libretto, then the score, then design the only theatre in which he believed it could properly be performed; then he would scrounge – there is no other appropriate word – the site on which to build it and the funds for its construction, with the avowed intention of playing his work only once before taking it down again? Everything, every stick, stone, piece of furniture, down to the music-stands and the orchestra seating-plan, up to the casting and conducting of the piece, would be his own work, paid for by others! Here is the mad musician, the crazy composer, a figure of fun. But wait! He was serious, a *practical* megalomaniac. He brought it off.

Being a man of rare sense with other folks' money, Wagner did not in the end dismantle his theatre but left it for us to enjoy. Many thousands have happily trekked off to Franconia for that purpose every summer since.

Among them are some who will listen to no music but Wagner's. This is silly, since every work of art needs a context, but the attitude is a simple inversion of the one which will not listen to Wagner at all, and this we accept as a matter of taste. Is the anti-Wagnerite so simply explained? In the case of the naive listener perhaps it is; the composer's sheer length demands a rare degree of concentration. 'Learning' the works, if indeed the listener ever learns music, can take a lifetime. Wagner, then, is difficult. Yet there are many musicians of experience who avoid him too.

Some, I think, refuse Wagner in self-defence. To most musicians music is a reassurance. Part of Mozart's universal appeal lies in a sense of secure inevitability, however great an illusion we know that to be. Wagner, on the other hand, is intentionally disturbing. *Tristan*, he said, was a dangerous work which would only be saved by its inevitably bad performance; played well it would be prohibited. One famous critic, admittedly a Wagner-susceptible, fainted during the *Liebestod* at Covent Garden. I have seen people helped in tears from the theatre at the end of the work. It is our Richard's most potent disturber of the psyche, one among many.

The Wagnerite displays some of the symptoms of the drug-addict, and the Wagnerphobe's objections, conscious or otherwise, are remarkably like the ones society advances against drugs. Wagner unbalances us, he distorts perspectives, and once hooked he leaves us little time or energy for anything else.

The orchestral musician is rarely a phobe nor a Wagnerite. Because the antidotes are too regularly applied, neither condition develops. So he is in a position to enjoy Wagner, to accept without reserve when the occasion arises. Those who cannot do so should keep away from Bayreuth. Everything about the Festspiel and the nice, ordinary little town in which it lives will increase his reserve. Every shop-window – well, perhaps not the greengrocers' – contains Wagner; his face is everywhere, on pottery, on paper, on record-sleeves. Even the street-names are Wagnerite.

Bayreuth seems almost to have forgotten its considerable pre-Wagner history as the home of the Margraves and of the Margravine who built the Hermitage. For the tourist this, together with the Margrave's theatre of 1748, is the chief place of interest. It was this delightful little House which first attracted Wagner to Bayreuth. It had the capacious stage he needed for his *Ring* though it was wrong in every other way. Still, he liked Bayreuth and the authorities there seem to have liked him, an important factor in his choice of site for the Festspielhaus.

Shaw has written entertainingly of his journeys to Bayreuth; of the Channel crossing and the slow train across Belgium and Germany to a town apparently unprepared for tourists. To this day there are so few tourist hotels in Bayreuth that the Festspiel must run its own accommodation service. This works well — what in the Fatherland does not? — and a bed is always to be found. Since this is often in some rural spot — the green fields begin half a mile from the town — one must be mobile. The best thing is to drive there. London to Bayreuth is possible in a day by road, though only for the energetic and single-minded who can resist the sirens en route, Würzburg and Bamberg included. The journey back is one I can easily face in the same time.

The trip is best planned with teutonic thoroughness. If you think you know the pieces, think again. Shaw's *Perfect Wagnerite*, the plain man's guide to *The Ring* and Karl Marx, with Irish wit thrown in, is surely the best possible way to do so. (I have often thought it surprising that Wagner, a prolific pamphleteer, did not beat Marx to *Das Kapital*; but perhaps that is what *The Ring* really is after all?) For some Wagner commentaries a thorough grounding in psychiatry might be useful. Donnington's *The Ring and its Symbols* is supreme, though one needs a thorough knowledge of the work *before* reading it.

Ideally, go first to *Meistersinger*, and first spend a day in Nürnberg. See the two great churches (like most of the city, these were once götterdämmerunged by our bombs, but that fact is not apparent now) and the beautiful fountain in the square, the Hans Sachs statue and the carvings in wood and stone made by Wagner's cast of masters. Have supper in the restaurant under the Rathaus and taste the wine of Franconia. It's not much exported; the Franks know a good thing when they drink it. Then drive north and find your Gasthaus. There are no bad ones hereabouts.

In the morning you have time for a walk about the town before a light lunch, then a nap (an investment this) before making your leisurely way to the Festspielhaus.

The approach up the green hill from the town is famous, and worth walking. The audience will be found promenading in the courtyard if the sun shines. They are a well-turned-out lot, many though not all in evening dress. This is not a house for dressing and being seen; there are no foyers. If it's wet there is nothing for it but to buy a beer and sit in one or other of the restaurants across the open space. For Bayreuth an umbrella is essential.

With twenty minutes to go a small procession of black-suited men carrying brass instruments is seen approaching through the crowd.

It enters the building and presents itself on the portico balcony, where at fifteen minutes to curtain-time it plays – with reliable intonation and precision – one phrase from the first act of the work. This will be repeated at ten minutes and played three times at five, by which time the prudent will be in their seats. So we cross the small cloakroom area and climb the stairs, through the door noted on our tickets into the famous theatre, a large, steeply raked fan without aisles. There are many doors, so access is easy. The rows are very long so it is vital to approach from the end nearest one's seat. Don't worry; the usherettes, young ladies from many countries, know their business. The custom is for each half-row to remain standing until it is full to the centre, so that we don't have to bob up and down for each new arrival. General consent for sitting is signalled by an almost-imperceptible unanimous nod. All sit together. Such unsmiling discipline! Bayreuth is for serious people. Perhaps, as Karl Böhm memorably observed, music really is no laughing matter.

As a listening-machine the Festspielhaus is very nearly perfect. Every seat has an identical acoustic and that acoustic is crystal-clear. The audience contributes; I've never met such a *positive* silence. The hard seats are legendary. Wagner originally furnished with woven cane, but this was abandoned because it made a noise when one 'turned the other cheek'. For many years we had plywood, simply. Now there is a sponge rubber cushion, about a centimetre thick! No-one complains. Is the capacity for suffering in silence a prerequisite here, or are these seats more comfortable than they appear?

A perfect acoustic? Not quite, I think. For me the orchestra is too remote. One gets used to it; the mental amplifier is turned up. We listen harder and that is no bad thing because our world is certainly too noisy. But at first hearing the *Meistersinger* Prelude seems to be the product of an offstage band. By its end we are naturally adjusted to this. The curtain rises and we are into the church chorale, sung as we have never heard it sung. Only a small part of the Bayreuth chorus is here, of course, an appetizer, an indication of the feast in store in the third act.

Just how good is this orchestra? The question is ungracious, since the performance as a whole is so admirable. My *Meistersinger* was a Wolfgang Wagner production, simple, unpretentious, lifelike and entirely effective. It presented nothing new of the producer and released everything of the composer. Here this piece is so often free, too, of conductor-fashions. Bayreuth gets hooked on names from time to time and it is easily possible to hear there conducting which does little for Wagner; but *Meistersinger* is often given to the House-conductors and they deal especially well with it.

The orchestra is enormous. Fifty-two violins are listed, with eight trumpets and twelve horns, all chosen out of a wealth of experience by Wolfgang Borkmüller of the Berlin Radio Orchestra. The scores demand such numbers; the same players cannot be expected to play such a repertoire every evening for so long a season. Yet to my ears the changes are rung a little too often. British players — hardy souls — would not thank a manager who planned to take out a player after an act, or even two acts, bringing in fresh muscle to finish the work, even for *Götters*. Our British first horns like to think they have lips enough for Wagner. They expect at most a 'bumper' to help out with the heavier stretches. At Bayreuth we can often hear the changes in sounds between acts. But perhaps these changes are essential? The 'cave' acoustic, as we have found here in the UK from our limited experience of such things, can be killing to the player. The clear but subdued orchestra which emerges is often but a fraction of what is produced inside. At great climaxes the internal condition at Baureuth is paralysingly loud. Can one bass trumpet make enough sheer noise to register its effect? No indeed; nor one first horn, nor many others playing singly.

What I dislike about Bayreuth is the orchestra's inability to contribute fully to climactic moments. Wagner's pit defeats it. When the Holländer's ship sails, when Brünnhilde rides into the flames, we miss the orchestra's potential. The Rhine-journey and the Funeral March are, for me, disastrously understated. I cannot believe that Wagner would fail to exploit the resources which are now available to remedy this. Those vast covers which suppress so much sound could move, surely? Solti, in his Ring year at Bayreuth, was granted a temporary modification of the great cowl. Perhaps only he could have achieved that; lesser men must have wished for it many times, knowing that to suggest such a thing would be to risk excommunication. Solti was right of course; it cannot be a good thing that the *Ring* orchestra is heard better from the Decca Company than in the Festspielhaus. But it is, certainly.

A colleague of mine who served on the music-staff at Bayreuth in the early 'thirties had a clear recollection of extra material being added to the structure to counter the increasing dynamic of the modern orchestra. If this is true then Wagner's theatre has already been significantly changed. Whether this justifies further change is debatable. What is certain is that the family will not for a moment listen to these ideas. So if you wish to have your hair raised by the Wagner orchestra you must hear the works in an Italian-style theatre, under a conductor who knows about balance. You need not, after all, watch the pit.

The invisible orchestra is naturally a bonus to the drama. Richard Strauss argued against it, saying that he thought it did no harm to watch the orchestra and its conductor. I think it does no good either, but I am one who can happily listen to the *Ring* in the dark. I believe Wagner was right to hide his vast orchestra.

It is always a shock, meeting a conductor-friend for a cup of Earl Grey between acts (Bayreuth does everything well, down to the tea-bag), to find him in tennis togs. Toscanini is said to have enjoyed Bayreuth because it gave him eight weeks without a bow-tie, in the days when curtain calls were 'out'. Nowadays one of the necessary skills of the Bayreuth conductor is that of getting into some superficial imitation of evening dress in time to take a curtain.

But let's return to our *Meistersinger*, which progresses through the song-trial in the first act, the philosophy and riot of the second, and the astonishing quintet of the third. Now enter the Guilds, the Mastersingers last, among a wildly cheering throng. Here we become aware of the sheer resource of the Bayreuth machine. The huge stage is full of people, and they are about to show us that they can all sing. Their *Wach auf* chorale is surely the finest choral achievement available on this planet. Precise, unanimous, balanced, perfect in intonation, beautiful in sound, and simply vast. A sound to bring tears of joy — one is thankful for the dark sometimes — to the eyes of anyone who has worked in even the best of opera houses. Such choral quality is impossible to assemble anywhere else. Whatever the glories of singing, playing, or conducting during the evening, it is this simple chorale which crowns the performance for me. I would go to Bayreuth just to hear it.

I have always loved *Meistersinger*; uniquely among Wagner's output it provides such a *happy* evening in the theatre; but until I heard it at Bayreuth I did not fully appreciate its importance to the German audience. No doubt my day in Nürnberg had had its effect; but the final scene of the opera that evening took on a new perspective for me, one contributed by the audience rather than by the performers.

The key lay in Sachs' monologue. I had always thought this rather a waste of time. Far better, surely, that Walter should collect his medal immediately so that we could all pop off to the tube five minutes earlier and none the worse for the cut. But here in Bayreuth the truth is made clear. Sach's lecture is the core of the piece, and it is for this that the German audience attends. Our Richard here argues that it is upon German values and German art that the future of civilisation depends. The audience, or at least the German part of it, sits up straight and listens. Here, for five minutes, I feel as much an intruder as a Catholic in a synagogue. There is, for me, an overwhelming impression of a culture worshipping itself: a culture from which I am excluded. I prefer not to think too much about this; I would like Wagner to belong to me too, and those old pictures of the dreadful corporal arriving at the Festspielhaus come only too readily and disturbingly to mind. All this is unfair to Wagner, who died so long before the late unpleasantness and who showed his concern for art above race by giving the first performance of *Parsifal* to Hermann Levi to conduct. Germans are entitled to national pride in their composer and the national art he represents. But the shiver is there, nevertheless, and a Bayreuth *Meistersinger* is not complete without it.

I have been told that my German friends feel the same way on hearing our *Rule, Britannia*. If this is true then their misunderstanding of the British is total. The last night of the Proms is fun, and with Arne's tune we make fun of ourselves, an achievement of which our German friends seem to be incapable.

I repeat: if you cannot give yourself up to Wagner for a space then avoid Bayreuth like the plague. If he bores you, or irritates, this is no place for you unless you wish for the final inocculation, an over-dose of the 'hair of the dog' which will send you screaming down the autobahn to the nearest airborne escape.

I love it all. But as readers of this book have seen, the Army developed both my sense of humour and the ability to discipline it.

CHAPTER 29

Frank and other friends

My working life has abounded with friends and colleagues as memorable for themselves as for their performance. There were, and still are, marvellous artists in the brass band. Mortimer was a player of near-genius, and seated behind us there was a player of supreme artistry on an instrument of fiendish difficulty, the soprano cornet. A country lad of no education, his Cheshire accent nearly impenetrable, he made his instrument talk and sing. His sense of humour, too, enlivened many an afternoon spent huddled under our mackintoshes near wet bandstands from Aberdeen to Plymouth. Then, an aged player of the flügelhorn with a sound of purest gold and phrasing which would have done credit to Kreisler. One of 'nature's gentlemen', he taught me much about music by example and kindly, restrained comment. Vaughan Williams, who fell in love with the flügelhorn much too late, would have written a concerto for the instrument had he heard my friend play. As a lad of fourteen I would ask him how he thought he'd played today and he'd reply always 'Well, like the curate's egg: good in parts.' Fifty years on I find myself using the same evasion at the opera, and never without a nod in the direction of his shade.

In the orchestra, above all, Denis Brain. I met his father, the first horn of the BBC Symphony, when the orchestra came to the Rhondda during the war; the first symphony orchestra I ever heard 'live'. A child looking for autographs, any autograph, I collected his without knowing who he was. His son was such a *nice* man; so nice that when he was told what the *Rosenkavalier* prelude represented he was almost too embarrassed to play it. Denis was the first British player to make friends with the horn. Before Denis cracks were allowed – nay, presumed. After him they became bad manners. But he was not merely a note-getting technician; he was a natural musician of rare distinction, his phrasing so Mozartian simple that no-one else could have imagined it, let alone deliver it. After having heard it, nothing less will do.

His technique was apparently a hundred times that available to any of his contemporaries. Nowadays, when the science of note-getting is rapidly replacing music as a performing skill, he might not be thought so technically remarkable, but he would still be as good as any.

My best memory of Denis is of a near-disaster. He was to broadcast two concertos with the CBSO, before an invited audience. He was late for rehearsal, and we waited for him in the sunshine outside. He trundled up in a magnificent old Lagonda. The thing was boiling up, he said, hence the delay. Opening the impressive radiator-cap he peeked inside, and the scalding water inevitably blew up in his face.

Denis was rushed to the infirmary while the BBC made plans for an alternative artist, but he appeared in good time, his face an interesting contrast of colours — half red burns and half zinc and castor oil cream — with his horn tucked under his arm in that practical way of his, to deliver the two pieces. What agony the mouthpiece caused his lips we cannot know, but he gave us perfect Strauss and perfect Mozart. What a player, and what a professional.

He was a marvellous driver. It was his way of unwinding. Perhaps if he had kept the Lagonda with the dodgy radiator he would be with us still.

The finest player by far in my CBSO was the timpanist, Ernest Parsons. He was even then an old man; orchestra jokers used to say that he'd played in the first performance of *Elijah* under Mendelssohn. An authority on all matters orchestral and on much else, Ernie was easily upset by the young, as many players of experience are. He found our youthful brass section, seated immediately under his timps, pretty hard going, and the appearance of any young conductor — which in his terms meant any stickwagger under fifty — meant almost certain trouble; trouble which seemed to be magnified at certain phases of the moon. There would come a point in rehearsal when mutterings from the back reached semi-audible level. 'Amateurs!' was usually a starter. Then 'children … fools … idiots' in a crescendo while we fumbled for diaries to check the theory. In the end there would come a great thump of timp-sticks crashing down on the drums before our star turn walked out. He always came back, and we always made allowance for him. How Ernest was explained to visiting conductors I don't know. Probably his fame went before him.

He was a superb timpanist. He liked to play the classics and early romantics on hand-tuned timps with calf heads, from which he produced sounds of inimitable quality and infallible pitch. Like that other timpanic marvel Alan Taylor, of whom we are so proud at Covent Garden, he'd studied other instruments before coming to the timpani. He added immeasurably to our work. What a magical thing to hear, at the start of the Beethoven Violin Concerto, four singing, phrased Ds from the drum, and at the end of the *Emperor*, when the six-eight galop is slowed to a walk and then to a stop, to hear the *Walküre*-rhythm so perfectly timed that great pianists would look up in surprise, then in amazement, to find themselves playing a duet with a timpanist rather than fighting one; adopting his *rallentando*. Who would grudge the old man a tantrum or two? Not I!

Among woodwind players, Janet Craxton was an inimitable oboist. She'd been a Hallé player too, but we'd never met before the day she telephoned to ask about our first-oboe vacancy at Covent Garden. Typically, she did not announce herself, merely enquiring about conditions. Then, eventually came the admission 'My name is Janet ...' Janet gave us evening after evening of delight until the awful day when she was taken from us. She was a marvellous colleague, though I felt always that Janet managed me rather than I her. If that makes her sound presumptuous, this is far from the truth. Her sense of fair play and of responsibility to the orchestra made that impossible. She was the complete professional, one for whom support and encouragement for less talented colleagues was part of the professional obligation. Her natural reticence was a delightful cover for a musician and a personality of extraordinary dimensions.

She was a very traditional English oboe at a time when the cosmopolitans were ironing-out orchestral sounds everywhere. This dubious trend produced two famous conversations between Janet and her conductors; the first with Dorati, a conductor of transatlantic taste who had taken over at the BBC. His dislike of the Craxton sound was immediately obvious, and matters came to a head very quickly. One day our friend went to her Chief Conductor and said 'Mr Dorati, I think you are not enjoying my work?'

Dorati, an honest man and musician, admitted that she was right.

'In that case, since I'm not enjoying yours either, it's best that I go away now.' And away she went, to please musicians of more open and receptive disposition.

The other conversation was in the same vein, though happily not terminal. It happened at Covent Garden. Zubin Mehta was rehearsing *Salome*. Janet anticipated his taste in oboes and did everything possible to help. Reeds were prepared and much work done in the good cause of the American sound; one which came very hard to her. Still, as she had feared, Zubin was not pleased. He did not complain; Janet was hardly a complainable player. But his face betrayed him; so one day, meeting him in the orchestra passage, Janet asked 'Mr Mehta, you don't seem to enjoy what I do for you?'

Zubin politely and kindly explained that he was so used to the other sound (he is a great expert on orchestral sounds and the means of obtaining them) that the English oboe was quite hard for him to take. Janet listened very carefully, then she asked 'Tell me ... if orchestras sounded exactly the same all over the world, would there be any point in you people travelling?' Zubin, marvellous sport that he is, began to smile and then to laugh. After that every Craxton entry was rewarded with a big grin.

I got quite used to the fact that foreign conductors were surprised by Janet. One day, after a Muti rehearsal, I asked him how he liked our oboe.

'Like? What do you mean, like?'

'The sound, Maestro. Do you enjoy the sound?'

'Mr Gay, when I meet a musician of such quality in the orchestra I just thank God.'

Perhaps the last word about Janet belongs to Karl Böhm, who asked me to send for her at the end of a *Figaro* rehearsal. At first I feared that after demands for the American oboe we were about to be pressed for a Viennese one. So, I think, did Janet. But no: the old man had something very different to say. 'Madam: never in my life have I met an oboist of such quality. You are not just a very good oboist; not even just a very good musician. You are a true friend to Mozart, and it is a very great privilege for me to work with you.'

It was a very great privilege for us all, Janet. And a lot of fun too.

Among the colourful membership of Barbirolli's original Hallé was one Sidney King, an old soldier in every sense, having learned in the Lancashire Fusiliers even more than I'd been taught in Birdcage Walk. Sid joined as second trumpet and rose to principal, a job for which he had more than adequate talent but perhaps not quite the temperament. By the time of my arrival he had become third player and an admirable backup; a superb practical orchestral musician, his talent and taste extending to all sorts of music. It was no secret that had he wished he could have become an important part of the 'big band' scene of the 'forties and 'fifties, rising even to the Heath Band. I'm glad he did not; his presence enlivened the Hallé Galley for a working lifetime.

Sid was JB's straight man, a nearly-essential part of the rehearsal atmosphere and a necessary tool in the relief of the considerable boredom endured by wind and brass while the old man meticulously organised every horse-hair on every bow. For this purpose he was allowed considerable latitude, often amounting to *lèse-majesté*. He had acquired an infallible judgement of JB's mood, and we learned to watch the King barometer very carefully. Sometimes when Barbirolli seemed at his most affable our friend would sit very quietly, saying nothing. Sure as morning, someone would try his luck too far and there would come a JB explosion. On other occasions, when JB seemed to be under intolerable strain, Sid would deliberately provoke him to what seemed professionally-suicidal lengths, until the ice broke and the stick would be slammed down on the score and the old man would shout in desperation 'Sidney! Shut up!!' Then the sun would come out.

If by chance Sid was late, JB would immediately ask 'Where's His Majesty today?' Meeting him at the Free Trade one day with one of the King family there came a famous exchange: 'Hello, Sidney. Is that your little boy?'

'Yes, SIR John', Sid had a habit of emphasising the title in a way which would have seemed impertinently ironic in anyone else.

'Can he play the trumpet yet?'

'Not yet, SIR John.'

'I suppose he's got to learn to give cheek to conductors first?'

Some of Sid's sayings are part of Hallé history. There was the intolerably long rehearsal day when we'd been locked up together since dawn and the evening was closing in outside the dusty windows. Concentrating hard, JB was disturbed by a distant train whistle — Central Station, round the corner, was a living, steaming entity then. 'What's that?' he asked. Came the reply in sepulchral tones 'It's the free world outside, SIR John!'

It was not customary to laugh at these achievements of Sid's. The knack, as in the Guards, was to chuckle with a straight face.

It was Sidney of course who furnished JB with his famous 'Telegraphic Address' as previously described. No-one else could have made that remark and survived. Coming from Sid, JB thought it terribly funny, which it was, and let it go. This was only possible because of the mutual respect in which these two lived. The player's respect for the conductor was not in doubt. JB's respect for Sid was total. The extraordinary thing is that this, in some ways the least personally secure of conducting personalities, could so cheerfully face so potentially lethal a threat to his authority in rehearsal. But then again, they both knew exactly when to stop.

Compared to players, their managers lack colour. Among the notable exceptions was the assistant to the orchestra manager at Covent Garden, one Francis Stead, a Yorkshire trombonist turned manager. Of all the unsung heroes who have helped to build our profession I think Frank to be among the most remarkable.

Frank first played at the House in Bruno Walter's *Ring* cycle in the 'twenties. His association continued through the prewar period, when the London Philharmonic played there. He had been Chairman of the LPO Board, supplying the casting vote, he told me, when the ownership of the famous headquarters in Wigmore Street hung in the balance; a decision which, had it gone the other way, might have meant the extinction of the LPO some years later since the house was the asset which kept LPO finances just on the side of credibility then. He had been in the box at the Leipzig Gewandhaus during Beecham's German tour of 1936 when, Frank insisted, Tommy did not shake hands with Hitler, faked photograph notwithstanding.

It was inevitable that Frank would join the Garden orchestra at its formation and equally inevitable that eventually he would lay down his 'bone and join the office. Frank never left the orchestra nor joined management. He occupied a critical niche poised between them, free to play merry hell with any aspect of either which failed to measure up to his amazing level of professionalism. He and Honor were an incomparable team.

His job, formally that of 'Orchestra Assistant', began when the office closed and before the players arrived. That line is not nicely drawn because the Orchestra Office light never goes out between eight thirty and curtain-down; but at about half-past-five each evening Frank would appear round the Nag's Head corner dressed, whatever the weather, only in sports jacket and flannels, to assume control; and the redoubtable Miss Thackrah would cover her typewriter, pick up her carrier-bag and groceries, and disappear. By that time all the contingencies and emergencies of the day must be solved and the orchestra secured for the evening.

Frank's first step on entering the office was a scrutiny of the orchestra list to discover what today's problems had been. His analysis of the situation was often entertaining. 'Oh', he would say, 'I see Mr So-and-so is taking the evening off with a headache. I thought that was due about now, with no overtime to be got this week. And Miss Thingummy (this with a pitying look in my direction): whoever gave her a free Monday morning with a free Saturday morning? You should have known she would be "down" on Saturday night! She'll be off to see mother of course.'

Frank was never sick; he did not believe in it. He never accepted illness as an excuse for absence while the patient could stand up. This was a residual effect of the freelance system where non-attendance meant non-payment, the routine of the big four symphony orchestras in London in which he'd spent his early life. Under this system concerts have been played by dying men. Frank would have thought that professionally correct, without a doubt, and he was not about to accept tummy-trouble as a reason for missing the ballet. We all knew that it was near-fatal to 'telephone-in' sick personally, in case Frank answered. The consequences could be severe. The conversation usually went something like this:

'Oh, sick, are you?'

'Rotten, Frank.'

'Where are you now?'

'On the phone of course.'

'But where's the phone?'

'On the hall table, why?'

'You can walk, then? You're not stuck in bed?'

'Well ...'

'If you can walk to the telephone you can get your clothes on and walk to the tube. It's hardly five minutes' walk to the tube, is it?'

'Well ...'

'Just get your things on and come. We'll find you an aspirin or some Collis Brown (Frank's infallible cure for the collywobbles — when he himself had stomach trouble he drank it like pop, straight from the bottle) and you'll be all right!'

Why these tactics worked I know not. No other manager in the world would have dared employ them; but on occasions when they failed the victim might be treated to a one-liner on the subject of professional responsibility, the sort no other manager would venture on pain of formal response from the Musicians' Union.

The orchestra of the evening safely memorised — Frank rarely produced Honor's list when checking personnel — our friend would settle down in the bar-corner of the canteen with his famous Barley Wine, to await the arrival of the mob.

Frank was more than an anachronism: he was a managerial dinosaur. His attitude to women in the orchestra was that of the prewar LSO and LPO — women were not suited for the job, not necessary, and not a good thing. His misogyny went deeper, even; he was never happy on ballet evenings when the canteen was heavily populated with young ladies in a state of partial undress. The growing habit of dancers coming down for tea without first donning a wrap brought him out in spots. 'This place gets more like a butcher's shop every day', he would complain in a voice loud enough to reach every dancer present. 'Madam (Dame Ninette de Valois was always 'Madam' in the House) never allowed it. Disgraceful!' Why, in the face of such an attitude, every lady member of the orchestra cherished a soft spot for Frank we will never know. He was certainly never aware of it.

His contempt for union activity was total, and partly explained by his trombonist background. Brass players are independent souls, preferring to fight their own battles with managers. The best of them are great successes in that way and often go through a professional lifetime without once playing for 'the rate'. Frank always referred to our splendid shop-steward, a dedicated and responsible colleague, by the name of a famous secretary of the TUC, pronouncing it in tones normally reserved for Adolf Hitler.

How did this holy terror survive in the climate of today's industrial relations? Surely by virtue of his total integrity; the fact that he served with the absolute dedication he expected of everyone else, and because his life was completely given over to the good — as he understood it — of the Royal Opera House and its orchestra.

It helped, as it always does in our business, that he had a wonderful dry sense of humour and that he was afraid of neither man, beast, general director, nor conductor. Generations of international names learned to treat Frank with the same care that we did, on peril of public reprimand. To a self-satisfied conductor of Wagner leaving the pit and asking (of me, not of Frank) 'How was that?' he immediately replied 'TOO FAST!' And when the poor chap asked him 'Too fast for what?' Frank replied that it was 'Much too fast for Dr Walter!'

No-one was safe from him. His most successful conductor-squelch, and the one most enjoyed by the orchestra, was at the expense of Carlos Kleiber. Coming on Frank one Thursday evening giving out pay-slips to the orchestra, CK asked politely whether there was 'one for me?'. Now Kleiber is famously expensive and this fact is no secret below stairs. Frank fixed him with a basilisk stare and replied 'No; Securicor is bringing yours – IN A TANK!'

The great man laughed with everyone else.

Our friend was a walking archive of information on all matters relating to the opera orchestra and its repertoire. Even the make-up of stage-bands, the exact placing of stage music around the set with advice about what worked and what did not, was instantly available off the cuff. The setting of a stage band, beginning with the retrieval of the players from the pub and ending with the manouvre of sandwiching them into the available small space backstage, was a highlight of Frank's week. Heaven help the brave repetiteur who made waves for Frank's stage band. Very short shrift he would enjoy.

Once the act went up (opera does not begin and end; with its curtain it 'goes up' and 'comes down') he would depart for the bar with a more precise estimate of its coming-down time than any stage manager. If he was occasionally caught out it was naturally because the conductor was too fast or too slow – for Frank! Texts, too, he could remember accurately. I've seen him give advice to a worried bass-trumpet over the bar in the Nag's Head, writing difficult passages from memory on an envelope-back with complete fluency. To Frank the great players of the past were friends lost only yesterday, and the great conductors too.

To this extraordinary man the Royal Opera House and I owe a great debt. As a player, newly arrived at Covent Garden, I was nursed and encouraged by him, as were all those players for whom he felt fraternal respect – and they were, when the chips were down, the great majority. When, years later, I became a very wet and green manager he looked after me like an uncle. Curiously, despite his surface toughness he was always quick to caution me when I seemed likely to go the hard-line route. He knew very well the difference between canteen rhetoric and practical management.

We tried to pension him off when the work was plainly getting beyond him, to no effect; Frank simply couldn't stay away, so we found him things to do and we enjoyed him as ever. He achieved the respect and − well, I suppose love is an odd word but I can find no other − of us all by the unique method of giving us all a very hard time.

He went suddenly, one Sunday morning, after more than 60 years at Covent Garden. The house gave him a famous memorial service, replete with a worthy tribute from his friend the Orchestra Manager: an honour which it reserves for its most loved servants. Never was one better deserved.

CHAPTER 30

Opera in Disneyland

Our three weeks in Los Angeles in 1968 were the happiest I have ever spent on tour. With a fine theatre, a comfortable hotel only ten minutes' easy stroll away, good food, wonderful weather, repertoire to revel in, some of the finest playing and singing we have ever delivered, and inexhaustible hospitality, LA had everything; well, nearly everything.

Los Angeles built for us a brilliant new *Turandot*, a typically lavish present from California which has delighted the home audience ever since. We brought our famous *Grimes*. *Zauberflöte*, not an especially remarkable production but under Colin Davis sure of very special performances, completed the repertoire.

Turandot, with its big and difficult offstage band and its percussion-packed pit, is a problematic piece for orchestra management. The gongs, xylophones, vibraphones, and tamtams and their eight players so beloved of Puccini are not regarded with the same enthusiasm by those who move them about; nor, incidentally, by the players who sit uncomfortably near them in a crowded pit. For *Turandot* we would need space. I enquired about this.

The reply from Los Angeles was that the pit had been big enough for Maestro Giulini in his opera performances and was therefore big enough for Covent Garden. The unspoken implication was that it would be enough for anyone else on earth. I love Giulini too, but this response was not reassuring. Marvellous though the LA Philharmonic was and is, its management had then little experience of opera. I asked what it was that the Maestro had played and learned that there had been one opera only – *Falstaff*, which is not a big score. I asked again and learned that Giulini had used only four double basses. This implied a small body of strings.

This can work; Giulini could organise a small-scale *Falstaff* in perfect balance if that was necessary. But would he play Verdi with a small string orchestra if he had space for a large one? I thought not. Responses from LA continued to be opaque. I voiced my disquiet to

Sir John Tooley, and he sent me, with our pit manager Malcolm Kinch, to LA to see for ourselves.

That trip taught me what jet-lag can really be. Four days in LA takes seven, effectively. Why four days? Because the theatre was working at ballet and the only time we two could get into the pit was in the very early morning, before it was set. Thirty minutes of each day was our limit. Malcolm is a virtuoso at pit-placing but the number of chairs one can move in 30 minutes is limited. Allow minutes for thinking and head-scratching — very necessary when trying to get the orchestral quart into the pint pot — and the job becomes a hilarious jigsaw played against time.

The Dorothy Chandler Pavilion, known to TV audiences world-wide for the annual Oscar ceremony, is a wonderful modern building, nearly twice the size of our own. Every seat enjoys fine acoustics and sight-lines. Sadly, Mrs Chandler was not an opera buff and had not equipped her magnificent gift with a pit to match. The pit would be fine for Mozart, but Britten would be possible only with unacceptably reduced strings. *Turandot* was out of the question.

All sorts of remedies were suggested. We could play at stalls level, bringing up the pit floor, or extend to the sides with screens and use that space for percussion, and so on. Good solutions perhaps for a British regional company touring small towns with tiny theatres, but hardly ways to present the Royal Opera in a city with a fine symphony orchestra of its own.

Still those on the spot were charmingly dismissive. There was in the air a distinct suggestion that I was being precious; that Sir Colin, an old friend and colleague of the LA management, would accept these conditions if that were necessary, as it would be; that opera was not, after all, about the orchestra.

We returned to London and reported to John Tooley and Colin, who promptly announced that since LA could not accommodate his orchestra, he would not go there.

Conductors who threaten are a commonplace of life in management, and it was some time before LA realised that our Music Director was serious. Then, perilously late, things moved with incredible speed. Though the building was in constant use a pit was designed and built. We were told that it had been done over a weekend, at a cost of some millions of dollars. I believe it; of LA I believe anything. And the pit at the Dorothy Chandler Pavilion is now by far the biggest, the most comfortable, the happiest acoustically, and in every way the best I have ever played in. If there is a better one it is in an operatic heaven.

In this superb environment we rehearsed for almost a week before opening. From the outset it was clear that *Turandot* would be a runaway success. The stage-pictures were gorgeous, the cast was superb and Colin had made firm friends with this last work of Puccini. Since we had not played the piece for some years, there was an atmosphere of enthusiasm and excitement all around. *Grimes* could hardly fail; the production was bomb-proof and the cast was largely the original one, with Jon Vickers, Geraint Evans, Heather Harper, Tom Allen and the whole motley crew straight from the Borough. In *Zauberflöte* the Queen of the Night was a problem. There are so few good ones, and all the available Queens of quality were citizens of communist countries, not eligible for US visas. We were still experimenting with Queens a week before the work opened.

The press conference before the opening was presented in a magnificent salon in the Chandler, the casts seated in a shallow circle centring on John Tooley. The room was large and full. The Americans present were taken aback to see seated next to JT a small, plump, bespectacled lady of advanced age. The US Press Corps was about to meet Dame Eva Turner, always an impressive experience.

Dame Eva was the first British Turandot at La Scala, where she sang for Toscanini, and Covent Garden never failed to commemorate the fact whenever *Turandot* opened, when traditionally a box was found for her. The Royal Opera is not so old nor so rich in tradition that it can afford to discard one just for the sake of a few thousands of miles, so our famous nonagenarian was with us in LA. She and our Turandot, Dame Gwyneth Jones, became inseparable.

Dame Eva sat mouselike while Sir John and the cast replied to questions about the Company, the operas, the roles, and all the other predictable concerns of the press. Her face, I noticed, grew animated when the *Turandot* production was discussed. Ours would be the first by an important company to discard the huge staircase at the top of which the Princess traditionally enters in the second act to sing the famous *In Questa Reggia*. This might disappoint those Californians who knew their operatic onions. It was not until the very end, though, that someone asked whether perhaps Dame Eva had something to say.

The first lady of British opera rose to her full five feet two and addressed the gathering in clear bright tones, projected to the back of the room with the same ease as in days of yore to countless amphitheatres.

'It is with the greatest possible pleasure', Dame Eva began, 'that I find myself once more upon the West Coast of the United States of America [a wonderful 'America' that was; an elocution-lesson in itself], where I have spent so many happy hours singing, teaching and relaxing with my many Californian friends.' For five minutes she riveted her audience with a demonstration of that which the local folk call 'star quality', effortlessly justifying the famous change we had made in her very own opera. How I wished that I'd had a tape-recorder with me. I hope that someone had, and that this remarkable off-the-cuff speech has somewhere been preserved.

The applause was thunderous. It was an achievement hardly to be believed unless one knew Dame Eva, who did nothing by halves. That she died before reaching her centenary must have been a matter of regret to her chiefly because of its untidiness. She had promised in her speech at Covent Garden on her ninetieth birthday, to 'see you all again in ten years' time!'

So to the *Turandot* opening, preceding by impressive renderings of *The Star-Spangled Banner* and *God Save the Queen*.

The early bars of the opera provided an unexpected insight into the Californian attitude to opera as our Calaf – on this occasion Placido Domingo – made his entry. This is not dramatic, Calaf being among a huge crowd here. He was instantly spotted, though, with nearly-fatal operatic effect. The auditorium burst into a holocaust of applause which took half a minute or so to die down while Colin and the company battled on, inaudible. At once it was clear to us that opera here was about stars first, last, and always. It was not necessary for Placido to sing. To be Domingo was enough. At this rate the opera would be largely unheard, since all the roles were in the hands of people of star quality. What would happen at the production's great surprise – Turandot's entry in act two, where our Welsh witch was required to walk around the stage in a breathless hush? We need not have worried. Whether the silence was due to Gwyneth's amazing presence – and we have not seen this silent entrance equalled by any other Turandot '– or to her lack of a properly organised fan club I cannot say, but we were grateful for it.

What would Gwyneth have done, given a noisy welcome? If anyone could have coped it is she; but our *coup de theatre* would have been wrecked, certainly.

The LA custom of cheering people rather than performance was demonstrated again two days later in *Grimes*. The piece begins with a brief orchestral statement ('accidental circumstances' in the wind) before the coroner calls three times 'Peter Grimes ...' The entry of Jon Vickers in sea-boots literally stopped the show. It would have been impossible for Grimes to 'Take the oath, after me ...' without utter destruction of the scene. We stopped.

Fortunately for Mozart there were no California-publicised figures in the *Zauberflöte* cast, Tom Allen, our wonderful Papageno, having not then reached the artistic stratosphere. The piece was wonderfully sung and incomparably conducted by Colin. Throughout the first evening we knew that the orchestra was giving something really special and the cast played up to that. Played at that level the work is irresistible. Colin remarked afterwards that this was probably the best Mozart he had ever conducted. Remembering that he had just finished recording the *Flute* in Dresden, we were grateful.

So, success assured, we settled down to enjoy California and the hospitality of the many friends of opera in Los Angeles who, lacking an opera company, adopted us. Each morning the foyer desk presented a list of available events: a cruise here, a barbecue there, lunch at the beach somewhere else, golf and so on. We had only to choose and the limo arrived as though by magic. Southern California, it seemed, was peopled almost entirely by the enormously wealthy and the down-and-out. Even the artisans of Silicon Valley had pools in their back-yards.

The pool, we soon learned, was hardly a luxury in this climate, and it was the only sensible way to use a back-yard where there was little possibility of cultivation. Our friends told us that Northern California had the water while the South had the money. If the two are equally balanced, then the northerners must be fine swimmers.

Our hosts were not just opera lovers but opera nuts. We were sucked dry of every scrap of information and background relating to opera in London. There was nothing our friends did not know about the personalities and lifestyles of the great singers. I lunched one day in a dining room decorated almost entirely with photographs of these, every second being of *dear* Placido. On the other hand, they seemed to understand the art not at all. To them it was simply a voice-vehicle; they were frankly puzzled that we had brought our own orchestra with us because LA was the easiest place in the world in which to 'pick up a band'.

But what hospitality! Whether spending a quiet day around the family pool, cruising in luxury off Santa Monica or at a beach party we were royally entertained. The most spectacular event was an evening at the home of a famous surgeon who entertained the entire company of 300 in his garden. His pride and joy was a collection of antique cars garaged underneath his tennis courts. There I renewed acquaintance with the model T Ford, having last seen one used as a coal-delivery truck in Cheshire in the 'forties. There was a beautiful Austin Seven, 1929 vintage, in some sort of mechanical trouble which had defeated Californian expertise for some years. A member of the chorus, drawing on skills remembered from his youth in Glasgow, put the thing right in ten minutes. Alan Taylor, our celebrated timpanist who doubles on the Rolls-Royce, found his spiritual home in that underground garage and left Los Angeles with instructions to notify our friends if ever he should find a purchasable Silver Ghost. The condition, it seemed, was immaterial, so long as some original scrap of the immortal Rolls existed. All else could be Californian-built from drawings.

The critics were kind. I little realised how important this was until over lunch one day my hostess remarked that she was puzzled by the *LA Times'* account of last evening's *Grimes*, which opera she had not enjoyed. That the critic of the *Times* obviously had done so was a source of embarrassed puzzlement to her. The *Times*, she knew, must be right. Her failure to react well to the piece meant that she had 'missed something'. As an intelligent listener – and such the lady certainly was – she felt she had failed. I asked whether she would have been equally worried if the *Times* had disliked *Turandot*, which she adored. Yes, she would. This is a reality of life in the arts in the USA. People believe the critics. On Broadway a new production may be killed at its premiere by adverse reviews. I could do no less for my friend than to give her a recording of the opera and suggest that she put a little time into it. Then again, she might cheerfully tell herself, like many thousands of British opera lovers, that Britten was simply not for her. This last suggestion fell on deaf ears. The *Times* liked our *Grimes*; her duty to do likewise was inescapable.

We are luckier in London. There is no surer guarantee of a good house at Covent Garden than a typically foul review in the *Guardian* comic. We pay our critics to entertain us; Americans believe theirs.

Los Angeles taught us some salutary lessons. I was arrested for crossing the street in the wrong place, despite there being no traffic in sight. Some of us failed to gain access to the theatre, having come without the essential pass; I believe those large gun-totin' fellers would have excluded Colin Davis and the President of the USA had they arrived together without that piece of paper.

Then there was Disneyland, a crash course in excellence from which every showman must learn, be he Sir John Tooley or Billy Smart. At Disneyland everything works and failure is unthinkable. The whole monstrous thing is squeaky-clean, every worker presenting himself immaculately, haircut (on the premises to Disney requirements, compulsory and on a timed rota) and smile equally reliable, shoes shining and trousers (forgive me, pants) machine-pressed; a complete establishment of all-American workers dedicated to the success of Mickey Mouse and friends. Stepford-clones? On Disney's premises, yes, certainly. If they scream with relief once outside the gate, within it they conform. The second customer-complaint, we were told, is the last.

Disneyland seems to aim at a mental age of nine, and the secret of its success lies in convincing us that we are all aged nine and that nine is the best age to be. Amid the perfectly organised fun-technology are impressive human achievements too. The Sousa-Band which parades at regular intervals is perfectly turned-out; it drills better than the Guards did in my time, and its performance is highly professional. This sounds easy. It certainly would not be easy to turn out a wind-band so many times each day, so many days of the year, without a slip in standards, in London, crammed though it is with unemployed musicians, because the job, like so many at Disneyland, must be utterly boring. Yet the standard, like the smile, never slips. I enjoyed best the smallest trick of all, Alice. Alice walks all day around Disneyland in her blue gown with the Mad Hatter, the Queen, and the rest of the tea-party. Alice and her friends *talk Lewis Carroll all the time.* They are delighted when a visitor tries to get into the act, and will happily build one into the conversation, inventing Carrollisms galore to suit the new arrival. Alice is rather older than the original, but so perfect is the trick that this is soon forgotten. Here is professionalism on a National Theatre scale and more.

I once saw in a New York street a young man wearing a tee-shirt printed with the words *I live in New York where only the toughest survive*: words which summed up for me the reason I loathed the place from my first five minutes in it, not because one had to be tough to survive — a man has to be fairly tough to survive in my business anywhere in the world — but because those who live there are proud of the fact and because such pride makes life still harder and tougher. Los Angeles is nicer; southern Californians don't boast of the abrasive society in which they live; but they are, I think, even tougher than their compatriots on the East Coast. Certainly they set higher standards and tolerate failure even less. LA is a giant Disleyland where failure is simply not 'on', and if opera, as we all hope, takes root there it will have to be foolproof, seamless opera. Nothing less will do.

On a free day we flew into Colorado to see the Grand Canyon. This I cannot describe nor, I believe, can anyone else. But it was a useful reminder that neither Disney nor John Tooley could produce the Greatest Show on Earth. Gazing fascinated across that immeasurable chasm, watching the ever-changing light and colour on the ageless rock-faces, one suddenly realised that *The Ring*, comparatively, is the soundless squeak of an ant.

CHAPTER 31
A Royal Occasion

Covent Garden really is a Royal Theatre. Quite substantial provision has been made for the Royal Family within it: a dignified dining room behind the Royal Box, with The King's Smoking Room below, specially provided for King Edward VIII. A special treat for distinguished guests is a visit to Queen Victoria's magnificent loo, complete with mahogany seat, splendid brass chain and ceramic handle.

Somewhere in the archive is stored a message from King Edward asking that we delay *Rigoletto* from Wednesday until Thursday next week so that he might stay longer at Biarritz. This was duly done. It was easier then than now but we'd try, no doubt, should Her Majesty ask. Sadly the Queen has little enthusiasm for her Royal Opera; not so the lesser royals, who seldom miss a new production or an especially fine revival. The Prince of Wales, a good amateur cellist and enthusiastic singer, is more than our nominal Patron. He's a real opera buff.

His visits are usually informal; sometimes very informal indeed. It's not hard, with the aid of a practised House Management, to arrive in an end seat a second after 'House lights down' and vanish just before the interval; much more fun than an evening on display in the Royal Box, where the sightlines are awful anyway.

At the end of formal evenings presentations are the rule, with cast and representatives of the House lining up for a brief word of congratulation and thanks from HRH. It was at one such that John Brown and I made a remark which eventually produced a unique honour for the Orchestra.

HRH seemed glad to see us that evening, perhaps because we were last in a long line or perhaps because we were familiar faces. Whatever the reason our chat was more than the formally brief one. I was asked how I felt about giving up my trumpet. Surely this must have been a trial? 'The worst part of my job', said HRH, 'is that they won't let me play nor sing these days.' How we summoned up the nerve to pull the Royal leg about the long-delayed marriage I cannot imagine; John Tooley must have been well out of earshot, and perhaps he had reinforced our morale en route with a quick one in the Crush Bar. But the Prince took our jokes very well; so well that in the end I said 'Tell you what, Sir — just let us know when the time comes and we'll pop in and play the music.' His response seemed genuine: 'I won't forget. What a good idea.'

We gave this project hardly more than a ten per cent chance of survival, knowing (and after the event we know even better) how many factors form these decisions and what power-games manoeuvre around royalty. But when after the announcement I went to John Tooley with a reminder of the Prince's words the Palace was telephoned, the promise remembered and the Princely command given.

The time could hardly have been worse. We were entertaining a visiting ballet company at Covent Garden that July. Extra rehearsals at St. Paul's were the last thing we needed. The redoubtable Kinch had booked his holiday; so had Honor, leaving the ROH before the season's end for the first and only time. Having got myself and the orchestra into this thing I was obliged to attend to every detail of it solo, aided only by Cliff Corbett, then our second orchestra porter and now our Orchestra Manager. He and I went through hell, high water and much worse together in the interest of the Royal Wedding. Heaven forbid that we will ever be asked to provide the orchestra for a Coronation. Vivat Regina say we, and not for patriotic reasons only.

That spring we played a season in Manchester and it was at a distance of two hundred miles that I first became aware of subterranean rumblings of discontent emanating from Ludgate Hill. The Church had not expected an orchestra at the wedding; it was not a state occasion but a family one. The Church expected to provide all the music needed. In any case, why an *opera* orchestra? Surely a symphony orchestra would be more appropriate? The theatre, even the Royal Opera House, was still not quite respectable, it seemed! This availed nothing; the Prince had decided and there was an end of the matter. A few days later, though, the earth began to tremble in earnest. We were not the only orchestra under the Prince's patronage. What about the English Chamber Orchestra? What of the Philharmonia? Then again, what of the Bach Choir and Sir David Willcocks?

It quickly became clear that if all the people now clamouring for standing-room on this bandwagon were to climb aboard would be impossible to wangle the vehicle through the doors of the church.

What a happy thing that we were out of town and that the whole problem was now in the hands of Sir John Tooley, diplomat. By the time we arrived home all the decisions had been made. Our numbers would be reduced to permit the addition of members of the ECO and the Philharmonia. I was to negotiate the fine adjustments. JT had added a refinement. Kiri Te Kanawa was now to sing Handel's *Seraphim* aria: a gesture to the Commonwealth which the Prince would very much enjoy. Kiri is among his most loved voices.

My colleagues the orchestra managers were co-operative. We built in the ECO's splendid string nucleus. Extra brass being useful on such an occasion, we invited the Philharmonia team.

The big headache was the choir. There were rather a lot of them, and space was the great problem. We made many visits to the Cathedral to plot the best way of getting the orchestral quart into the ecclesiastical thimble. As the early planning had envisaged no orchestral music at all, and no choir other than the Church's own, this entailed hilarious discussions with those in charge and with the Clerk of the Works, whose job it would be to build the seating. These problems were never solved. Players and singers were simply crammed in. To the very last, people added to our difficulties by simply adding themselves and their gear. Arriving for the final rehearsal on the wedding eve we found a chamber organ sitting in the middle of the cellos. For a time it seemed that we were about to lose five players in the lost cause of Handelian authenticity, but somehow space was found.

The rehearsal schedule was enough to give any orchestra manager an ulcer. Had it not been for the ingenuity and energy of the players the rehearsals could never have taken place at all. In theory the schedule worked; we had nearly always ninety minutes to get ourselves and our gear from the House to the Church and the same to get back. I knew from years of military experience that the timetable would genuinely run to time; to the Palace the minute really is Kipling's unforgiving sixty seconds. The problems arose when our own work ran over, and they became really formidable when Ludgate Hill was closed to traffic for the later rehearsals. Given that our van could run down Drury Lane to the Strand, down Fleet Street and up the Hill without hindrance all was well; but just try that trip in a three-tonner by any alternative route, arguing with the police at every street corner!

Our greatest fright was caused by the difficulty of getting out of St Paul's, rather than in. One evening, with an hour to go before curtain-up on the ballet, the team was ambushed at the Church door by a posse of Special Branch, who insisted that none of our boxes was to leave without being thoroughly searched. This hardly seemed reasonable. A bomb in a cello case coming in, possibly; but going out again? Hardly! As I was already at Covent Garden holding the fort, I cannot vouch for the means used to solve this impasse. When I enquired I was reminded that a six-foot double-bass box travelling at high speed is a difficult object to stop, even for the largest Bobby.

After one late-evening call, Cliff Corbett almost failed to get out at all, narrowly escaping a long cold night locked in the crypt. Eventually he was discovered and nearly arrested by a prowling Special-Branch officer, alert no doubt for a latter-day Guy Fawkes.

At this time I rediscovered many long-lost friends who, having no hope of a seat at the service, telephoned to ask that we take them with us to one or other of the rehearsals, preferably one which HRH and the Lady would attend. Never before had I realised my immense popularity. Alas! The Cathedral was as tight as Fort Knox, so I was able to refuse each and every one with a clear conscience. No doubt I will hear from many of those folks again before the Prince's next wedding.

Our music was to be exclusively British. There was Elgar, Walton, and Handel, Purcell too; the Prince had asked for his *Trumpet Voluntary*. This was 'arranged' anew for the wedding, to no good effect. Henry Wood did it best, long ago. Still, the *Voluntary* suffered less than did the National Anthem, similarly revamped. Why, knowing the existence of so many fine versions of this tune by great composers from Weber to Britten (there is a Rossini version, too, in *The Journey to Rheims*, and a splendid score it is) did we invent yet another? Ah well! If every musician present, from the leader of the orchestra to the youngest choirboy, was entitled to a television fee (there was a rumour that some members of the clergy were giving the BBC a hard time about 'the rate for the job' but of course no-one believed this), why not a bob or two for 'the trade'?

Came the great day. We were up and about very early. I slept in my office and walked to St Paul's, clocking in at about 7.30 and passing en route some of my friends holding a champagne breakfast at the White Lion in Floral Street. We were all in the crypt in good time;

and that meant two hours before we could reasonably be expected to go up into the Church, an age before the service. This situation was unnerving. We were all pretty hard cases, but the occasions when we play live to half the world are rare. Things got a little edgy. Relief was needed. It was Kiri who cracked the problem.

Breezing up to our corner of the crypt with a cheery 'Hi fellers!' this marvellous lady asked Colin Davis whether he had any experience of back-combing ladies' hair? Colin had not. 'Well', said the Maori nightingale, 'it's about time you learned. I'll show you how!' So, at nine o'clock in the morning in the crypt of St Paul's Cathedral, on the day of the wedding of the Prince and Princess of Wales, the Music Director of the Royal Opera created the coiffure of our leading soprano. Needless to say the pair were immediately surrounded by a large and admiring group of players, the ladies giving advice and the men cheering Colin on.

We entered the Church in procession, forming a long crocodile with me at its head; not the sort of thing I do, generally, and a source of amusement to my friends. We entered immediately behind the Gentlemen at Arms. These are very large people; I suspect that any object less than five feet ten inches tall is invisible to them. They were, as always, gorgeously clad and stately of tread. We were obliged to adopt their pace and tempo; not an easy matter for many of us, and very hard indeed for one with my short legs. When, at the tail of these gullivers, I appeared in Church leading the members of the three orchestras, the Bach Choir produced what can only be described as a choral giggle.

The service went beautifully. Kiri sang her Handel with John Wallace as ever a paragon of a trumpeter. Colin conducted, as part of the outgoing music, a splendid *Crown Imperial*. We were back at the factory just in time for our matinee.

Some weeks later the happy pair were at the House for a gala performance of Ken MacMillan's *Romeo and Juliet*, to Prokofiev's music. I was again presented, with my wife. They were really delighted to see us again and full of enthusiasm. 'Wasn't that absolutely splendid?' asked the Prince. I replied carefully that it had been a good evening. He laughed. 'Not the ballet — the wedding! Wasn't that perfectly splendid?' and both laughed heartily.

I told them that we had enjoyed the wedding very much indeed and that if either of them ever felt like doing it again we would be happy to ...

CHAPTER 32
Where there's muck ...

In the late 'seventies I was distracted for a time by an involvement in the affairs of the brass band, the medium which provided my earliest musical education. I'd never lost sight of its activities; folks with that background rarely do; but for twenty years past my dealings with it had been at arms-length, through publishing and through adjudicating at home and abroad. Now the Cory Band, a famous old ensemble from my home valley, struck a conducting difficulty and invited me in. The temptation was irresistible, and I spent two exhausting, exhilarating, and finally frustrating years with these wonderful chaps, conducting three rehearsals each week in South Wales while working in London. This meant two nights weekly on British Rail and eight hours' driving each Sunday.

I cannot bring myself to regret this time, life-shortening though it must have been. It taught me a great deal, showing me how my conducting technique had rusted up — it had not been exercised since my Birmingham period, when I'd had much more time for such things — and how impossible it is to learn repertoire under pressure; British Rail is no place for study, despite its encouraging advertising. The period also reminded me of the vast difference between professional and amateur management. It takes a degree of discipline, after driving two hundred miles before eleven o'clock on one's only day off, to smile at the news that a vital tuba will be missing today owing to a baby-sitting problem. These things, I was often reminded, are sent to try us. They tried me.

We gave many fine performances to audiences all over the UK. I enjoyed those close to home best, finding much to enjoy in my compatriots both as players and audience. There was a marvellous occasion in a neighbouring valley where our concert was introduced by the local mayor. After the overture this worthy produced for the audience my curriculum vitae, listing in glowing terms my entire professional life since leaving the valley 20 years earlier and ending with the masterly punch-line 'Well, ladies and gentlemen, I don't know what more he could have done. You can see he's too small to play Rugby!'

We toured the USA in its bicentennial year, a memorable two weeks, with audiences ranging from universities to parks. We played Byrd in Wall Street on the great day itself, and on one hilarious day in Colorado Springs we delivered Berlioz in a skating rink; no, not an ice-rink but the noisier sort. Having been presented with this prime example of British culture, the USA had sometimes very little idea of what it was or of what to do with it.

The bandsmen loved it all. Some had travelled very little and one had never seen a big jet before. As our coach left the Heathrow tunnel, seeing one rise over the tower he exclaimed 'Good God, I never knew they went up as far as that!'

It was a moving experience to meet America at home, and to discover the extent of Welsh culture there. We had a marvellous evening in Central City, Colorado, playing in the opera house built by miners from Wales and Cornwall brought in for the gold a century ago. It's a tiny building, complete down to the primitive technical equipment, very like that of Drottningholm. In Central City I was installed as an Honorary International Bellringer, an honour I share, I understand, with Leonard Bernstein. I have a bell to prove it. The barbecue following that concert is one of the great memories of the tour.

In Denver we played in a concrete plaza, hot enough to fry an egg. We bought stetsons in a nearby store, odd hats for the band's uniform but the only solution in that heat and much enjoyed by the audience. Only at the end of that concert did we understand, lumps in throats, how very Welsh Colorado is. It seems that every one of the thousands present was singing *Land of My Fathers* in Welsh.

The inescapable 'contest' activity I enjoyed much less. I've never approved of it, though I recognise the amateur bands' dependance on it for the keeping up of their tremendous head of steam. The competitive instinct is not part of my makeup; I'm always happy to listen to anyone who can 'do it better' than I can. Perhaps this is why we won few first prizes, though we were never far out of the running and often very close.

Conducting at the great brass band festivals was never as great a matter for me as for most people in the field. I've played in those buildings too often, and under far greater pressure than the band festivals can generate. On the other hand, I suffered every bit as much, and perhaps even more than my friends, from the let-down at the end of the day. I remember returning to the changing-room at the Albert Hall after collecting a sixth place, sitting down on a bench head in hands and asking out loud 'Why the b...h... do we do this?'

From the other side of a row of lockers (we were separated in that way from the Brighouse Band) came a sepulchral Yorkshire voice in reply: 'We do it because we loov it, Bram lad!'

I suppose that sums the whole crazy business up.

I shook the disease off after two years, recognising the impossibility of conducting well on my schedule, and after wearing out three cars in the process. Now I conduct only in summer, with proper preparation and very much better. It has provided me with splendid Scandinavian holidays, the Swedish attitude to music, a thorough and thoughtful one, being something I enjoy. At home I limit myself to adjudicating at festivals, where the music played is occasionally worthy of the people who play it and the technical level is really stunning. The conducting, too, is often very fine.

The day of the brass band is yet to come, I believe. We will see the finest of them break away from their eight-hour day in pit and factory to become professional, much admired (as they are already copied) all over the world on the rare occasions when they travel.

The brass band gave me so much; to plough some back, even at considerable cost, seemed the least I could do. If I have a residue of energy left when professional music chucks me out I will offer it again.

CHAPTER 33
From Russia
(with love)

I've never travelled in Russia. Among my colleagues this is usually considered a matter for congratulation, orchestral visits to the Soviet Union having all too frequently produced a catalogue of primitive hotels, missed meals, icy trains, and botched arrangements: a manager's nightmare. When negotiating the contract of a distinguished player for my orchestra some years ago I was faced with a final point-blank condition: rather than tour again in Russia, he said, he would resign.

I'm sorry, though, not to have seen something of that land to which the musician owes so much. Which of us has not enjoyed a youthful affair with Tchaikowsky, to be left in maturity with a balanced and reasoned admiration? And Moussorgsky! *Boris Godunov* – in all his versions, and happily we have come at last to understand that the composer was right first time – is an operatic essential. We need more Russian opera. It will come, despite awesome difficulties for the chorus in memorising new repertoire in Russian.*

Nicolai Malko was a lesser light among the conducting luminaries of my first season in Birmingham. An expatriate then in his seventies, he'd spent most of his years of exile in the USA. A very small man, with little hair and high cheekbones supporting rimless spectacles, he was quite unlike the received picture of the maestro. His rehearsal tee-shirt – very much less usual attire then than now – had four pockets, one for each of the day's miniature scores. These rarely emerged.

His programme began with the prelude to *Lohengrin*. Then there was Mozart; flexible, perhaps too flexible in tempo, with drastic slowings-down for trios and so on, the hallmark of the German school

---

*For the chorus, Russian pronunciation is a nightmare resolved by phonetics. The extent to which this succeeds varies. A Russian visitor to *Boris Godunov* once asked me whether perhaps our translated surtitles were 'for the Russians'.

of a certain period. Rudi Schwarz' orchestra took to it with reluctance softened by appreciation of the old man's sure technique and apparently infallible memory.

The Shostakovitch symphony he chose was just six months off the press, but his score left its pocket only for rehearsal figures, and not always then. Not a stitch was dropped. Touring conductors rarely find time to learn new music, let alone memorise it. Taking Malko's age into account, this is among the more impressive feats of musical memory in my experience. He was a charming old gentleman too; we enjoyed his company no end.

I knew no more Russians — few of them were allowed out in those days — until the Hallé met Arvid Yansons in the early 'sixties. Yansons was an adopted Russian; a native of Riga, trained partly in Germany, as were so many important Baltic musicians before the Second War, and finished in Leningrad. He succeeded Eugene Mravinsky at the Leningrad Philharmonic too late in life for the establishment of a comparable reputation. Yansons brought to Manchester its first experience of the excitement of the Leningrad school.

The style suited us perfectly. Arvid knew how to stoke the Hallé boiler and release the famous steam. Curiously we didn't discover this during his single rehearsal day — all the Hallé routinely afforded before sending a visitor out to conduct his first concert, often in a distant town. The Fifth Symphony of Prokofiev, new to us, was the big piece that week, and our visitor's dismay on discovering the brevity of his rehearsal period was obvious. After telling us that he spoke no English and must rehearse in German — and he might as well have worked in Latvian for all the use either language would have been to him — he immediately suggested that we abandon the symphony because there simply was not time to prepare it. Martin Milner, who'd heard this before and would hear it many times more, tactfully suggested that he at least try the work. By tea-time our visitor had discovered that six hours in Manchester could achieve as much as six days elsewhere. Or so he told us.

That first day, partly because we disliked the symphony, became something of a depression. Only next day did we discover the lucky match of this extraordinary conductor to our orchestra, the basis of a long association which was to give us all such pleasure.

We were to play in Hull. I arrived late, having had a small motoring mishap en route, and I entered the hall from the front. Rehearsal had begun perhaps a minute earlier, with a run-through of Glinka's *Russlan and Ludmilla* overture, a routine work which had not been rehearsed on the previous day since we 'knew' it. The sounds which stopped me in my tracks in the doorway owed nothing to routine. The tempo was extreme, the playing breathtaking. Here was an orchestra hypnotised, hanging on to Glinka by supreme concentration as the notes flew by. When the overture ended, eighty players smiled. Arvid smiled back. It was as though conductor and orchestra had shaken hands.

He limited himself to the Russian repertoire on his first visit. Prokofiev apart – and he was superb in the *Romeo and Juliet* music as well as in the symphonies – his Tchaikowsky was a new and refreshing experience.

It is hard to explain to the listener how fed up an orchestra can become with the three great symphonies of that overpopular master. They are not easy pieces, and their constant flogging in the vital cause of bums-on-seats has done nothing to endear them to us. The performing advantage of familiarity with the text is ultimately cancelled out by routine, and the conductor's task becomes less one of technical and musical direction than of motivation – a much harder business. Yansons achieved motivation in one great leap through the conviction of his approach. So often in the West we *condescend* to Tchaikowsky, this self-pitying Russian who wears his heart so embarrassingly on his sleeve. Yansons, like other Russian conductors in my later experience, had none of this attitude. We hear sentimentality; the Russian feels *passion*. One can gain some idea of the essence of Yansons' Tchaikowsky from Mravinsky's recordings – recordings no collector ought to be without. I was grateful to Yansons for reopening my ears to the potential of those works; I am, still.

He was with us for two weeks that season. The Hallé wisely employed him for much longer periods thereafter and he became a visiting uncle with whom we communicated on many levels. His English, improving with almost comic speed, vanished completely at the end of the first week when Igor Oistrakh arrived to play the Tchaikowsky Concerto. It reappeared, further improved, when he left. Our friend, once allowed out, was taking no chances for the future.

When I asked him about that extraordinary tempo in the *Russlan* overture, he told me that it was printed 'only 132 to the minute' but the original in Leningrad said one-fifty-two and so he always played at one-sixty-two, 'just to be quite sure.'

Yansons had a great gift for driving fast tempi to the orchestra's technical limit but miraculously never over it. His finest achievement in that way was again in Tchaikowsky, the *Francesca da Rimini* overture, where the coda, with its dangerous cross-rhythms and orchestral collisions, was whipped to a frenzy which left us all winded, surprised to have finished together, awed by the pressure he exerted and by the enormous sound he produced.

Here is a peculiarly Russian phenomenon: the characteristic gritty, grainy delivery, a unique national combination of intelligence and muscle. To hear *Onegin* from the Kirov is an experience utterly different from a British performance, however polished. It's a new sound, a language very different from our applied Russian, almost as though the orchestra learns Russian vowels. It can be reproduced to some extent by their best conductors with our orchestras and it makes their performances very special. Part of the Hallé's love affair with Yansons related to his tendency to play flat out, muck or nettles as the Lancashire saying has it. There was no reserve in the man. That was very much in tune with the attitude to music of JB and his orchestra. Yansons was impeccably clear, too. He made playing very easy.

Arvid enthused constantly to us about musical Leningrad. No lover of the Soviets, he nevertheless admired Soviet Russia's musical achievements. Leningrad he considered the musical capital of the world, its resources unmatched anywhere. His orchestra, he told me, was big enough to play a concert, an opera, and a big choral work on the same evening, and the supply of string players at the highest level was practically unlimited. 'If we lost them all today,' he said, 'we could replace them in three days.' The Conservatory tradition, founded by Brodsky, first performer of the Tchaikowsky Concerto — who afterwards became the Hallé's Leader and Principal of the Royal Manchester (now the Royal Northern) College of Music — supplied strings beyond the dreams of most orchestras in both quality and numbers. The difficulty, he told us, was that of persuading those people to go away to distant parts of Russia. They preferred unemployment in Leningrad. I drew the obvious parallel, that with London and the regions, and he laughed. 'Mr Gay, from London to Manchester is two hours only. From Leningrad to these places in Russia is five thousand kilometres, with snow all the way, and when you get there the lavatory doesn't work!'

Since *glasnost* there has been an exodus of players from Russia to the west. The Leningrad — forgive me, the St Petersburg — Philharmonic is not what it was, and its rebuilding is taking rather longer than Yansons' predicted three days, but already the Kirov orchestra, under Gergiev, is rejuvenated. The tradition is not extinguished.

Among my regrets on leaving Manchester was missing Yansons' performance of the First Piano Concerto of Shostakovitch, with its writing for solo trumpet. When we met years later in London, just before he died — in Manchester, after a Hallé performance of Mahler's Fifth — he told me that he'd meant it for me. It would have been a delight, I know.

Why this splendid artist and delightful man failed to impress our colleagues in London I will never understand; but fail he apparently did. It was left for his son to become an important guest conductor with the London Philharmonic. This, I fancy, will not be Mariss Yansons' peak achievement. The Covent Garden Orchestra awaits his opera debut with intense interest and with regret that the first House to invite him was not, alas, our own.

Quite soon after my arrival at Covent Garden I met the genius known to the London orchestral player as 'Noddy', Gennadi Roszhdestvensky. Noddy escapes Russification in the way that Abbado escapes Italianisation: they are both so good at whatever they conduct that national identity is cancelled out — almost. That 'almost' really counts, and more in the case of Roszhdestvensky than of the other man because his Russian repertoire is truly extraordinary. But what draws the player to him is his hands. Superlatives among artists are for fools, agreed; but if there is a better equipped technician than Roszhdestvensky then I have never seen him.

Noddy is a sort of Russian Boult, sharing his confidence that the hundred musicians before him are all competent, all know the repertoire and all understand the art of orchestral playing. He knows conducting to be a craft as well as an art, and accepts the obligation of clear direction. That being the case, he expects to be able to perform on very little rehearsal. Like Boult the Russian maestro occasionally goes too far in that way and meets something very close to catastrophe. It serves them both right. Each ought to know where to draw the line; the orchestra sometimes needs more help than they imagine. But to the player with his wits about him and his eyes and ears open Noddy is a delight.

His reluctance to lecture the orchestra — another Boult characteristic — is almost comic. He will go to almost any length to avoid stopping. At our first meeting, over *Boris* at the Garden, I was able to watch his reaction to indeterminate brass chording under a recitative. He made no complaint. On the following day he looked across a little earlier, prepared a little more clearly, and tried again. Still our attack was not incisive enough. Yet again next day he tried, this time by quite extravagant over-encouragement. Now at last the thing was done, but — reading the look on his face — the dynamic was over the top. Surely, I told myself, the man must now discuss. But no, the thing was left for the performance itself. This time his encouragement seemed even greater, the preparatory beat even clearer. Then suddenly came the whiplash — perhaps a fifth of a second earlier than his preparation had indicated. The attack was perfect, and because it had come unexpectedly soon it was delivered without the full support of the lungs. The delivery was ideal. He responded with a broad smile. That *is* conducting.

He has come to us, from time to happy time, with our Christmas *Nutcracker* ballet: for the orchestra a considerable compensation for a spoilt Boxing Day. For this work, on the first occasion, he cautiously asked three calls with the orchestra alone. Half-way through the second he sent us home, cancelling the third. These are characteristic Noddy tactics; but he was not so incautious as to leave himself without a margin until he'd heard the orchestra play. It had been ten years, or even more, since the last time. Coming back for the following Christmas he was disappointed, he said, that I had not given him the same orchestra as last year. No, there was nothing wrong with this year's people, but it would have been possible, he pointed out, to dispense with *all* rehearsal. Well, he seemed serious enough.

He likes to entertain. During *Nutcracker*, in a passage needing no control from the box, he once put down the stick and picked up the miniature score which had remained closed during all rehearsals and performances, leafing anxiously through it as though searching for a lost detail. Somewhere along the line of that passage there comes a short single-note interjection from muted brass, an incident which must have direction. He seemed oblivious of it. Closer and closer came the pitfall. Absentmindedly his hand fumbled for the stick, raising it limply to his right. Suddenly it was energised by an electric wrist, producing a flick as though at a fly. The brass spat the single note. Still his gaze was riveted on the little score, as the stick once more fell to the desk. The orchestra, naturally, was convulsed with silent laughter.

His *Boris*, in the '92 season, was masterly, even surpassing for some of us Abbado's wonderful performances some years earlier. To one player who broke protocol by making the comparison in his hearing he remarked: 'Well, it is my own language ...' This is obviously true. What is equally true is that while few Russian conductors are first-rate in any other, Noddy is just as good in German, in Italian, and even in English.

The orchestra's admiration made all the more sad the catastrophe of the '93 season when, reacting to an unfortunate word spoken by a producer, Roszdestvensky walked out of a production. The cause of this collision between pit and stage – neither the first, the last, nor the most spectacular in Covent Garden's history – was obscure. The orchestra, always ready to back the conductor as one of its own, felt that the problem, whatever it was, could and should have been spotted and defused by adroit management. So did I. What is certain is that the House managed the ensuing public brou-ha-ha with less than its customary aplomb and that damage was done to its relationship with this fine artist. The Orchestra waits anxiously for his return.

Yevgeny Svetlanov came to conduct *Khovanschina*. That opera, with *Boris* and the indispensable *Onegin*, were the extent of the Royal Opera's Russian repertoire then. It was the last *Khovanschina* of my time because the staging had aged to the point of physical disintegration and it was not thought sensible to replace it with another, the opera being long, expensive, and unpopular with the public.

I fell foul of Svetlanov long before he met the orchestra, at the meeting in John Tooley's office called to discuss his requirements. His demands in orchestral time were spectacular. Exotic visitors like this one are not accustomed to the speed at which London players assimilate music, and this one was measuring his schedule so safely as to be silly. We tried, we really tried, to reduce his demands, remembering that while he prepared *Khovanschina* in luxury some luckless ordinary mortal would be preparing something else on his time-leavings. In the end, braving JT's wrath − Sir John always preferred to skirt round such collisions to find a solution in his own quiet way − I told the maestro that our orchestra was 'not really so bad as all that. And although *Khovanschina* is long, it is not really complicated.' My remark, translated into Russian, produced raised bushy eyebrows and a reduction of one rehearsal.

In the event his demand was almost justified. I was reminded of Boult's remark, that when he was obliged from politeness to rehearse *The Planets* for four days in Vienna the work 'actually improved.' In this case it was not merely the performance which improved but the orchestra too. And when he discovered the quality of the orchestra he relaxed, showing his true warmth and humour.

Perhaps the best joke ever seen in the Royal Opera House Green Room was the one he played on our percussionists during his last performance. He'd made extraordinary demands for bell sounds for *Khovanschina*. Covent Garden is not equipped, as is the Bolshoi, with a built-in belfry behind the stage, stocked with the bells of generations of closed churches. Our bells have to be carried in, a job for engineers. Our percussionists, never loth to discover new ironmongery of all shapes and sizes, had done him proud. Every bing and bong in London's capacious hire systems had been produced for his approval. Then, on that last evening, he asked me to bring the entire percussion department to see him in the interval. Such a request usually bodes ill, and not unnaturally the players expected some sort of complication to their work tonight. The atmosphere when they entered was guarded.

Svetlanov rose with a smile, his English carefully prepared and nearly correct. 'Gentlemens, you have give me very much bells. I thank you. Now I give you ... BELLS!' With a whoop of delight he reached behind his chair and produced seven bottles of the golden liquid, one for each player.

We have not seen Svetlanov since. That is a pity. He is remembered with admiration by the orchestra and with affection by its management.

New times are producing new people. Among the young men of today Gergiev, the architect of the renaissance at the Kirov in St Petersburg, is the most exciting conductor to come out of Russia for many years. He is very much today's man, leaping out of the Fabergé egg ready-armed with perfect English: something we could not have imagined in a Russian conductor ten years ago, when to speak English well was politically incorrect. When he arrived to prepare *Onegin* he immediately showed, too, that he understood more about us than the language. 'The orchestra knows the opera', he told me to my infinite relief, 'and it is only necessary to find the right sound, make an understanding with them. Then it will all come quickly.' Orchestrally, he said, he need not even rehearse the entire piece.

This is an attitude only available to the perfectly assured technician who has done his homework on the orchestra in question. Gergiev had done that very thoroughly. He is an enthusiast of the orchestra and he loves the animal in all its varieties, as do I. To chat with him is to gain background and opinions, invariably positive, about the condition of the world's orchestras. Already he's conducted almost everywhere and heard almost everyone – part of his immense learning process, the fruits of which he takes home for the benefit of the Kirov. About that House and the work of rebuilding its resources he is confident.

His new orchestra, he says, is already less negatively Russian. The dubious characteristics of the old Russian orchestra must go, to be replaced by the best of what is heard internationally. The Russian orchestra as we know it certainly has its drawbacks. A very negative description was given to a group of Hallé players over a drink in Athens in the 'sixties by a famous American violin virtuoso who'd recently played in Moscow. 'The winds are German style,' he said. 'The brasses are French style, but much louder. The strings? Well, they ain't got no style ...'

This was very unkind. The strings were at that time technically as fine as any on earth. Slow to rehearse and learn, yes, but Parkinson's law applies: give people time and they'll consume it. The winds were heavy-German, agreed. The brass – well, the brass never played below a British *mezzo-forte*, its extreme *forte* being simply earsplitting. Mahler's exclamation on seeing Niagara for the first time – 'At last, *fortissimo*!' – perhaps sums it up adequately. But Gergiev's young brassmen are as accomplished and as civilised as any in Europe.

His handling of our own orchestra was extraordinary. His sound, the intense Russian variety needed for *Onegin*, came quickly, partly a matter of method and partly of attitude. He worked intensely but for short periods, handing back lots of rehearsal time. His hands could be pinhead precise but often were not – he knew when direction was necessary and when good things would come by allowing the ensemble to find its own way. Not for a moment was he uninstructive, yet the orchestra never felt itself to be driven. He had the knack, given to only the greatest of conductors, of accepting what the orchestra had, of its own, to give. The results were very exciting for audience and players, something of the old Kirov Tchaikowsky with the best of British added.

Here perhaps is the most important young conductor of his age, the first truly cosmopolitan Russian conductor since the revolution. Such is the quality of Russian teaching that we must expect more like him. Many more? No; such olympian gifts are never prodigally bestowed. But someone remarked on his leaving that we'd seen the future, and that it worked.

CHAPTER 34

To the Rising Sun

Each year Japan entertains a catalogue of visiting artists which is the envy of concert and opera-goers anywhere in the world. Every major opera and ballet company has been there, and every important performer. Hardly a year passes without a visit from a British symphony orchestra, and of the seven excursions abroad of the Royal Opera since its foundation three have been to Japan. Japan is that rarity, a country which can afford us.

It's a very long way away, though not so far since our Russian friends opened their airspace to us. Our first trip to the Far East — we spent a week in Seoul in South Korea before settling in Tokyo for four weeks — was made the hard way, flying over the Pole and stopping to refuel at Anchorage, Alaska. Three hundred bleary-eyed people were bussed at 5am from Floral Street to Gatwick for a twenty-three-hour flight. They were very nearly minus one; taking every precaution I slept overnight at the Adelphi in the Aldwych and woke at 4.50am. From bed to bus took seven minutes, the fastest sprint of my life, encouraged as I panted into sight at the foot of Bow Street by the cheers of many throats, some of them highly trained. I need not have panicked; the flight was so late I could have bicycled to Gatwick and caught it.

We were spared the planned change of planes at Narita, Tokyo. Only when we were safely in Seoul did we discover that though we had not changed planes our instruments had done so and were waiting in Japan. Paul Findlay, with nonchalance born of many minor catastrophes surmounted during international tours of the Royal Ballet, shrugged off this small difficulty with ease. Within the allotted span the gear duly arrived. We were able to deliver our *Tosca*, our *Grimes*, and our *Flute* to the delighted Koreans. Colin Davis, by a miracle of conducting stamina, conducted every performance of the tour, the only performer of the company who didn't take a night off.

That troubled country was a unique experience; not that it inflicted its troubles on us, but there was no escaping them. Domestic politics were unstable. The President, on his visit to the opera, huddled against the wall of his box out of any possible line of fire, while the boxes opposite were packed with large men with short hair. Invasion from the North, highly unlikely though it seemed to us, was expected daily. We were forbidden to photograph landscapes facing North, our high-rise hotel windows being fitted with charming but immovable venetian blinds on that side. An entire complex of shopping arcades, corresponding with the streets above, ran underground so that life would go on regardless of bombs, and each night the streets were disturbed by the rumble of tanks. Yet the only real evidence of antagonism between North and South was some miles to the North at Panmunjom, where the apparently everlasting truce talks were held. I was reminded of the 1984 scenario; of a government frightening its own people for its own ends.

Seoul will long be remembered by the Royal Opera for the Lotte Hotel, named after its builder, a manufacturer of chewing-gum. The Geraint Evanses, trotters of some experience, thought it the best in the world. Staffing, the great problem of hotel managers, was not a problem in Seoul. Watching a team of ten old ladies polishing the Lotte's acres of marble foyer *by hand* one morning, I suggested that one youngster with a Hoover polisher could have done the work in half an hour. I was told that the ladies could be paid for a year for the price of the polisher, and that they needed the work much more than Hoover needed the money.

Under-paid and underprivileged they may be, but the Koreans are delightful folks, communicating easily with visitors because of the Korean alphabet, the creation of their King Seijong, of the 17th century. Realising that Mandarin — Korean education then owed everything to the Chinese invaders of centuries — was beyond the reach of the masses, he formed a royal commission to design a phonetic alphabet. With its aid the Korean can write and pronounce almost anything, in any language, with amazing accuracy, unlike the Japanese, poor chap, who rarely knows his Rs from his Lbow linguistically. We quickly learned the trick of the lapel badge which could say, in Korean characters, 'I am... of the Royal Opera Company.' This procured instant help in the street, at the small cost of having every second person one met say 'Good morning Mr Gay of the Royal Opera Company' in perfect English. In Seoul one had only to produce a street-map to be surrounded by helpers. Wherever we wished to go we were not so much directed as taken, though if our destination was a shop we might well be shown a better one, often owned by the brother-in-law of the guide.

We saw something of the Korean countryside, of its folk-crafts and folk-arts. Particularly marvellous were the Korean dancers in their national costume, the flowing sleeves part of the choreography, dancing to wonderful drums. Lady members of the chorus were attracted to those graceful gowns and a number came home. They were not much seen afterwards. Perhaps national costume travels badly; perhaps, too, one needs a national shape to go with it.

We were soon away to Japan. Overflying Tokyo one is stunned by its size; at 15,000 feet the city is a black ant-hill stretching to the horizon. Japan is not a big country, and since very little of it is habitable, teeming millions of its people are crammed into the coastal strip. From a hotel window high above the city it's hard to resist the conclusion that most live in the capital itself, an area stretching perhaps from Watford to Croydon, every inch of which is continuously as busy as Oxford Street on a December Saturday. The Japanese are a small race, a very good thing to be in Japan.

Korea is merely exotic; Japan is on another planet. Without experiencing it the complete 'difference' of Japanese life and attitudes from our own cannot be understood, if ever. The isolation of the Japanese for so long has created a mentality which its recent headlong plunge into Western culture seems to have changed only superficially. I read, while there, James Clavell's *Shogun* and I recommend this to first-time visitors to Japan; not that there is now much danger of one being boiled alive on arrival, as in the book, but many attitudes survive and they condition everyday life to a surprising degree. To read the book in the gardens of Osaka castle, where its climactic events are set, is a special experience.

If the Lotte Hotel in Seoul impresses by its design and performance, then the New Otani in Tokyo gets the medal for size. The grounds, with Japanese gardens and waterfall, are roughly as big as Soho, and the hotel contains twenty-eight restaurants ranging from the serviceable to the superb and from the Italian to the Japanese via India and New York. There are many fine shops and indeed a department-store and supermarket in the basement. The Otani Tower is the only restaurant in my experience which provides as part of its buffet breakfast free gin and vodka for adding, *ad libitum*, to one's breakfast fruitjuice.

The Otani, like every important Tokyo hotel, has facilities for weddings, and each day produced another bride. Marriage in Japan is an interesting illustration of the national tug-of-war between western and traditional ways. Each bride is married three times: once in a civil ceremony, once in a white veil, and lastly, in the wedding kimono, by Shinto priests. In this garment, surrounded by her family and friends similarly dressed, she is a gorgeous sight. Western fathers bemoaning the cost of their daughters' nuptials don't know their luck. The *obi* alone, circling the lady's waist, may easily cost a thousand pounds.

We had many opportunities in the course of our work to observe the Japanese attitude to theirs; management especially, since we worked with Japanese crews in adapting the various theatres for our use. They are fine theatres with excellent acoustics, lacking little in the way of equipment or facilities. Only details were missing and these were supplied with awesome speed and efficiency. At the first rehearsal Colin complained that the desk provided would not do; it was too small, and too little lit. The technician arrived and asked for a drawing of what we needed. Ninety minutes later the desk needed only paint.

Each morning we saw the theatre staff standing in a circle around its manager, listening to what seemed to be a lecture. We were told by our interpreter that they were being reminded of the privilege of work and of the need to give of their best today for the satisfaction of the Royal Opera Company and the honour of their employers.

When in Japan we were expected to do as the Japanese did, as our pit manager, Malcolm Kinch, discovered to his discomfiture. After some days, when routine was secure, he told his Japanese team that he would arrive late next morning, and that they knew what was to be done without him. Before he could escape he was confronted by our interpreter, a diminutive but determined Japanese girl graduate, who said politely but firmly 'Mr Kinch ... privilege of management brings with it very great responsibility. It is not possible that manager can begin after workers ...' We were amused. But are these ideas so foreign to us? Surely they are a Japanese expression of what we used to call the Protestant Work Ethic, that principle which taught that work was honourable and to be done with pride, for its own sake rather than for the money? It was this which took my grandfather down the pit, gasping for breath, within months of his death from the dust. Didn't the preachers of my own Welsh valleys, paid as they were largely by coal-owners, exhort their congregations to give to God that which was God's, to Caesar that which was Caesar's, and to their employer what was his? Perhaps when the lessons of the Japanese success have been learned the Royal Opera House will sing each morning at nine its own workers' song, with words set to a chorus of Verdi? Perhaps.

We had, thankfully, free time in which to enjoy the more popular tourist sights of Tokyo and later of Osaka and neighbouring Kyoto, where for so many years the Sons of Heaven reigned, protected but powerless. These buildings are wonderfully preserved, or in many cases — like Osaka Castle, perhaps the most famous example — have been completely rebuilt after the toll of centuries. They are fascinating, though more picturesque than remarkable, remembering that few go back more than four or five hundred years, at which time many of our own finest cathedrals were already weathering nicely.

Japan, a country of earthquakes, was built until recently mainly of wood and as lightly as possible. Among Tokyo's high-rise blocks are still found a surprising number of Madame Butterfly sets, complete with sliding screens and tatami mats. Old Japan in the true sense I never saw. Those who were not 'in' an opera were able to make extended trips to the countryside, even to the Inland Sea, by means of the Shinkansen train. I envied them. Only once did I venture forth, and that was on a tightly-scheduled trip to Mount Fuji, where we were promised a cable-car ride close to the summit. It rained like a bad day in Manchester, and though we passed within a hundred yards of the great mountain, high on our cable, we saw nothing of it in the mist. All I remember of Fuji is the stench of sulphur. The mountain is volcanic, and not to be blamed for its smell. The next morning was bright and clear. Emerging from the lift into the restaurant for breakfast we saw Fuji outside the window, apparently close enough to touch.

The famous Shinkansen, the 'Bullet Train', is a total disappointment, defeated as a travelling thrill by its own total success. The monster is smooth as silk and silent as a ghost. There is no sensation of travel at all. One has more fun in an ancient MG car at 50.

Modern Tokyo has the feel of modern America but it is so very much cleaner. Despite the awful congestion the Japanese maintain an incredible level of city cleansing and maintenance. The people, too, seem to scrub themselves harder and oftener than any others. Cram as they may into their urban trains — and rush-hour in Tokyo is something to be experienced — there is no feeling of discomfort from proximity. These are surely the world's most considerate people. It seems to come naturally to them, but it is essential anyway; they live one on top of the other, and any general loss of temper would surely produce mayhem. So disciplined are they that despite crowded streets their traffic flows freely. Dented cars are not seen. Old ones are rare.

More than anything else the Japanese fear failure. That's old Japan coming out, and it can make for comic happenings like the afternoon when Montserrat Caballé, coming by cab to the theatre to rehearse *Tosca*, was driven for an hour and a half around the city before an increasingly desperate cabbie gave up and returned her to the hotel. This is one of the results of the city's size; no-one can possibly know where everything is. But that driver, Miss Caballe told us, was humiliated by his failure. Whether he went home to join his ancestors in the traditional way we will never know. I hope not.

In Japan, true to form, we played splendidly. The cast of the original performances of our *Grimes* was still intact, the audiences reacting there as everywhere to John Vickers' overwhelming characterisation, a performance which transcended language. We had fun with the *Flute*, which Tom Allen enlivened with Japanese jokes. Unrehearsed, they created as much hilarity in the pit as in the audience. The audience loved the children in the piece, tiny tots drawn from the offspring of the Corps Diplomatique.

Among the major problems of the *Flute* are the Three Boys, difficult parts often sung by small ladies. For Colin nothing will do but three hardworking kids, their struggle with the notes becoming a characteristic of the piece. We toured nine of these children, lucky kids, for safety. We were obliged to travel their schoolteachers too.

The Royal Opera Company was happier within itself during the first Far Eastern tour than I ever saw it before or since, high spirits snowing in everything we did on or off the stage. Colin's birthday was celebrated with a 'Happy Birthday' curtain call from chorus and orchestra, and the arrival of his youngest child was announced, after a *Flute* performance, by the public presentation of the biggest teddy-bear in Tokyo. How well the audience understood our high jinks, or indeed how well they understood these complicated operas we couldn't know. Musical taste in Japan is not in doubt, the Japanese orchestra being highly developed; some important European conductors spend months of each year in Tokyo, so highly do they value the playing there. It's curious that after so many years of highly skilled orchestral playing, and with Japanese singers performing in Western houses, there is no permanent opera in Tokyo. It will come.

Our trip home was the longest ever. There was fog at Gatwick, and shortage of fuel meant that we must put down at Frankfurt to wait for the weather to clear. Soon it did so. But alas, some members of the company had passed through customs and security in search of a telephone, and the ever-thorough Polizei would not permit us to board until we'd all been through the mill again. Three hundred people, literally too exhausted to complain, were duly processed. Away we flew, to land at Gatwick in the middle of a Customs work-to-rule. Those officers had a field day, opening and searching every bag and box. Cameras, kimonos, and small souvenirs apart, there were a hundred-and-fifty hi-fi outfits on that plane. Some of us were at Gatwick from 8.30am until the middle of the afternoon. My last recollection of the first Far-Eastern Tour was of a five-a-side football match in the customs hall with Colin playing in goal. One of my colleagues, whose early experience like mine was gained in the Brigade of Guards, wisely remarked that he and I had been trained for disaster on this scale, but it tried my sense of humour, that I'll admit.

We've been back twice since. Japan changes little, though it grows more expensive and more westernised. This seems a pity. There is much to be admired in Japanese tradition, in the beauty of kimono, the grace of the tea-ceremony, the studied depth of the bow, depending on the status of those involved on either side, the infallible good manners of the people. Japan has shown us an enviable degree of civilised discipline. If we are to compete with Japan we must equal it. More: we must learn how very different from us that extraordinary nation really is. Under every neat blue suit is a kimono still.

CHAPTER 35
I Maestri

The Latins have produced only one really fine orchestra, that of La Scala, Milan. This cannot be excelled in those part of the opera repertoire which are its own province. In Italy music means opera. Neither France, Italy nor Spain has yet produced a great symphony orchestra, though Paris has tried hard and typically expensively, and has come near the mark from time to time. There is no shortage of fine players in any of the three countries, certainly not in France, where the conservatoires are superb; an evening at the Paris Opera proves that the individual talent in the pit is splendid. What is lacking, then, that their great orchestra never arrives? Barbirolli, the son of an Italian father and a French mother, insisted that the Latins lacked the corporate discipline without which individual virtuosity amounts to little.

A conductor-friend now dead told me that he carried on his visits to Paris a postcard bearing the words *Think of the money.* This he placed on his desk as a restraint on the instinctive wish to abandon rehearsals, a reaction not to the playing but to the very poor prevailing discipline. To a greater or lesser degree this seems to be a characteristic of orchestras in France and Italy. JB once told me of an occasion when a Roman orchestra drove him to a total loss of temper. His command of the language enabled him to achieve this with panache, addressing to the players an epithet which cast aspersions on the virtue of the mothers of each and everyone present. The resulting shocked silence, he said, had been very impressive. During the rest of the week he'd had two worries; what superlative insult to use next time, and how to leave Italy alive.

All this hardly squares with the attitudes of the great Italian maestri, who have the reputation of hard men in matters of orchestral discipline. But each of these, from Toscanini through Giulini to Abbado and Muti, has done his best work abroad. None has succeeded in creating in Italy the instrument he needed. A very great pity, this, and an important challenge for the younger generation of Italian conductors.

Toscanini conducted little in London, limiting himself to the BBC Symphony of the middle 'thirties and, 20 years on, the Philharmonia. The latter saw the great conductor in physical decline, his faculties failing; the BBC Orchestra met him in his prime and loved him in spite of a technique which they found unclear. The famous tantrums were few though the tension was very high. What should be said of this great man is that his famous rages, one of the most famous of which was illicitly recorded for posterity and has enlivened orchestra parties for decades, were never used to destroy a player but rather to dissipate the Maestro's own disappointment. I think such behaviour would have done the man little good with today's great orchestras; by the end of that tirade there would hardly be a player left in the room, and those would probably have stayed only to give him an ironic round of applause. I may be wrong; it's just conceivable that an artist could be of such quality that the orchestra would stand for absolutely anything from him, but I've never met such.

A distinguished member of the BBC Orchestra described Toscanini as 'supreme; the one conductor of whom every player approves.' Perhaps his explosive temper has been as much exaggerated as has Beecham's wit? In any case he was for most of the time utterly charming in London, as even the worst of conducting monsters usually is. Perhaps because the orchestras of *The Land without music* are remarkably disciplined, musically and otherwise, compared with many of those in Europe, visiting conductors often seem to pick up nicer personalities with their bags at the Heathrow carousel.

Orchestral standards in London today owe much to Claudio Abbado and Riccardo Muti. The difference in personality between these two was described to me by a member of the Scala music staff when Muti succeeded Abbado there. Claudio, he said, was a practical man of the theatre, one who knew how to work within the limitations of the house, how to deal with the internal problems of the orchestra and the company. His gift for necessary compromise had been very valuable during a problematic time in Milan. Muti was very different, a man without compromise. This would make life much simpler for him, because that was an attitude La Scala understood. It was in the Toscanini tradition to refuse to concede. Already Muti was nicknamed *Riccarturo.*

Abbado's readiness to compromise, though, is tempered by a shrewd assessment of what is truly possible. He 'knows the business' and he can distinguish between the impossible and the very difficult. If he is told of a production crisis which demands the use of the stage today, making it necessary to move his rehearsal into a room with a very bad acoustic, he may weigh one need against another and perhaps concede, knowing that the production is part of 'his' evening. If on the other hand he is told the very sound reasons why he cannot be given the enormous string numbers he asks, he will merely tap the score and say 'Mr Gay, here is *my* problem. The orchestra budget, the problems of seating in the pit, and so on, these are yours. You cannot give them to me.'

I first met Abbado in the 'sixties, in Manchester. We didn't take to him. Orchestras seldom take to the young conducting genius, fresh from school, touring the world with a meticulously prepared but tiny repertoire, and there was a certain handsome arrogance about the young Claudio which we found less than endearing. He had, too, a common flaw of the man with the 'toured' repertoire in that he brought to rehearsal the expectation of failure where he'd experienced it elsewhere. The 'bits which would go wrong' were carefully registered in his mind for correction, and when they didn't go wrong he was disconcerted. My trumpets had the pleasure of disconcerting him at least once. We were not expected to get that passage – in the *Chout* ballet of Prokofiev – right first time, and it showed. This was inexperience and it amused the Hallé, but the young man put us under considerable pressure nevertheless. We rose to the challenge with fine performances of the Bach Third Suite, the Prokofiev, and the Second Symphony of Brahms. All agreed that if this chap could learn some things about the nature of the British orchestra he would be very important indeed. Well, he learned and he is.

Abbado's visits to Covent Garden have been rare but enormously valued. He came first with *Un Ballo in Maschera*, soon after my translation from the pit to the office. It was a splendid occasion, the first night a state gala during the visit of the French President, M. Giscard d'Estaing. The Queen attended, the House was glorious with flowers, Domingo and Caballé sang. It was all marvellously done, but at the cost of a great deal of hard work on the part of the conductor. The orchestra was well below form then and Abbado's unhappiness during rehearsals was obvious to me, though much less so to the orchestra; he was then, as always, concerned not to hurt players and reluctant to complain. He got the fine performance he deserved, but he didn't come back for a long time.

His return was a splendid occasion, a wonderful new production of *Boris* which won a famous award for Covent Garden. When he came next, in 1993 for *Pelléas et Mélisande*, his confidence in the orchestra was obvious from the outset, a heartening demonstration of the respect in which we were now held by the great conductors.

The youthful arrogance, probably a product of nerves, has long since been replaced by real security. Abbado is unusual among the important conductors, and especially among Italians, in that he makes no attempt to impress by his physical presence. Toscanini − even from his photographs − was a walking hand-grenade, the only available film of his work with the NBC Orchestra showing a hundred mesmerised players sitting transfixed before the tiny bundle of energy. Giulini's entrance to the theatre is something between that of a film-star and the Pope, while Muti radiates tension enough to stop the conversation in the Nag's Head pub; but Abbado is a man one could pass in the street without noticing, one not out of place on a football terrace (he's very happy there; he played soccer for La Scala) or in a supermarket on Saturday morning. Only the eyes give evidence of the acute brain, constantly alive and alert, weighing people and possibilities. Not a man to worry a manager unnecessarily, but not one to take for granted, either.

His hands are superb, with the ability to turn from the flexibly-expressive to the pinhead-precise in a flash. Sometimes he combines the two extremes, dropping exact instructions into an expansive and elastic bar with the ease and certainty of Kleiber. This is a great asset in Debussy, where clinical precision can produce clarity of a sterile kind, but where a lack of ensemble makes a vague and woolly mess. His knack of producing the right sound, too, is uncanny. Most fine conductors produce a personal sound, and the lucky ones are those who can make most music work within it. Abbado has escaped this limitation, or if he has a sound of his own it has so far escaped me. Within five minutes of beginning work on his Debussy *the composer's* sound had arrived, a sound utterly different from the cold, dark drama of his *Boris*, and a different orchestra apparently from the one which had played Stravinsky on the previous evening. It was not, for Abbado, a matter of reproducing the precise text of *Pelleas*, as Boulez had done here 20 years before, but of creating Debussy's

[223]

orchestra. 'The orchestra is fine' was his only comment. 'The sound must come, that's all.' And so it was.

His voice is never raised, though a colleague who worked with him at La Scala assures me that when he 'blows' the effect can be extraordinary. When the hands stop the music immediately stops, and he exchanges a few words of advice or comment in a conversational tone. He's heard by everyone present, a rare knack in our dead acoustic. People listen, as orchestras always listen to conductors who say necessary things. Otherwise they pass the time by fiddling at difficult passages or — in case of extreme boredom — by games of chess passed by note across the pit, a trick which once, according to Garden legend, drove a temperamental Hungarian screaming from the rostrum.

That was long before my time. I never saw that trick, and there was certainly no chess-game under Abbado. The work was absorbing and amazingly easy to bring off under those interested eyes and that informative stick. Nothing was conducted which need not be, and nothing left which must be shown. Great art, this.

For *Pelléas* he called the cast to very early orchestral rehearsals, not because they needed to work — he'd played the work with them before — but because in this opera the voices are not so much accompanied by the orchestra as woven into the fabric of the score, instruments with words. Voices and instruments play as one ensemble, stage and pit perfectly merged.

Between calls he is very informal. Those members of the orchestra who were members of the European Community Youth Orchestra, his particular pride and joy, come for a chat about old times. All are remembered, and absent friends enquired about. Where are they, where is so-and-so playing now? And then he will turn to last night's football. 'Did you see Milano on TV on Sunday? Good, eh?' I pointed out that Lazio had nearly beaten them. 'Ah! But only nearly!' He is delighted, and dismissive of the efforts of our Paul Gascoigne to defeat his team. Clearly he did not give up Milanese football with La Scala.

Talk turns to the work. He is pleased. It goes well, he says. Such a fine production, and well played. There is always something, of course. He complains in the mildest way. 'This player, you know ... always he plays a little late? Is it possible to say it kindly perhaps?' I assure him that it is possible and that I will do it. 'Good. I don't want to hurt, you know ...?'

He goes back into the pit to restart, and I ask myself again how it is that the best conductors are the nicest, how they get such results without 'hurting' and why some chump long ago confidently announced that security is the enemy of orchestral performance. It's taken conductors a long time to reach an understanding of the rest of the human race, but they've made it, the best of them.

Abbado memorises. The orchestra has mixed feelings about this. We have risks enough without the added one of the conductor forgetting the work and selling us a dummy, and memorising is often a party-trick, meant to impress, without positive performing advantage. But Abbado's memory is colossal. I've seen a few remarkable specimens, but nothing to compare with his. To memorise *Boris* we thought a great feat, but in Moussorgsky we have a relatively simple structure with clear melodic lines and logical sequences. Where would one begin to memorise *Pelléas*, a web of spun impressionism conveyed through the subtlest orchestration? If ever mind boggled, this is the time. Every entrance, every dynamic, every infinitely subtle phrase, is conveyed. Repose becomes drama, soft string sounds develop sonority and bite instantly at the command of confident hands. The one undeniable advantage of the genuinely memorised performance, the constant eye-contact with the players, is wonderfully exploited. So often the memorised conductor 'receives' the performance, to some extent guided by the orchestra, but Abbado conducts in the most positive way, controlling every bar. There is time even for a glance, some bars before an entry, at those who have been resting for a long time, to make sure they are awake and aware. The man knows the work and he knows how to make it happen.

On the first night of *Pelléas*, too, his memory was put to the ultimate test. The question of how he, without a score, would cope with unforeseen disaster was conclusively resolved when during performance the pit lights went out. The orchestra stopped; *Carmen* we might play in the dark, but *Pelléas*? Hardly. There was a tense two-minute silence while our friends in Technical found the fault and cued it. The lights came up, Abbado gave a quiet bar-number *from memory* to the orchestra, the music restarted, the cast found the place ...

Abbado is not characteristically Italian at all. Yes, he is especially fine in the Italian repertoire, and never happier than in the pit with Verdi or Rossini, but he is without the limitation which so often marks the Italian conductor, the lack of instinctive sympathy with the classic symphonists. Abbado is cosmopolitan. In Mozart, Beethoven, even Brahms, he is utterly satisfying. *Even* Brahms? Yes, Brahms is the hurdle, the Becher's Brook at which so many fall. We have only the recordings by which to judge Toscanini; but since they are now the evidence on which his case rests in all repertoire, and since in so much he is inimitable, I think it fair to say that I cannot listen to his Brahms, nor even his Beethoven. Brahms was the composer in which I least enjoyed Barbirolli, and many of today's Italians share this vulnerability. They live for melody and for the colours which lend emotion to it; sometimes music which depends on structure defeats them. It is no accident that the classical work for which the old hands of the BBC best remember Toscanini was Beethoven's *Pastoral*, not that the Moussorgsky-Ravel *Pictures at an Exhibition* or the Respighi *Pines* – or *Fountains* – *of Rome* so often come with Italian maestros on tour. These people are at their best with pictures, and when the colour is lacking they apply it. The best of them do so with skill and grace, but Brahms is a black-coffee man, not to be taken with grappa. Abbado knows this well.

Far be it from me to suggest that my other great Italian, Riccardo Muti, is a mere colourist either. His long years with the Philharmonica gave us proof of a musical taste extending to every corner of the repertoire. Yet first and foremost he is an Italian conductor, positively and delightfully so, his enthusiasm and dedication in the cause of Italian music fundamental to his musical personality. To mention a neglected Italian work to Muti is to produce an enthusiastic lecture on its importance. A ten-minute conversation with him can send the unwary away to the nearest record-shop to buy – of all things – *Semiramide*, in his opinion Rossini's neglected masterpiece, perhaps the greatest Italian opera of all. But wait; tomorrow it may be Bellini.

A little *Semiramide* goes a long way with me. But of course, he would say, how can the British feel these things? He sits at the piano in his Covent Garden green-room, thumping out the 'um-chuck' pattern of early Verdi and asks with a chuckle 'What is this, to you? A cliché, naturally! To me, to Italians, an act of faith!'

I think Muti enjoys the Maestro image. If, as Barbirolli used to say, Rome's customs-officers still salute when presented with a Maestro's passport, I have no doubt that Muti like Barbirolli thinks the salute appropriate. He would think it right that he should be noticed, not because he is Riccardo Muti but because he is The Maestro. This is, for him, an office and a responsibility. Music, and especially Italian music, is in his hands.

In private he's a man with a ready chuckle. Why he finds it necessary to present on the box the unsmiling face of the hard man I cannot tell – unless it is a cover for the smile which might undermine the serious- ness of his work. If so it's been a mistake and a handicap to him. Some players just can't take it; they think it a pose, or perhaps an attempt to intimidate. Neither can possibly be true. Muti needs no pose and he is the last to intimidate, a warm, understanding human being with a great affection for those with whom he develops a working relation- ship and in particular for his old colleagues of the Philharmonia. We've seen his attitude soften during his visits to Covent Garden. On his first, for *Aida* in '75, he was distant, cool, detached, almost dismissive. True, he worked with the same under-par orchestra as did Abbado in *Ballo*, and he is a little less able to conceal his reaction to failure than is his compatriot. After that, with *Macbeth*, there was a warming. The orchestra warmed in response, and fine playing resulted; fine singing from the chorus, too, at a time when it was generally under form. When he came again with *I Capuleti* things went splendidly, helped by a characteristically Irish icebreaker from our leader, Hugh Maguire.

I preferred leaders to introduce conductors to the orchestra. They have to work together; in the last resort I'm a spectator. So I first introduced Hugh to Muti. They'd never met. 'Well,' said Hugh to the great man, 'isn't that strange now! We've never met – and I've played for absolutely everyone else!'

This took Muti aback; but Hugh was not finished yet. Standing on the box he clapped for silence and said 'Ladies and Gentlemen, here's Mr Muti. I've never met him before. They say he's a terribly hard man but he seems a nice enough feller to me ...'

The resultant laughter would have thawed an ice-cap. Muti's response matched it. 'No, I am not a nice man. You will all have a terrible time for two weeks!'

From this beginning he went on to discuss the opera. 'We have a big problem. Bellini is not interesting for the orchestra. But to make him sound well we have to take great care, work at the sound. It will be boring, but without this care Bellini is nothing. So I have to ask you for really special patience with this score.'

Uphill work it was. There was really nothing to play, yet to dismiss the task would have been to wreck the piece. Bellini got his due and the work went so well that we were able to record it, live during performances.

It is true that the ability to compromise has been left out of his makeup. In some people this amounts to an ordinary nuisance, a pose adopted merely to demonstrate maestro-power. In Muti's case it's nothing of the kind; he simply will not permit any removable obstacle to come between his audience and the music. A notable example was his argument with the House 'tabs', the great red curtains decorated with the Royal monogram which conclude every performance at Covent Garden. We love those curtains. They are the most beautiful drapes in the operatic world, and much admired by our visitors, but they have a vice: they make a whirring sound as they come down, caused by the running of twisted steel cables through steel rings. Usually the sound is not heard, as opera and ballet have an obliging habit of ending fortissimo. At the end of *Aida*, though, the sound has always been audible. This we tolerated as inevitable. Then our tabs met Muti.

I was summoned to the pit one day at the end of the fourth act. Why me I cannot guess, except that the Maestro knew me and had not met my friend the technical director. 'Mr Gay ... how can I stop this terrible noise?' he asked.

What was he talking about? 'This noise, of the curtain. Verdi says at the end of the opera [here he showed me the score] that the curtain will come down; but not that the curtain will make a noise. All the noises in this opera are mine. This noise I don't want!'

I was sure the problem was insoluble, but there seemed little point in saying so. We could have ended without the tabs, dropping in our red runners instead, but the effect would have been much less. So I referred Muti to my friends in technical, sure I would hear no more of the matter. I was wrong. Two days later I was again summoned to the pit, this time empty except for the Maestro himself. He invited me to sit. He was rehearsing the curtains solo. 'Up... down... up... down'. The silence was absolute. He looked pleased, whether at the silence or at my own amazement I don't know. I asked him how it was done. He had no idea. But it was done and that was what mattered to him. *Aida* would end in silence except for the *pianissimo* which he would create.

How had it been done? Using very long ladders the crew had wrapped each curtain-ring in bandages, which were then soaked in lubricating oil. Some of those rings were very high indeed. It had been a tricky job. It worked though. Technicians at Covent Garden react as do musicians to uncompromising conductors. They compete.

We've seen Muti only in Italian opera. Here his concern was for the quality of the sound above all, striving to eliminate all hardness from the strings and to blend the wind and brass with them until he achieved a perfectly mixed organ-like balance. His reminders about these things were constant, sending me sometimes to the canteen in a performance interval to remind an errant string principal of his need. The result is very distinctive quality, a rich, dark string sound quite different from that obtained by anyone else. Rare indeed are the conductors who can make any orchestra sound entirely different from its norm. Muti can and does. For this quality he will sometimes sacrifice audible detail. Once I pointed out to him a loss of internal figuration in middle strings in a great chorus of *Macbeth*. He asked me for a solution. Reluctantly, knowing I was about to be taught a lesson, I suggested a little more 'off-the-string' in repeated patterns in seconds and violas. He would have none of my solution. The sound would immediately become hard and unmusical, he said. 'Besides, over such a chorus that detail will never be heard unless the strings are twice as big. In the first bar, before the chorus begins, the audience will hear the figure. After that *they will see it, and think they hear it.*' As always he was well ahead of the game. A lesser man might have struggled for half an hour with that figuration, all for nothing.

His chorus in that opera was enormous, one hundred and forty; a figure which caused alarm among budgeteers when it was demanded, a year before he arrived. John Tooley, chairing the meeting, suggested that we 'might perhaps compromise', a suggestion which Muti seemed to let pass. As he left the room at the conclusion of our discussion though he turned with a smile and said, 'And yes, let us compromise about the chorus. Perhaps one-hundred-and-thirty-nine?'

That, I think, is a typical Muti compromise.

We've not seen him for some years, since he joined the Philadelphia Orchestra. Now, as Music Director of La Scala, he's even busier, more's the pity. He is all the harder to secure because he will not divide his time. If he conducts at Covent Garden that is what he does; nothing else. He asked once – half in fun, knowing John Tooley's horrified reaction at the sheer length of the piece — to be permitted to conduct Rossini's *William Tell*. A complete performance would have absorbed eight weeks of his life, though, and he just hadn't eight weeks to spare. He loved to reminisce about his Florentine performances of the work, the first complete ones ever. 'We began at eight-thirty', he said, 'and still we were playing at two! What a piece!'

I told him that for a work of such length he ought to have two orchestras, and he replied with a laugh that for *Tell* one needed two maestros too. He's repeated the feat at La Scala. Perhaps one day...

It was always such a joy to be with him, and to meet Mrs Muti, who always arrived for his first night with the Muti bambini until they grew up. They are a marvellously matched pair, Mrs Muti having been a successful singer. 'Then', she told me, 'we had to decide. He was here, I was there, you know how it is. So now *we conduct*.'

Who will come next from Italy? After a period when we all suspected the vines to have withered, a new vintage is appearing, much to the relief of those who value the Italian tradition. Rizzi, the talented young Music Director of Welsh National Opera and a Covent Garden discovery, will in time make a mark comparable to those of my prize maestri, I believe. And now his close contemporary, Gatti, is to become a part of our own house, contributing the Italian element which some say we have lacked since our foundation. His input so far has been impressive. Even as I write, new Italian talent rises over the horizon. That's vital. Italy has something unique to give, especially to opera. And now there are reports that Italian orchestras, too, are rising to the demands of their conductors. We hear great things of the Santa Cecilia Orchestra in Rome, and the opera in Bologna is producing playing at international level. I think we have not yet heard the last from Italy, nor the best.

CHAPTER 36
Voices

My home was, and I hope still is, the Land of Song. Those classrooms of singing children, those chapels bursting with decibels – a man could walk from end to end of the Rhondda on Sunday evening without once being out of earshot of a singing congregation – are heard nowhere else. And what other street in the world, like that humble row of back-to-backs in Cilfynydd, can boast of having raised two world-quality opera singers, Geraint Evans and Stuart Burrows, one born at each end? It's entirely appropriate that I should have found a home in the opera house. Few Gardeners have more enjoyed the wonderful voices heard there.

My early cornet-lessons borrowed heavily from the vocal style. Harry Mortimer pressed the matter further. He'd learned so much, he said, from the fine singers at the Hallé; they, and the great string players, were the models on which to form phrasing and style. My first meeting with such people took place in Yorkshire, in a church in Silsden near Keighley, where Mortimer sent me to deputise in a performance of *Messiah*. *Messiah* was part of the Christmas ritual of such towns then, sung annually by every self-respecting choir, and it had long been what today's trumpeters would call 'a nice little earner'. This was still true as late as the 'sixties, when my colleague in the Liverpool Philharmonic was said to replace his car annually on the proceeds of as many as twenty-nine performances over the Christmas season. *Messiah* contains a celebrated trumpet obligato, as I described earlier, to a wonderful bass aria *The Trumpet Shall Sound*.

It was this fearsome piece which I met for the first time at the age of thirteen, in the first of almost two hundred performances. Fashion dictated that I play it upon a 'long Bach trumpet', a machine which owed nothing to Bach but everything to the commercial instincts of trumpeters of nineteenth-century Germany. It was introduced to England in a performance of the B Minor Mass – a much more formidable piece of writing for trumpet than *Messiah* – by Herr

Kosleck of Berlin. The long trumpet was part of the North-Country Messianic ritual; the money came as much for the machine as for the sounds. It was hell to handle, especially for a diminutive boy, but in the right hands, such as those of Mortimer himself, it sounded wonderful.

In Silsden, then, I first encountered The Voice. It was not the operatic voice of today, though many of its best exponents had trained for opera in Italy. These were of a generation of unspoiled, unforced voices which I think — though I am no expert on the voice — died when the jet-plane was born. Listen to the *Walküre* recording made by Bruno Walter in Vienna in the middle 'thirties for perhaps the most wonderful demonstration of what singing then meant. Every note is the right note and every word sung with the clarity of a linguaphone course, yet nothing is lost of dramatic intensity. Such total commitment to the work in hand is only possible given *time*. When the *Ring* Cycle is the only one of the year for the singer, when the performance of *Figaro* is the last appearance until the transatlantic liner docks in New York three weeks later, then the voice, like the intelligence controlling it, is properly rested, refreshed and exercised. The great voices of today sing too frequently for their own survival. Their owners are not to be blamed; their singing lives are short, and they are shortening them wilfully in order to secure their old age, that's all.

But back to *Messiah*, in the traditional Yorkshire fashion. Our solo quartet owed little to the opera stage, whatever its training. We had so little opera then, that these artists would have starved but for Handel's oratorio and a few more works like it. Their approach to the piece was wonderfully simple. They sang from primitive editions, with none of today's textual expertise. Those Rip van Winkle Handelians who knew the man personally were still asleep, only to wake when authenticity became a profitable vogue. Handel was less complicated in the 'forties and 'fifties.

There was, in those days, a *Messiah* first team. The contralto might vary, but Isobel Baillie knew that her Redeemer lived, William Herbert exalted Every Valley, and Norman Walker sounded the Last Trump. These folks could not sing *every* performance of the piece, though at least one had sung it twice in a day one profitable but exhausting Christmas. Praise be, they sang in my first hearing of it, and their style left an enduring mark on mine. We had no orchestra of course; just the organ. That would not be thought good form today, when only the authentic will do; and since the authentic is very expensive, the thing is done much less often. It's a solution, I suppose; but there ought to be a better one.

Messiah was good business for the brass band cornetist. Many legends surround the greatest amateur exponent of the Bach trumpet, one John Paley of the Black Dyke Band. John was a very large man, celebrated for his presence as for his sound, and in Yorkshire in the 'twenties he was thought indispensable to the work. Met at the station by the secretary of the choral society for which he was to play with the question 'Have you come to play *Messiah*?' John once replied 'Young man, I AM THE MESSIAH!' That fine baritone, Owen Brannigan, battle-scarred veteran of many encounters with trumpeters of all kinds, told me of his first meeting with Paley, long trumpet in hand, at the door of York Minster.

'Thour't Maister Brannigan?'

'I am.'

'My name's Paley. John Paley. Th' hastna' sung i' t'Minster before, hast?'

'No, I haven't had the honour.'

'Well, I've played *Messiah* iv York Minster forty year, man and boy, and I allus likes t'ave a word wit' bass before t'start, tha' knows.'

'Very wise.'

'Well, there's some as thinks *Troompit Shall Sound* is a bass solo wi' troompit obligato ...'

'Yes?'

'It's not, tha' knows. It's a troompit solo wi' bass obligato.'

There being little point, as Owen put it, in arguing with so large a man with so powerful an instrument, that was the only way to play the piece that day. The story taught me, as no doubt Owen intended, to give the piece more thought than Paley seemed to have done. A solo trumpeter can make life hell for the bass in *Messiah*, the aria being high and windy and the trumpet a formidable opponent. Happily Mortimer had shown me a civilised approach, one much appreciated by basses over the years. On the last occasion when I played the work for the Birmingham orchestra the bass was the same as on my first in Yorkshire, fifteen years earlier: Norman Walker. It was the closing evening of the Three Choirs Festival in Worcester, when *Messiah* was played for the Town rather than for the Festival, unrehearsed; a secure enough operation given good enough singers, players, and conductor, and a sensible approach to the music. Concerned to make my aria secure and the bass comfortable, I lay in wait at the door, Paley-fashion, for the great man. He held out his hand with a warm smile. 'Oh', he said, 'It's you. Thank God!' We did not discuss the work.

Walker had a fine way of half-turning to the trumpeter, with his first announcement, and raising his hand in a commanding gesture which said 'Come along, friend, wake the dead – but only between my phrases please!' It was a great privilege to play with him.

Baillie was a wonder; she made the work sound so direct, so easy, so simple as to render today's authentic stylists – whether they are right or wrong – a sort of synthetic. When Baillie sang *Gknow*, we knew that she knew. For a few minutes every atheist in the audience knew too. That was perhaps the ultimate use of the soprano voice in that repertoire. Happily one can still hear it on record, and once heard it is impossible to resist the search for Baillie's *With Verdure Clad* from Haydn's *Creation*, made with the Hallé between the wars. It is a treasure.

Opera sopranos capable of such clarity are uncommon, though not extinct. In that repertoire the classic British soprano of my time has been Heather Harper, who brought to her work the accuracy of a fine wind player allied to perfect diction. Again, Gundula Janowitz, in Karajan's recording of *Creation*, comes close to Baillie. In Kleiber's *Freischütz* recording she is Baillie's equal in quality and style, so the art is not dead; there are still people who provide on the opera stage the honest notation we demand in the pit.

What of my two compatriots, Geraint and Stuart? Musicians both! More than can always be said of the great voices? Sadly, yes. A famous conductor, faced with awful stupidity on the Covent Garden stage, once reminded the orchestra that 'These people have very special equipment in their throats, but it is a mistake to assume that there is always something equally valuable immediately above it.' Well, it is not surprising that the orchestra prefers a musician to a mere singer; and for musical intelligence the Cilfynydd pair have been hard to beat. Stuart was refused admission to his father's male-voice choir because he 'had no voice', a miracle of misjudgement which, because of Stuart's determination, gave us the finest British Mozart tenor of my time, and one of the most delightful of collegues. In *Onegin* his

Lensky was of such quality that I found myself wishing he'd been a better shot, so that we could have enjoyed his voice in the third act as in the first and second. At the other extreme, I enjoyed him too in his famous renderings of Victorian ballads, a style achieved only by those who *believe* in the pieces — few indeed in these disillusioned days.

Geraint is the classic example of success deservedly achieved in the absence of the freak voicebox, his skill as an actor so great that there is some danger of the voice itself being underrated. A greater opera singer than a baritone voice, yes, but a fine singer nevertheless. His Wozzeck, perhaps the greatest test of musicianship for the baritone voice, was peerless, and his stage skills rendered it overpowering. His Balstrode in *Grimes* was a masterpiece, like his Figaro, which I just caught. His Falstaff was for me quite perfect. Yes, Gobbi and others gave us better voice in the role, and there were some who turned up sophisticated noses at Geraint's gift for comic and pathetic characterisation. I've met one great Italian conductor who did not think *Falstaff* a funny opera anyway. But he is certainly wrong and the nose-turners are ungrateful people. Geraint's was a gift polished by sharp observation, and the result of hard work. 'A fat man', he once reminded me, 'is not a thin man in a basket (that being the way my friend was made fat for Falstaff). *He is a different man entirely.* When you go through a door, Bram, you open it just far enough, and slip through it. A fat man has to open it all the way, come back from it, walk through it …' He used to wear that basket at home, to think himself into a fat man. Here was the same total dedication which made Gobbi wear shoes a size too small all day before *Tosca* to make himself an evil man, not just a nice one playing an evil one.

The unique thing about Geraint's Falstaff as in his Beckmesser was his ability to make us like the two men while laughing at them, being irritated by them, almost hating them. Well, one can hardly hate Falstaff because he is so obviously about to bite the dust and wash it down with Thames water, but it came as a surprise when, watching him shiver with fright under Herne's oak in Windsor Great Park, we discovered that we were actually sorry for the poor chump and cross with the Windsor ladies for leading him such a dance. When he began to dance to his own *Tutto il mondo e burla* in that wonderful finale he reminded me irresistibly of a grandfather dancing with the kids around the maypole in Treorchy park. Oh well, say blood is thicker, if you must.

[235]

His Beckmesser was the finest example of operatic *acting* I have ever seen or hope to see, and never finer than in the famous scene in act three where he entered the cobbler's shop, bruised, creaking and groaning from the riot of the second act, to rummage for Sachs' song. Here, for two minutes or so, there is nothing to sing; a matter of reacting silently to Wagner's score. No other singer on earth could have used that time as he did. Watching a very famous contemporary in the role at Bayreuth, I suddenly realised how much *Meistersinger* owed, in my mind, to Geraint. For me the piece was about the poor deluded self-important keeper of the rules, who would discover that talent and truth could defeat the book and all tradition. And Geraint's Beckmesser could, at the end of the opera, appeal to us with a small silent gesture which made us wish that he might, after all, find a lady who would comfort his old age. Not a bad man, Geraint's Town-clerk. A talent which Chaplin would have applauded, allied to a formidable musical intelligence.

In the 'seventies we made with Giulini a famous recording of *Don Carlos*, still the choice of most critics today. It was splendidly cast, the names all gilt-edged and perfectly matched. Our Elisabetta, Montserrat Caballé, has often expressed her admiration for our Orchestra, and that admiration is returned. She was the first of the great ladies I heard in that role, and I have yet to hear a better. The final scene of the opera is all hers, and her performance then was phenomenal. It was all the more remarkable because the lady was ill and in a hurry to go home for surgery of some kind. Of this worry there is not the smallest sign in the recording. Here was a great voice making the most of a great opportunity and rejoicing in a role utterly suited to it. The last scene of the opera, in that recording, must be my choice of all the Verdi I've ever heard.

Miss Caballe ('Mamma' to the trade) was with us in Japan, where she partnered Carreras in *Tosca*. On the final might she threw a massive bouquet to John Brown as a gesture of thanks, and when José was about to leave the stage with his flowers the lady hauled him back (she would not mind my saying that she found this easy because of her weight-advantage) and suggested that he throw them to the principal cello. Caballé is one of the few foreign artists − Jose is another − who seemed to *join* the Royal Opera while with us. No doubt her generous heart has found room for other companies, but we are glad and grateful to have been her friends.

What of the tenors? 'They are more trouble', as JB once remarked, 'even than horn players!' Indeed they are, and scarcer too. Three names will spring to every mind. I would add two others. Carlo Bergonzi and Alfredo Krauss have each given me more pleasure than the big three. Bergonzi I caught very late, but little the worse for that. The great aria which concludes *Lucia* is a fearsome test for the tenor. For canary-fanciers the show is over, Lucia being dead. The scene changes, and the finale is short. Now Donizetti throws the vocal book at the poor tenor, exhausted though he be by the evening's work. The best one can expect is honourable survival. Yet Bergonzi took the piece over, capping the evening with glorious sound. A master indeed.

Krauss survived, as did Bergonzi, by careful husbanding of the voice, without overwork, and by intelligent choice of repertoire. He's been known to inveigh against the modern school of opera conductors who 'imagine they are conducting symphony concerts' and create conditions in which singers cannot survive; an indication of the disciplined way he has paced himself through a long and glorious career. I first heard him in *Rigoletto* in the early 'seventies. It is impossible to imagine a better Duke. He looked the part, and he sang the role then with the polished ease of the aristocrat. This Duke was impossible to hate. He was so splendid a figure as to be desired by every lady of the court and not a few in the audience; a Duke less an exploiter than a victim of his own natural talents.

Of the 'big three' nothing remains to be said, since they themselves have said it so often and so loudly. What is surprising to the musician is that *they really can sing*. A cynical lot down in the pit, we expect overblown fanfares to end with a fart; but no – wonderful people they are, and essential to the work of a first-rate opera house.

We thought we'd lost José, but no; inside that slight body is the heart of a fighter and a winner. I like him best of the three simply because he makes least palaver and sings somehow for the composer rather than for himself. Placido, wonderful artist thought he is, enjoys his lovely sound a little too obviously for me, congratulating himself on every splendid note. The big man we see less frequently. However often he is heard in the theatre, though, the result is the same: sheer astonishment at the vocal resource available to him. Here is a tenor to whom all other tenors listen in amazement, his Covent Garden stage rehearsals liberally peopled with other tenors in the dark stalls. There is no justice, we think. An artist who advertises so enthusiastically deserves to fail, but no; we are instantly entranced. Whatever these chaps are paid … well, what would opera be without them? And how will they be replaced?

Among the basses and baritones one figure stands apart in remembered performance: Boris Christoff, and for one role in which he was incomparable, Boris Godunov. This performance I was privileged to hear twice, beginning with a splendid run in the Rimsky version of the score with Roszdestvensky conducting. In every way Christoff *was* Godunov. This is not easy; one cannot make a Tsar just by dressing a man up in a gold cloak and a crown. Unless he carries the dress well he becomes simply ridiculous. Then again, once placed centre-stage in that outfit with staff in one hand and orb in the other there is a vital need to produce something sizeable from the voice. These needs Christoff fulfilled and to spare; a Tsar more credible, I fancy, than most born to the job. Was anything more moving than Christoff's last speech to his son, with its hopeless encouragement to the little boy, now obviously at the mercy of the Boyars who waited behind the door for the old man's final disintegration? And in the awful last seizure, the Tsar refusing to die *because he is the Tsar*, tumbling horribly from the throne to die at the feet of the Prince, he was terrifyingly real. The court crept towards him, still afraid, unbelieving, as one might approach a dying tiger. We held our breath — why? Was ours the opposite fear, that Christoff had finally gone over the top *and died*? I know of one princeling who was helped from the set at the end of the opera in a state of weeping collapse at Boris's almost too-successful death.

Are the great singers, like the great conductors, the ones who have gone? Nonsense! What of the past can compare with Tom Allen's Billy Budd? With Te Kanawa's's Countess? And these are our own people. We are far more successful at singer production than in the conducting field, a surprising thing when we remember that to sing one must first have a voice, and there are few.

We are teaching better of course, as in most fields of music, and in the USA too great things are being done. Hardly a year goes by without some new voice crossing the pond to demonstrate that fine singing, even in the Italian repertoire, is no longer an art restricted to Latins, and that Wagner is global — as witness the incredible Wotan of James Morris. Surely there must be a future for opera despite its awful economic problems, otherwise why would the world be turning out such talent?

CHAPTER 37

Finale and Coda

It's been fun: almost certainly more fun than life would have been had I not taken to my infant cornet. Yes, I might have been a happy coal-miner; I was a cheerful enough foundry worker. The quality of life does not depend on a clean pair of hands; but the employment of innate talent is a promising base for a happy existence. I know of few talented and successful musicians who are miserable people.

The risk entailed in professional music, on the other hand, is considerable. Would I encourage a talented youngster to have a go? I've never done so; the safe advice is the negative, because only the best can succeed, and these cannot be deterred. The important thing is that he or she should know from the outset that the job is a hard one, undertaken in a competitive environment where throats are sometimes cut without conscience and where the inadequate may become miserable, stressed, ulcerated people.

Much has been said and written of late about stress in musical performance; so much that one begins to wonder whether this is not becoming a fashionable excuse for the failed player, a stick with which to beat orchestral employers, and a specialised career for doctors who have nothing more profitable to do. Of course the stress is real: in which skilled occupation is there none? Is there less stress, for instance, among doctors? Is it useful or fair to present us to our public, as sensational journalism sometimes does, as overworked, exhausted, nervewracked automata kept moving by alcohol and beta-blockers?

Some years ago I attended a conference in New York where people from all over the world debated the causes of stress in the performing arts. It was a depressing experience. My colleagues were not, as I'd hoped, a gathering of performers discussing a general problem; more a collection of stressed people seeking escape through one or another of the theories being propounded. There were, happily, people with good ideas, like the experts in the Alexander technique, a theory of better health through better posture. Their teaching needs no commendation, its wisdom being obvious. But many were the speakers who tried to the limit the patience of the few professional players and managers who'd come to contribute.

The soundest advice of the week came from the manager of the New York Philharmonic. He pointed out that the commonest cause of occupational stress in music, as everywhere else, was the forcing of square pegs into round holes. Music teachers, he suggested, carried a great responsibility here. Economics obliged them to take pupils who would learn little, and to suggest to those who showed even the smallest talent that they might play for a living. Arriving at the Juilliard, where he taught, many entrants suffered a terrible culture-shock, meeting talent on a scale of which they'd never dreamed. They would not give in, their personal investment being already irretrievable, so they worked and they slogged, they graduated by the skin of the teeth − not that a certificate ever got anyone a job in a professional orchestra − and they started on the long circuit of auditions, looking desperately for 'an opening'. The lucky inadequacies, in his opinion, were those who *failed* to get work. For them there was still hope for some other job, with music as a relaxation. The unlucky ones, the unhappy ones, the people stressed out of their minds and into the bottle, ought never to have been encouraged into the business. Their catastrophes were the responsibilities of their early teachers.

This view was not a popular one except among the managers attending. Half of those present were music-teachers, is seemed; but we visitors from what my colleague aptly described as *the real world* knew that a genuinely talented youngster, capable of self-discipline and properly taught his profession − and not merely his instrument − need not be unduly stressed and rarely is. If we're on top of the job, any job, we usually face the day with confidence; if not, then life can be hell.

Let's be fair: one cannot ask that a village music-teacher should detect, at a distance of years, the lack of personal balance which will come between the student and success. Teachers are paid to teach, not to design lives, so in any walk of life there must be misfits. Saddest are those who in another field might have been famously successful. A fancy for the violin or a knack for the trumpet, encouraged by a gifted and energetic teacher, may be a lifetime trap.

Naturally the influence in the orchestra of frustrated people, their personal potential so much greater than their musical talent, can be devastating. Such a man must prove himself, somehow, to himself; if not with a concerto at the Royal Festival Hall, then sometimes in less constructive ways.

Let me say immediately that among the ranks of MU representatives are a majority who serve their colleagues with justice, with integrity, and with industry far above the call of duty. As a manager I've had cause to be grateful to several. But still — and sometimes against the advice of the union itself — the members of an orchestra occasionally behave with the manners of the car assembly line. Why? The answer is simple. We are the most motivated people alive. We'll play even where there is no money, sometimes, because we enjoy it. This makes us exploitable; and when we believe ourselves to be let down by our employers we react with the anger of reasonable people driven beyond restraint: a much more dangerous anger than that of the bored mechanic who, having little regard for his employer or his product, sometimes fights for fun or for what he rightly or wrongly believes to be political principle.

Music will never be a secure living. At best we're only as safe as last night's performance. Then too, however well we play, we have the arts-politicians to contend with. These are powerful people, often amateur musicians of more or less skill and background who sit in comfortable and secure offices in arts institutions or at the Arts Council itself. Their influence is immense, their personal accountability often small. Some are delightful people. They are not *all* failed and frustrated artists — though there are few personalities so dangerous to the professional, I find, as the subconsciously envious amateur; but the general effect of most is negative. They are expensive, subsisting in a degree of luxury from which their performer-victims are excluded. They give uninformed advice and apply wrong solutions to our problems. Their existence is only possible in a nation which once appointed a Minister of Transport who had no driving licence.

Fortunately my job has required very little contact with these folks beyond the politenesses of the Crush Bar, the House's contacts with the arts moguls being wisely left to colleagues with softer boots and much more patience.

It would be idle to pretend that the Arts Council itself is admired by those it finances. It is in a no-win situation, hopelessly under-funded.

[241]

This we all know and understand. I think, though, that it might lose more gracefully and effectively, a trick essential to the successful manager. For some years past its policies with regard to orchestras have seemed very silly indeed. After years of indecision over the fate of London orchestras a policy emerged which no-one of informed intelligence could take seriously. This was dropped, among howls of derision, and another quickly substituted. What is being attempted now is simply the starvation of three of the four orchestras in the expectation that the one with the smallest appetite will survive as the great London orchestra. This is very foolish indeed. Anyone who has the least knowledge of those organisations and the amazing resilience of those who play in them knows that our orchestral republics never give up. The experience of the Philharmonia, the London Philharmonic and the Royal Philharmonic — each in turn left to starve by its founder and each in turn surviving — shows that what they will do is to deteriorate, rehearsing less, with less expensive conductors and artists and worse pay, living somehow to tell the tale to some future hopefully better-financed and certainly wiser body politic than that of today. These policies do not serve British music; they assault it.

In the regions too the meddlers are busy. In Scotland an attempt has been made to amalgamate two orchestras, the BBC Scottish Symphony and that of Scottish Opera; an amalgam which would, if achieved, produce at best a ligon. The arguments for this policy are that each orchestra is under-employed and that public concerts in Scotland are waiting for a second symphony orchestra. This is nonsense, invented to justify joint economy by the BBC and Scottish Opera under what must be considered pressure from the centre. If parts of Scotland are starved of concerts, then the orchestra of Scottish National Opera is already equipped to supply them. That is what happens in Yorkshire, where the orchestra of Opera North does a splendid job.

This scheme is lying very still at the moment of writing, encouraging one to think that it may just go away, as it ought. Should it come to fulfillment then heaven help our friends in Cardiff and Leeds, where similar bad arguments may be as easily and as foolishly applied.

*   *   *

For me, what happens next? I go out to grass, lucky and unusual to have survived so long. None of my colleagues in other orchestras were in situ when I took up my job, which has something in common with football management: one scores a goal from time to time or – out! And the team is one's hardest critic. I've seen many good people, excellent friends, come and go; some falling foul of their boards, some crossing their music directors, but most removed by their orchestras, invincible once they become opponents. My friends insist that my talent been not for the trumpet nor for management but for survival. I do not dispute this.

It's an addiction, the Royal Opera House, and one that consumes lives. One of the hidden snags attached to a senior appointment there is the near-impossibility of going anywhere afterwards but down. I hoped at several points to make a move sideways but John Tooley effortlessly dissuaded me, typically without spending a new penny of the House's money. So it must be on the Floral Street doorstep that I end up. Indeed, I retired at the end of July 1995.

Well, what now of Covent Garden? Of the administration which replaced that of John Tooley it is too soon to write. My opinions throughout this book have been given with the perspective of time and perhaps with the tint of the rose. I think it unfair to discuss the work of my new colleagues and friends – for such they are and will I hope remain – since such a perspective is impossible and the tint, so far, not discernable. What can be said is that our poor, starved old House is singing, both cast-wise and chorally, dancing, producing – oh well, most of us hated the '94/5 *Ring*, but in general – and certainly playing better than ever before in my time. True, we lack our Kleiber, our Muti, our Abbado, our Zubin Mehta from year to year. We have, however, our uncle Georg, happier and even more welcome now than ever, and – miraculously – he records *live* with us now; a tacit admission, surely, that the present orchestra is up to scratch in a way his never was. We have, too, Christoph von Dohnanyi of the infallible ear and encyclopaedic mind, and the new talents of Daniele Gatti, Carlo Rizzi and Christian Thielemann. The sand falls in the glass and older talents drop away with it. Some among my younger colleagues react to the young men as I reacted to Van Beinum and Beecham. Happy am I to have known them all.

Above all we are fortunate in Bernard Haitink, surely the master-conductor of the big orchestra among all his contemporaries. Bernard approached the House through its orchestra, and that body has rewarded him with loyal enthusiasm and wonderful playing. The

Meistersinger of the '93 season was, for me, the apogee of orchestral performance at the Garden during my twenty-five years – though I bow to the *Otello* of Carlos Kleiber which was, as they say, *something else.*

The emergence of the Orchestra on the concert platform has been the great joy of my time with it. Bernard knew, as I had for so many years insisted, that without that experience and that exposure his instrument could not achieve the self-respect and public acclaim which it deserved and must have. Opportunities for concerts are limited, and will remain so; in this sense at least it is true that London has too many orchestras. Wisely, then, our Music Director has devised exciting programmes, thoroughly rehearsed to illustrate the capabilities of his players. Critical response to these rare excursions has been highly encouraging. Perhaps the scribe we most enjoyed was the one who observed, following a performance of Strauss' *Alpensinfonie*, that even in London there was room at the top.

Given a secure financial base – and today even the parlous finances of Covent Garden seem paradisical compared with those of most symphony orchestras – I believe the Orchestra of the Royal Opera House to be capable of establishing itself as the finest in London. Many folks closely informed have believed this to be the case for some time. The public will decide, if it is given the opportunity to hear it. It shows no lack of enthusiasm for us; we get more bums-on-seats across the river than most. We are, as the Festival Hall managers say, a special event, not to be confused with the routine concert. The difference, I think, is a matter of attitude; one can see by the way our people mount the platform that they are glad to be there, positively enjoying the evening. It's catching, enjoyment. There's not a lot of it about.

* * *

Well, I must go! How to entertain myself in what is commonly called retirement, and what I've always regarded as rotting-away, poses a problem. Possibly my enthusiasm for the brass band will provide some of the interest I need. Here is a field in which I can involve myself, at home and abroad.

Regrets? Well, I would like to have played the trumpet so much better, and any reader of sense will have understood from my fascination with the art that I would like to have conducted. I look at close friends and collegues who took that road, sidelining their instruments, and I think that I might have done so; but what fulfilment in a life of planes, hotels, and mediocre orchestras in obscure places, month by month, year by year, wondering just what it is that Kleiber has that one has not? No; it was just as well.

Some ambitions I have, still. So much music I've heard from the inside, and now perhaps I may find time to hear it as audiences do. Opera too I may be permitted to enjoy, setting aside the critical hat for the first time in a quarter-century. Perhaps my heirs and successors will permit me a seat, now and again, for that purpose, for as long as I'm remembered in Floral Street. That, I fancy, will not be for long. The footstep in the sand vanishes with the turn of the tide and, as Peter Grimes has it, who can turn skies back?

Index